Public Policy and Politics

Series Editors: Colin Fudge and Robin Hambleton

Important shifts are taking place in the nature of public policy-making and government at both the central and local level. Increasing financial pressures, the struggle to maintain public services, the emergence of new areas of concern, such as employment and economic development, and increasing partisanship in local politics, are all creating new strains but at the same time opening up new possibilities.

The series is designed to provide up-to-date, comprehensive and authoritative analyses of public policy and politics in practice. Public policy to us involves the implicit or explicit mediation of social and economic forces by the state, is determined by political action as a result of conflict or consensus, and leads to specific patterns of response and activity by government, by non-governmental and private agencies, and by the public.

Two key themes are stressed throughout the series. First, the books link discussion of the substance of policy to the politics of the policy-making process. Second, each volume aims to bridge theory and practice. The books capture the dynamics of public policy-making but, equally important, aim to increase understanding of practice by locating these discussions within differing theoretical perspectives. Given the complexity of the processes and the issues involved, there is a strong emphasis on inter-disciplinary approaches.

The series embraces not only governmental activity, but also central–local relations, public-sector/private-sector relations and the role of non-governmental agencies. Comparisons with other advanced societies will form an integral part of appropriate volumes.

Every effort has been made to make the books in the series as readable and usable as possible. Our hope is that it will be of value to all those interested in public policy and politics – whether as students, practitioners or academics. We shall be satisfied if the series helps in a modest way to improve understanding and debate about public policy and politics during the 1980s.

Public Policy and Politics

Series Editors: Colin Fudge and Robin Hambleton

The Politics of Privatisation

Contracting Out Public Services

Kate Ascher

**MACMILLAN
EDUCATION**

First published 1987

Published by
MACMILLAN EDUCATION LTD
Houndmills, Basingstoke, Hampshire RG21 2XS
and London
Companies and representatives
throughout the world

Typeset by Latimer Trend & Company Ltd, Plymouth

Printed in Hong Kong

British Library Cataloguing in Publication Data
Ascher, Kate
The politics of privatisation: contracting
out public services.—(Public policy
and politics)
1. Privatization—Great Britain
I. Title II. Series
363'.0941   HD148
ISBN 0-333-40391-6 (hardcover)
ISBN 0-333-40392-4 (paperback)

Contents

List of Tables

List of Figures

List of Abbreviations

ABLC	Association of British Launderers and Cleaners
ABLCRS	Association of British Laundry Cleaning and Rental Services
ASI	Adam Smith Institute
AHST	Association of Health Service Treasurers
CAC	Central Arbitration Committee
CCMA	Contract Cleaning and Maintenance Association
CIPFA	Chartered Institute of Public Finance and Accountancy
COHSE	Confederation of Health Service Employees
DHA	District Health Authority
DHSS	Department of Health and Social Security
DLO	Direct Labour Organisation
DOE	Department of the Environment
EEC or EC	European Economic Community or European Community
EETPU	Electrical Electronic Telecommunication and Plumbing Union
GLC	Greater London Council
GDP	Gross Domestic Product
GMBATU	General Municipal Boilermakers and Allied Trades Union
GMWU	General and Municipal Workers Union (now GMBATU)
HGVTS	Heavy Goods Vehicle Testing Stations
LAMSAC	Local Authorities Management Services and Computer Committee
MMC	Monopolies and Mergers Commission
MOD	Ministry of Defence
NALGO	National and Local Government Officers Association
NFBTE	National Federation of Building Trades Employers

NHS	National Health Service
NUPE	National Union of Public Employees
OECD	Organisation for Economic Cooperation and Development
PI	Performance Index
RCM	Royal College of Midwives
RHA	Regional Health Authority
RIPA	Royal Institute of Public Administration
SHA	Special Health Authority
T&GWU	Transport and General Workers Union
THF	Trusthouse Forte
TUC	Trades Union Congress
UCATT	Union of Construction Allied Trades and Technicians
VAT	Value Added Tax

Acknowledgements

This book had its origins in my doctoral research at the London School of Economics. It developed more rapidly than expected, thanks to the cooperation of a great number of people actively involved in the debate over contracting out. I would particularly like to thank senior managers within the contract service firms, local and national officials of both COHSE and NUPE, civil servants within the DHSS, Treasury, and DOE and public sector administrators within both the NHS and local government. I have tried to use the information they have given me both discreetly and appropriately and hope that in doing so I have managed to avoid betraying any confidences.

A number of people have contributed comments on various drafts of the manuscript. Sue Budd and Duncan Eaton scrutinised those sections dealing with the health service; likewise, Keith Hickson offered detailed comments on the chapter on trade unions. Robin Hambleton took on the daunting task of reading a very early draft and emerged with a number of valuable suggestions. Special thanks are due to Patrick Dunleavy and Adrian Ellis, whose comments and queries throughout my research helped me to focus both my thoughts and my writing more clearly.

I am also indebted to a number of my colleagues at Harbridge House. Sue Cooper and Debbie Rose have put in a great many extremely unsocial hours in order to complete this book and have willingly suffered through countless amendments and revisions. Frances Airey and Tony Cooper cast a critical eye over the penultimate manuscript and helped root out both inaccuracies and redundancies. A debt of thanks is also owed to David Hussey, Managing Director of Harbridge House. In addition to providing me with an extended period of paid leave, he has offered constant encouragement throughout a long and disruptive year of research. His support for my academic efforts provides a good example for other private sector managers to follow.

One final note about the nature of the material which follows.

Contracting out is a diffuse and divisive issue, and any attempt to characterise it on the written page is bound to be fraught with a number of deficiencies and omissions. It is also a very topical issue, and the political and commercial environment within which it has developed is changing rapidly. While this book will no doubt fall short on a number of counts, it is hoped that the overall analysis will provide a useful and stable foundation for further research in this area.

London   KATE ASCHER

Guide to Reading the Book

Contracting out – the private provision of public services – has recently become a salient and controversial issue in British politics. Although many local agencies relied on private firms for a variety of services prior to the election of a Conservative government in 1979, the new government's espousal of a mandatory tendering programme for NHS hospitals brought the issue to the national political agenda. This transformation has provoked sharply divergent expectations. While supporters of the Government's policy have forecast dramatic cuts in the cost of delivering public services, opponents have predicted a serious deterioration in the standard of service provided to local citizens. Although it is too early to evaluate either of these claims comprehensively, it is possible to narrow down the range of probable outcomes by examining the implications of recent initiatives for different groups – private contractors, trade unions, local councils, health authorites and the Government itself. This book examines the impact of competitive tendering and contracting out in each of these sectors, and draws some general conclusions about the effect that government action has had upon local policy-making processes.

The first section of the book explains the rise of contracting out and competitive tendering in Britain. Chapter 1 sets the debate in the UK in its appropriate geographical and political context. It examines the growth of private provision on a worldwide basis, and considers the political environment in Britain which allowed contracting out to become a salient political issue. Chapter 2 offers a detailed chronology of the development of Conservative policy in three areas – the NHS, local authorities and central departments. It also explores the factors which contributed to the unusually rapid rise of mandatory tendering to the national political agenda.

The next section examines two of the most visible and most vocal interest groups in the present debate. Chapter 3 considers the position of contract service firms presently seeking work in the public sector. It offers an overview of the structure and activities of the relevant contract industries, placing particular emphasis upon their reactions to the new public sector markets, and analyses the recent commercial performance of five of the major contractors. Chapter 4 looks at the public sector trade unions. It considers the effects of tendering and contracting out upon unions and their members, and analyses both the strengths and weaknesses of the unions' campaign of opposition to government policy.

The third section of the book illustrates the interaction of these and other groups in local tendering exercises. Chapter 5 outlines the mechanics of the tendering process, and explores some of the more controversial issues surrounding the process itself. Chapter 6 examines the implementation of compulsory tendering for ancillary services in the NHS, and Chapter 7 analyses the scope and effectiveness of both competitive tendering and contracting out exercises in local authorities. Both Chapters 6 and 7 rely on case studies to highlight the dynamics of the local tendering process.

The fourth and final section, Chapter 8, examines in greater depth some of the key issues raised in earlier chapters and attempts to put recent events into an appropriate historical perspective. It contrasts developments in local authorities with those in the NHS, in an attempt to highlight both the true significance of contracting out and the dangers associated with current government approaches to local service provision.

1 An Introduction to Contracting Out

Between 1980 and 1985, the debate over private provision of public services rose to the top of the British political agenda. From its origins in a small number of Conservative-controlled local authorities, it spread rapidly to both central government and the National Health Service. The issue became particularly salient in the wake of the Conservative Government's decision to require in-house hospital workforces to compete with the private sector for NHS ancillary work, an initiative which has involved tendering exercises for three separate services at some 2000 NHS hospitals. Yet this substantial programme represented only the first manifestation of the Government's ambitions. Decisions to require both central departments and local authorities to go out to tender for an even wider range of services in the future were announced in 1985. These confirmed that the Conservative Government continues to view 'contracting out' – the private provision of public services – as an integral and important part of its campaign to introduce private sector discipline and efficiency into British government.

Coalitions for and against contracting out are, to a large extent, drawn along party political lines. Proponents include Conservative politicians in both national and local government and the intellectual 'new right' that has helped them to formulate Conservative Party ideology. These groups are supported by the private contract service firms, many of whom have already made inroads into the public sector market. Opponents of contracting out are less homogeneous in outlook and belief. Foremost among them have been the trade unions, whose 'save our services' campaign has provided the most visible evidence of opposition to the Government's policy. Support for the union campaign has come from the Labour Party and to a lesser extent from public sector administrators, many of whom are not opposed to contracting out in principle but are

1

hostile to what they see as unjustified interference by central government in their operational and managerial affairs.

These two sides have waged an active battle of words, in an attempt to influence both government ministers and the public. One has portrayed contracting out as a cure for the ailments of the state bureaucracy; the other has suggested that this particular form of treatment is unsuitable and will prove detrimental to the long-term health of the institutions involved. Unlike medical science, however, the evidence upon which these diagnoses have been based is in nearly all cases insubstantial. Both sides have supported their claims by documenting the experiences of organisations that have shifted from public to private provision, but the data employed in these exercises is uniformly partisan and highly suspect. 'Evidence' often focuses on very short-term phenomena, such as the level of cost savings or the inevitable hiccoughs which characterise the transition from internal to external provision. Many of the facts used by both sides are exaggerated or simply untrue. Trade unions have made false accusations about contractors' performance, while their opponents have been shown to overstate the level of savings achieved by individual authorities. These inaccuracies have rarely been recognised by the media who have used information supplied by one or another parties to quite spectacular effect, increasing the level of confusion and misunderstanding about the likely effects of contracting out.

Analysing the respective claims of the protagonists is not easy, as very little reliable information about private provision exists. Only a handful of new contracts have been operating for any length of time, and the information gathered from these is as yet inconclusive. Most if not all of these arrangements were born in an environment of poor industrial relations and high political tension. As a result, they are poorly suited to objective assessment by participating parties and could not be considered 'representative' of events likely to occur in less politicised environments. The only reliable work on the impact of contracting out comes from the United States, where a more significant volume of experience has been built up over a ten-year period. However, even in the United States, much of the evidence is contradictory and the most recent non-partisan studies have suggested that the general effects of contracting out are not yet known.

In Britain, the lack of comprehensive data has meant that

academic research into the subject has been limited to very specific aspects of contracted services, such as the deterioration in conditions of service or the financial effects of privatisation. But information about contracting out in Britain is now growing rapidly, thanks to the size and speed of the Conservative initiative, and the next few years should see increasing attention devoted to both the quantitative and qualitative impacts of the contracting process. It is thus important that some form of rigorous analysis is conducted at this stage, in order to establish a less partisan and more stable foundation for future research than that which currently exists.

This book attempts to provide part of this foundation by examining recent developments in local authorities and the NHS. In sharp contrast to the literature produced by interested parties, the intention here is not to make normative judgements about the merits of private service provision but to explore Conservative policy itself, highlighting and evaluating the impact that recent events have had upon the nature and quality of service provision decisions in locally-based public agencies. This first chapter provides the framework for this perspective by introducing the political, geographical and theoretical context of the current debate. It begins by describing the political environment which gave rise to contracting out in Britain and then moves to a more detailed analysis of the concept of contracting out – what it means, where it came from, and why it has become so popular in the past fifteen years. It concludes with a general overview of contracting out developments worldwide.

Privatisation in Britain

Although private provision of local services has existed on a small scale for many years, its popularity as an alternative to direct public provision grew rapidly in the early 1980s. This growth is generally attributed to the wave of fiscal conservatism which has characterised the rebellion against 'big government' in many industrialised nations of the West. In Britain, this change in public attitude underpinned the election of a determined and ideological Conservative government in 1979. Although the new Government signalled its approval of private provision as early as 1980, it was not until the Conservatives' firm commitment to privatisation was in place two years later that contracting out was elevated to 'policy' status. Any discussion of contracting out in Britain must therefore begin with a look at the context in which it developed – the privatisation programme of the early 1980s.

The word 'privatisation' itself is an umbrella term that has come to describe a multitude of government initiatives designed to increase the role of the private sector. In its most literal sense, as it is used by the Thatcher Government, it refers to the transfer of state ownership in nationalised industries to the private sector. The objective of such exercises is to introduce greater competition into these industries, thereby improving efficiency and reducing the cost to the public. By 1985, about a dozen asset sales had been completed and some 400 000 jobs transferred to the private sector. As one proponent noted recently, these exercises have 'achieved the largest transfer of property since the dissolution of the monasteries under Henry VIII'.[1] Receipts from these privatisation exercises, as shown in Table 1.1, have exceeded £5 billion and are forecast to continue rising between 1985 and 1987.[2]

Although asset sales have received tremendous media attention, they are generally considered only one type of privatisation initiative. Despite the Government's narrow definition of 'privatisation', a whole host of other exercises undertaken with the same objectives – to introduce private sector competition and efficiency – are considered equally important elements of a 'privatisation strategy' by many of the Government's strongest supporters. This wider usage of the term privatisation is best explained by Madsen Pirie in a pamphlet published by the Adam Smith Institute, one of the most active of the think-tanks supporting Government policy: 'Privatisation is a complex and subtle process. It is not a panacea or a formula. Instead, it is an approach which can generate and focus creative policy ideas. Overwhelmingly, the impression emerges that each case is unique and requires a different remedy.'[3]

To prove his point about the necessity for a 'creative' approach, Pirie goes to great trouble to identify numerous different methods of privatisation. These variations on the privatisation theme are shown in Table 1.2, alongside a recent example of each method. Some of these approaches, such as the sale of state assets, have been implemented on a substantial scale in the UK; others, such as the use of vouchers, have been limited to one or two local

TABLE 1.1 Asset sales: 1979–80 to 1984–5

Asset (% sold)	Sale proceeds (£m)	Annual total (£m)
1979/80		
British Petroleum (5)	276	
Others	101	377
1980/81		
British Aerospace (51.6)	43	
North Sea Oil Licenses	195	
Others	167	405
1981/82		
British Sugar Corporation (24)	44	
Cable and Wireless (49.4)	182	
Amersham International (100)	64	
Others	204	494
1982/83		
Britoil (51)	334	
Associated British Ports (51.5)	46	
International Aeradio (100)	60	
British Rail Hotels (91)	34	
North Sea Oil Licenses	33	
Others	75	582
1983/84		
British Petroleum (7)	543	
Cable and Wireless (22)	263	
Britoil (48.9)	293	
Others	69	1168
1984/85		
Associated British Ports (48.5)	50	
British Gas (Wytch Farm Oil) (100)	82	
Enterprise Oil (100)	380	
Sealink (60.6)	40	
Jaguar (100)	297	
Inmos (75)	95	
British Telecom (50.2)	1500	2444
Total		**5470**

Source: *Economic Survey of the UK* (Paris: OECD, January 1985).

TABLE 1.2   Methods of privatisation

Method	Example
selling the whole	Amersham International
selling complete parts of the whole	English Channel Ferry Services
selling a proportion of the whole	British Petroleum
selling to the workforce	National Freight Corporation
'giving' to the public	British Telecom discounts
'giving' to the workforce	Hoverspeed
charging for the service	NHS prescription charges
contracting out	local authority and NHS services
diluting the public sector	road funding
buying out existing interest groups	council house sales
deregulation via voluntary associations	aviation (CAA)
encouraging alternative institutions	University of Buckingham
making small scale trials	freeports
repealing monopolies	bus and coach services
encouraging exit from state provision	social security (private pensions)
vouchers	transport tokens
curbing state powers	private searches
divestment	British Gas
applying liquidation	hospitals
withdrawal	quango activity
right to private substitution	the 'right to repair'

Source: M. Pirie, *Privatization* (London: Adam Smith Institute, 1985).

situations. Pirie's point, of course, is not the utility or popularity of a particular method, but the variety of ways in which privatisation might be carried out.

Both the Government's narrow approach to the term privatisation and Pirie's very broad definition are extreme, however, and neither provides a very useful typology of privatisation initiatives. A more sophisticated approach, put forward by Heald and Morris, breaks privatisation activity into four classes.[4] The first might be called denationalisation, and refers to both the selling off of nationalised industries to the private sector and the gradual withdrawal from comprehensive public provision in areas like education, health and the social services. A second form of privatisation involves the substitution of customer fees for tax finance, an example of which can be found in the recent increases in the charges for NHS services. Liberalisation constitutes a third form of privatisation and refers to the abolition or relaxation of the monopoly powers of nationalised industries, as witnessed in the case of British Telecom and the telecommunications industry. The fourth and final form of privatisation in this typology is the contracting out of public services to the private sector. Under contracting out arrangements, public authorities continue to bear direct responsibility both for the provision arrangements and for the quality of service provided although the work is actually carried out by employees of private firms.

This last form of privatisation is the focus of our interest. Unlike several other forms of privatisation, contracting out does not signal an end to public sector control; state agencies continue to both plan and finance the services involved. For this reason, one might expect it to be less controversial an approach than those that do remove all traces of public sector participation. But quite the opposite has been the case: contracting out has been among the most divisive of the Government's approaches to privatisation. Much of the explanation for the controversy surrounding the issue lies in the nature of the specific policy framework in which it has developed. Although contracting out first appeared in local authorities as a remedy for particular localised service problems, it was soon captured and made the subject of a major national initiative designed to improve productivity and performance at local level in the health service. This tension between national policy and local needs has made contracting out a more controversial and indeed a more significant issue than it might otherwise have been.

Contracting out – what is it?

The term 'contracting out' describes the situation where one organisation contracts with another for the provision of a particular good or service. It is essentially a form of procurement, in the sense that contractors may be considered 'suppliers', but in common usage it has come to refer more specifically to the purchase of an end product which could otherwise be provided 'in-house' by the purchaser himself. In the private sector, contracting out is a common and growing phenomenon and is sometimes referred to as 'outsourcing'. The commercial reasons for contracting out vary, but generally include cost-effectiveness, lack of in-house expertise, the need to reduce overheads, greater administrative convenience and the need for increased flexibility to respond to changes in market conditions.

Contracting out is equally common in the public sector, where public agencies contract with a variety of organisations to supply products that they cannot or do not want to provide in-house. Most commonly an agency will contract with a private firm or individual, but it may also contract out to voluntary or cooperative organisations, or to other public sector agencies. The product provided externally may be required to maintain internal operations (for example, computers to process employees' pay, or window cleaning services); alternatively, it may contribute directly to meeting external output obligations (for example, the purchase of linen or the use of agency nurses by the NHS). Although the public sector regularly contracts out for both goods and services, the focus of the Government's recent interest is exclusively on the increased contracting out of services. Service provision is labour-intensive and therefore the more natural target for a government determined to reduce manpower levels and improve managerial efficiency.

The traditional structure of public service provision sees the state both planning and delivering a variety of services which are indirectly financed, in whole or in part, from taxes. Obvious examples of such comprehensive provision include schools, libraries, and recreational facilities. But there are numerous other less comprehensive forms of service delivery in which the state is active. One particularly useful typology was put forward by Sonnenblum, Kirlin and Ries, who outlined three different modes of service provision: 'regulated', 'grant' and 'contracted'.[5] Under a regulated mode, the state is involved in planning, but not in financing or producing a service; zoning enforcement is a good example of this type of activity. Under a grant mode, the state provides financial support for an activity, but does not plan or produce it; farm support, student grant, or legal aid systems fall into this category. Finally, under a contract mode, the state plays a financial and planning role but does not produce the service itself; building maintenance and road construction have traditionally been provided via such contractual arrangements.

This approach is useful insofar as it helps to explain why some public agencies have had significantly more experience of contracting than others. Because different services require different modes of service provision, the extent to which any one government agency relies on a particular mode will depend primarily on the nature and mix of the services it provides. If we take government departments in Britain as an example, departments like the Ministry of Defence or the Ministry of Transport will commonly rely heavily on contract provision; although they are responsible for planning and financing defence projects and road transport respectively, neither maintains the in-house expertise or staff to develop airborne warning systems or to build major motorways. In contrast, a department like the Department of Trade and Industry will rely on the grant mode to provide a variety of services to British companies, and may also assume a regulatory role in monitoring competitive behaviour in industry. The Department of Health and Social Services (DHSS) may provide many services directly, but it also acts in a grant-awarding capacity by distributing social security benefits, in a regulated capacity by monitoring the drug industry and prescription charges, and in a contract capacity by using agency nurses or private hospital facilities.

This typology deals primarily with service outputs and service delivery, and does not really address the issue of how an agency's internal operations are organised. It is important to note that different modes of service provision will also exist within an organisation. In the case of an internal finance function, for instance, an agency may retain its own accountants or it may employ a private firm of accountants; similarly it may employ cleaners directly or hire a contract cleaning firm. This represents another form of contracting out, but one that can be distinguished from that concerned with ultimate service delivery. Both forms of contracting out, one for internal and the other for external purposes, are involved in the present debate.

A useful way of putting both 'internal' and 'external' contracting out into perspective is to look at an agency's budget, which must include funding for both elements. Dunleavy has distinguished three different types of budgets under an agency's control.[6] The 'programme budget' refers to all expenditure which passes through the hands of the agency, even if some of it is destined for other public agencies; the Department of Environment (DOE), for example, has a large programme budget even though much of it is passed on to local authorities. The 'bureau budget' is a subset of the programme budget, and consists only of funding for programmes under the direct control of the agency; in the case of the DOE, this would include expenditure on major civil engineering projects. Within the bureau budget exists the 'core budget', consisting of expenditure on internal operations or what are often referred to as 'running costs'. In the DOE, this would include the salaries of DOE staff, the costs of services provided for them and any other overhead costs associated with DOE business.

Contracting out has traditionally been associated primarily with parts of an agency's bureau budget, or those items which are provided directly by an agency to its client body. Examples include the building of bridges and tunnels or the development of a metropolitan subway system. Although interest in these sorts of client services continues (for example, refuse collection), increasing emphasis is now being placed on the contracting out of core budget items such as cleaning, catering and computing services, all of which had previously been provided by a directly employed workforce. This change in the nature of contracting helps to explain the rise of an unusually and highly controversial form of competitive tendering.

Competitive tendering

The process by which private contracts are usually awarded is known as competitive tendering. The most common form of competitive tendering involves private contractors competing against one another either for contracts that had previously been in private hands and expired (for example, catering concessions at sporting events) or for contracts that had not previously existed (for example, contracts for building the M25 orbital motorway around London). However, in the past few years a different form of competitive tendering has become popular in Britain. As a result of increasing emphasis on the efficiency of core budget services, many recent competitive tendering exercises have involved services previously carried out by a direct labour force. In most of these cases, the in-house workforce has been asked to compete against interested private sector bidders. Where the in-house force has offered the most cost-competitive alternative, it has generally retained the service and the contract price has become its budget. In cases where a private firm has proved cheaper than the in-house service, the direct labour organisation has often been disbanded and the winning firm has assumed day-to-day control of service operations.

This particular form of competitive tendering, in which an in-house team competes against private contractors for a service it previously provided, is at the centre of the current debate. It is the only type of tendering exercise that can lead to switches from one type of labour to another, an event that raises a number of delicate questions. The first issue raised by a 'switch' in delivery mode is the future of the previously existing workforce. Unlike private contractors' employees, who when they lose one contract will be moved on to another, the switch from in-house to external provision signals the end of public sector employment for most of the direct labour force. It is for this reason that the unions have fought contracting out so bitterly. A switch in delivery mode raises a second and perhaps even more controversial issue – that of the most appropriate means of service delivery. Many supporters of contracting out, including many members of the Government, believe that private sector delivery is inherently more efficient than direct provision. In contrast, opponents argue that 'indirect' delivery reduces accountability, democratic control and quality of service.

The growth of contracting out

The question of the most appropriate means of service delivery has only recently become controversial; indeed it is only recently that it has even been asked. For years, in-house provision was accepted and indeed preferred as the most effective mode of delivery for a great many public services throughout the world. The origins of direct provision date back to the latter part of the nineteenth century, when local authorities began to assume increasing responsibility for the health and well-being of the local community. Over a relatively short period of time, these new activities of local government – ranging from social services to refuse collection –

became accepted and indeed defined as 'public services' by the majority of voters. There are a number of reasons why these services grew up in the public sector as opposed to the private, the most obvious of which is that there were simply very few private companies able and willing to provide the sort of services that citizens had begun to demand. But putting this 'practical' point aside for a moment, it is possible to identify two other sets of reasons why direct provision became the preferred mode of delivery for many public services.

The first set, drawn from organisational theory, suggests that all organisations – both public and private – will prefer to provide certain services in-house rather than resource them externally. One factor influencing decisions to internalise services is size. The general rule of thumb is that the larger an organisation, the more likely it is to internalise service provision; for example, economies of scale are an important factor in considering whether an internal catering, cleaning, or computer programming department is feasible. Another factor to be taken into account is the nature and variability of the workload; in catering, for example, providing a regular volume of pre-specified meals for company staff is one thing, but meeting the periodic needs of Board and senior management lunches is another. A third important factor is confidentiality: many organisations would not consider privatising cleaning services, for example, because it would put outsiders in a position of close proximity to sensitive competitive or client information. A fourth factor influencing service provision decisions is the indivisibility of many services. Computer programming and the processing of corporate data, for example, may need to be carried out by those with experience of the organisation's accounting or financial systems.

A second and equally powerful set of explanations for the development of in-house provision in this sector focuses on the unusual nature of public services themselves. Many public services are highly specialised with characteristics that differentiate them from those normally provided by the private sector. These characteristics would include:

● *Fairness* Public services must be provided fairly and equitably to all end-users. Such an obligation does not exist in the commercial world where suppliers are able to discriminate among, and negotiate independently with, individual clients.

● *Fail-safe risk* A high level of risk may be involved in the failure to provide adequate standards of public service. For example, regular refuse collection is necessary to minimise health hazards; frequent social service visits can be critical to the well-being of children, families and older people. While delays in provision of goods or services by commercial firms can have a detrimental impact on sales and profit, the impact upon 'clients' is generally much less dramatic than that resulting from service provision failures in the public sector.

● *Difficulty in specifying output* Few public services lend themselves to easy specification, due to the importance of quality in determining citizen satisfaction. While outputs associated with most commercial services are relatively easy to quantify and satisfaction can be measured through the marketplace, areas like education, water supply and personal social services present significant problems of measurement.

Many who accept the rationale behind direct provision of public services nevertheless believe that the rapid growth of the welfare state has led to diseconomies of scale and that specific services are no longer provided efficiently by the public sector. This attitude, often expressed in very emotive terms such as 'government is too big' or 'the need to cut red tape', has led to new levels of interest in alternative modes of delivery. These alternatives to direct provision have historically taken a variety of forms, not all of them market-based. In many countries, there is a tradition of voluntary provision of public services which predates contracting out and, in some cases, predates the welfare state itself. Lifeboat services in Britain and ambulance services in many American communities, for example, are provided voluntarily and have been for many years. A great number of services are provided by independent non-profit organisations; legal aid in the City of New York, for example, is provided by the Legal Aid Society – an organisation funded primarily by charitable donations. Other services are provided by private agencies who receive a grant or subsidy from the government and levy minimal user charges; many local bus services are run this way. While each of these arrangements are important 'private alternatives' to direct provision, none have taken off as rapidly as contracting out and they have therefore been excluded both from the discussion below and from the analysis contained in the remainder of this book.

The American experience

The first signs of real interest in contracting out as an alternative to direct provision occurred in the US. Although contracting for local services had existed in America for many years, it was not until the 1970s that it became a 'hot' topic in local government circles. The interest in contracting out which blossomed then was a function of several factors, foremost of which was the dramatic rise in the pay of local government workers in the 1960s and early 1970s. Traditionally, American municipal employees had received good benefits to compensate for low and uncompetitive levels of pay. With the rise of merit hiring, itself an attempt to do away with networks of local patronage, more qualified people were brought into local government service and pay scales had to be adjusted to compete with the private sector. Simultaneously, the unions successfully challenged the laws exempting municipal workers from unemployment compensation, social security, minimum wage protection and other benefits enjoyed by the private sector worker. The resulting increases in pay and benefits made public sector workers a more expensive proposition than ever before.

Concurrently, the economic and political environment in which American municipal decision-making occurred was changing. Emphasis on costs grew dramatically as a result of increased 'tax awareness' among citizens, economic problems resulting from the 1973 oil crisis, and new accounting and budgeting techniques. Computers allowed major improvements in financial and management accounting and programme budgeting came into widespread use. The trade union movement in local government grew rapidly, upsetting the paternalistic relationship which had existed between many cities and their employees. Whereas previously public employees had given municipalities total control over public expenditure in return for job security, trade unions in the 1970s began to demand a larger voice in local policy-making for their members. As a result, many local authorities gradually abandoned their protective attitudes toward employees.[7]

These factors stimulated reappraisals of service provision on a large scale throughout the 1970s. Keen to make visible cost savings, American cities tried a variety of techniques. Some negotiated new wage settlements with their existing service staff, others decided to put contracts out to private companies, and a few pioneered competitive tendering techniques which involved the in-house staff.[8] The approach chosen was always 'city-specific'. Some cities could not contract out, due to earlier agreements with municipal workers, and were therefore forced to negotiate with their in-house staff; others found that 'contracting out' to larger neighbouring authorities was the most cost-effective alternative. No consistent pattern of contracting out ever developed, although much of the activity was centred around large metropolitan areas with highly unionised workforces.

During this period, refuse collection was the most popular area for contracting out experiments. The ease with which refuse collection outputs could be quantified made it well-suited for private provision and also made it the focus of academic interest in contracting out. At least five cross-sectional refuse studies were undertaken in the US during the 1970s, one on a national basis and the others in the Eastern, Midwestern and Western parts of the country respectively. Each compared the costs of alternative modes of service provision in different cities, and each came to somewhat different conclusions:

- Two studies showed that contracting out was cheaper than in-house provision. One used data collected from 101 Connecticut cities between 1972 and 1974. A second, conducted at about the same time at Columbia University, considered data from 206 cities across the country. Both found significant differences between the costs of the two types of services.[9]
- Two other studies, both conducted in the St Louis area, found that no significant cost differential existed between the two types of service. The first was published in 1965 and relied on 1960 data provided by 24 cities in St Louis County. The second study, undertaken ten years later, covered 53 cities in the same area (excluding St Louis itself) and confirmed the earlier study's findings.[10]
- One study found in-house provision to be cheaper than private collection. It was conducted in 1974, and used data collected from 26 cities in the State of Montana. Whereas the Columbia study had found contractors to be cheaper in

communities with populations over 10 000, this study concluded that contractors were likely to be cheaper only in very small communities.[11]

The inconclusive nature of this evidence is not the only problem one encounters when considering the lessons that British local authorities might draw from US experience in the refuse collection field. The relevance of the studies themselves is questionable, as refuse collection in the US has traditionally been provided by a wide variety of methods including 'franchised' operations (whereby the city grants a firm the right to provide a fee-paying service to all citizens in a given area) and 'private' operations (whereby each household undertakes its own contract with the company of its choice).[12] Comparing municipal to contract operations thus gives only part of the picture and ignores the savings that have been made in switching from private or franchised operations to municipal provision.

Although American academics have focused primarily on refuse collection, the growth of contracting out in the US has not been limited to that service. Rapidly growing costs in the health care field have given rise to the contracting out of a number of services by private and municipal hospitals. Approximately 18 per cent of domestic services and 20 per cent of catering services provided by US hospitals are supplied by private contractors, and the number of private 'hospital management' contracts is growing rapidly.[13] Two American studies have looked at contracting out in hospitals. One study, undertaken by the School of Public Health at the University of California, Los Angeles (UCLA), examined the performance of hospital management contracts at 15 of 39 hospitals run by county government in California between 1973 and 1980.[14] No significant changes in service cost or efficiency were reported, but several hospitals found that better accounting and billing systems had resulted in increased revenue. However, 7 of the 15 hospitals terminated the contracts during the seven-year period as a result of either public opposition or a belief that the techniques of private management could be emulated by directly employed staff.

A second study, conducted at Kansas State University in the early 1980s, looked at the relative benefits of contract catering in American hospitals.[15] It found that the major advantages of contract catering included the private caterer's more extensive corporate resources (e.g. buying power, procedures), better back-up systems (e.g. personnel, purchasing, training) and unusual expertise, but noted that contracting also brought with it a division of employee loyalty, loss of control, poor relationships between old personnel and the contractor, and inadequate provision of modified diets. These findings, which suggest that the advantages of contract catering are primarily a result of the catering organisation's size and volume of experience, are not surprising, as most US hospitals are small and independent (only 30 per cent are organisationally linked or affiliated to others) and therefore cannot achieve significant economies of scale. The relevance of this study's findings to events in the UK is questionable, as the nature and the size of the NHS provide it with the internal corporate resources and back-up systems which many American hospitals do not have. Furthermore, whereas the system of health care in America is open-budgeted and rewards hospitals according to the volume of services performed, hospitals in Britain are forced to work within strict financial constraints determined by central government.

Other studies have attempted to document the effects of contracting out in the United States. A study published in 1978 by the Urban Institute, a nonprofitmaking policy research organisation, found that contracting out was not in itself a cheaper method of provision and concluded that nearly all changes in the existing mode – either from municipal to contract or vice versa – were likely to lead to cost-savings on account of pre-existing service inefficiencies.[16] A more recent study, undertaken by the California Tax Foundation in 1980–1, examined contracting out over a wide range of services in 87 local authorities (including cities, counties and school districts). It found that the major advantages of contracting out were a reduction in cost and the availability of special equipment and skilled personnel. Most prominent among the disadvantages of the process were greater difficulties in monitoring contracts and the unreliability of contractors.[17]

None of these studies, however, can be considered either comprehensive or authoritative. Despite considerable media coverage of contracting out in American local authorities, the number of all municipalities that has shifted from internal to external provision has remained small. Equal attention has been paid to a variety of other private approaches to the provision of services – franchise, voucher, volunteer and fee arrangements among others. A recent review of private approaches to public service delivery published by the Urban Institute concluded that,

> contracting has probably been the most closely examined approach to privatisation. The amount of independent, comprehensive evaluation of the effects of contracting, however, is quite small except for solid waste collection. Few trials of contracting, including the recent innovations, have been adequately evaluated to permit agencies nationally to learn under what conditions contracting works well.[18]

Developments in other countries

Like the United States and Britain, many countries in other parts of the world have well-established traditions of private provision of certain public services. Most countries in Western Europe rely to some extent upon private contractors. Denmark has a tradition of private provision of emergency services, with the Falck Company providing emergency fire services to nearly half of the country's population. In Switzerland and France, local authorities have had extensive experience of both contract refuse collection and privatised security services. In Germany, municipalities have employed private companies to maintain parks and perform gardening chores. Similar situations exist in other parts of the developed world. Many cities in Canada have had considerable experience of contracted refuse collection.[19] In Japan, nearly all public sector housing construction is contracted out, as are a wide range of other activities including refuse and tax collection, secretarial and computer support, and recreational services.[20]

Contracting out has not been confined to the local authority sector. Significant inroads into the hospital cleaning sector have been made by private firms in both Western Europe and Australasia. It is estimated that 50 per cent of hospitals in France and Belgium and 60 per cent of hospitals in Germany and Denmark use contract cleaners; in Sweden reliance on private contractors has risen to 70 per cent.[21] Contract cleaning in hospitals has become popular in New Zealand; indeed the largest contractor in the UK health service market, Crothall, owes its early success to developments in that market. Private sector provision of hospital services has also grown in Australia, though the introduction of contract cleaning has met with hostility from certain professional associations and the debate over the most suitable means of service provision continues.

Much of the locally-based contracting out activity outlined above predated the rising tide of fiscal conservatism that characterised the late 1970s and early 1980s. However, the recent economic climate has led to renewed interest in private arrangements and has helped to increase reliance on private contractors in most of these countries. This worldwide increase in private provision is best viewed in the context of a shift in the economic activity of developed countries from manufacturing to service sectors. The range of commercial services and the number of firms providing these services has grown rapidly in the latter part of the twentieth century. Fifty years ago, public authorities interested in contracting out mainstream services would have been faced with a small number of high-priced alternatives. Today they are faced with a large and growing number of suppliers and, as a result, very competitive prices. Given the present environment of tight financial constraints, it is hardly surprising that public agencies have given these low cost alternatives increasingly serious consideration.

Observations

The newfound popularity of contracting out is not exclusive to the public sector. Private sector firms 'discovered' contracting out long before their public sector counterparts, and their patronage of contractors during the 1950s and 1960s helped many fledgling service industries prepare themselves for the explosion of work which occurred in the 1970s. Today more and more private companies rely on outside firms to provide services they once provided themselves. Increasing specialisation of labour and more competitive pricing in service industries has meant that firms can often get better quality outputs at lower prices in the marketplace. Uncertainties in the economic environment have caused many firms to shy away from long-term investment decisions and to rely instead upon short-term contracts to meet their immediate operational needs. These arrangements offer them increased flexibility and enable them to react much more quickly to changes in the commercial environment.

The recent growth of contracting out in the public sector has had somewhat different origins. Though the immediate reasons for contracting out have generally been framed in economic or financial terms, the underlying cause has generally been dissatisfaction with internal provision. As the welfare state has grown, problems with internal provision have been magnified to the point where the benefits of direct provision no longer outweigh the costs associated with it in all situations. This has prompted interest in a variety of private approaches to the delivery of public services, including grants, subsidies, franchises and contracting out. All act to reduce reliance on internal provision and thus minimise the diseconomies of scale inherent in large bureaucratic organisations. Although these private approaches are unlikely to present a long-term challenge to in-house provision as the most popular means of public service delivery, they are important developments both for academics and municipal administrators.

The growth of contracting out is a particularly significant development as it raises serious questions of accountability and control within local communities. It is not immediately obvious, for example, how the electorate's wishes can be translated into action by a newly elected administration that is forced to honour the contracts of its predecessors and therefore has no control over the level or type of services provided. Nor is it clear what effect the agreement between authority and contractor will have on the former's ability to react to citizen complaints or changes in citizen needs. Contracting out also raises questions about the replacement of the public service ethic with the private sector profit objective. Profit is a complex and curious motive; it gives firms an indirect incentive to do good work (to keep the contract), but it also gives them a direct incentive to do a job as quickly and as cheaply as possible (to cut costs and maximize profit) and may open the door to bribery and corruption of public officials. The effect that the introduction of the profit motive will have upon the quality of service provided at the local level is unclear.

In summary, the worldwide growth of contracting out poses very interesting questions for democratic theory and its development in the British context poses some compelling ones. Whereas contracting out in the US, Europe and Japan has developed in a haphazard fashion in response to local needs and priorities, contracting out in Britain has grown up as a central plank of the national government's privatisation programme. It has been the subject of several major political initiatives and has been forced on locally-based public agencies, nearly all of whom resent increased central government intervention in their affairs. This unusual treatment of the issue, documented in the following chapter, helps to explain why contracting out has been considerably more controversial in Britain than in any other industrialised country.

2 Conservative Policy: Development and Dimensions

The popularity of contracting out as an alternative means of public sector service delivery grew dramatically between 1980 and 1985 in Britain. In local government, the number of authorities relying on private firms for provision of major cleansing services jumped from two to two dozen. In the NHS, the number of hospitals relying on outside cleaners rose from 40 to well over 100. And in central government, where the volume of contracted out services had been stable for many years, the number and value of such contracts grew considerably over this period. Central government and industry forecasts suggest even more dramatic increases in the frequency of contracting out between 1985 and 1990.

This transformation is remarkable, as methods of service provision have traditionally been resistant to rapid change over time. But in the context of the Thatcher administration's radical programme of privatisation, the transformation appears less exceptional. It is simply the result of one among many government initiatives designed to increase competition and efficiency in public service provision. Like other recent Conservative initiatives, competitive tendering and contracting out have developed at a speed that few would have thought possible in the 'consensus' environment of post-war British politics prior to the election of the Conservative Government in 1979. The following pages examine the origins of contracting out policy in three separate areas – the NHS, local authorities and central government – and consider the general political climate which has produced the 'tendering boom'.

The origins of contracting out

Private firms have always assisted government agencies in carrying out their duties to the public. Up until the end of World War II, however, most of the contracts awarded to the private sector involved fairly specialised or unusual services that the government was not competent to perform. In the 1950s, this situation changed due to the shortage of labour caused by successive governments' full employment policies. Public sector agencies found it difficult to recruit operational and managerial staff to perform key services and began to turn to private sector firms who were able to meet staffing needs. This period, the first in which private firms were asked to undertake work that the public sector could itself have carried out, really marks the beginning of contracting out as we know it today. Records from this period are patchy, however, and most of the firms which held these contracts have long been out of business; as a result, the total value of this early 'privatised' work is not known. But it is clear that a number of contracts for private refuse collection and waste disposal existed, based primarily in the South-east, and that the situation existing during the 1950s was dramatically different to that which exists today. Trade unions in local government had full recognition rights from contractors, and the rates of pay and conditions of service applying to contractors' staff were determined by the National Joint Council for Local Authority Services Manual Workers. There are no indications that the situation was politically contentious and no evidence of competition between in-house employees and external contractors.

In the 1960s, contractual work in local authorities dried up, possibly as a result of a more fluid employment situation. Work in health authorities, however, continued to expand with small but significant numbers of contracts won by catering, cleaning and laundry service firms. Indications of their success can be found in references offered by companies to health authorities during the mid-1960s. The Crothall Company's promotional literature, for example, claimed that the firm had provided cleaning services to hospitals in the UK since 1961 and that it had already established itself as the dominant company in the field. Both claims were true: by 1967, Crothall had contracts at 32 hospitals in the UK while less than a dozen other hospitals were served by Crothall's competitors. Similar inroads were made by catering contractors during this period and, by 1965, at least 34 hospital contracts were in private hands. The overall increase in private sector penetration primarily reflected growing competition in key service industries, but it was also a function of personnel management problems. Authorities continued to find it difficult to recruit supervisory staff, and many hoped private contractors would relieve burdens on existing hospital managers.

Contractors were rarely if ever cheaper than in-house provision, commanding premiums on the basis that they were more convenient than in-house labour due to recruitment problems. Many of these private arrangements were 'management contracts' whereby the contractor provided managerial staff only and workers remained employees of the NHS, retaining NHS wages and conditions of service. In some cases authorities contracted for labour as well as management, and NHS employees were 'rehired' by the contractor. Conditions under the private firms were generally slightly better than they were in the NHS, which served to compound hospitals' recruitment problems. In 1964, the Chairman of the Hospital Domestic Administrators Association, herself a domestic superintendent, wrote in the *British Hospital and Social Service Journal*,

> Any hospital management committee who may be considering a cleaning contract because of the difficulty of obtaining domestic workers should consider possible side-effects very carefully. Some contractors acknowledge that they pay wages higher than Whitley Council rates or offer variation and conditions of service that are not available to the hospitals. This position could have a disruptive effect on the attitude of other sections of the ancillary staff: workers today are quick to resent inequality. It is also possible that a contractor offering favourable terms or conditions will overcome a labour shortage in a particular hospital by attracting workers from other hospitals.[1]

The first major inroads made by private contractors into the public sector occurred in 1968 but, interestingly, did not involve either local government or the health service. Central government departments were asked to find private contractors to take over their cleaning services. The request came from Harold Wilson's Government, which saw contracting out as a convenient way to make cuts in the public sector workforce in the aftermath of the 1967 devaluation. Private cleaners were brought in for all but the smallest offices, saving an estimated 35 000 jobs and £500 000. Whereas previously contractors had held under 10 per cent of this market, this exercise allowed private cleaning firms to establish a dominant position in servicing government departments which they have maintained ever since.

But progress made by contractors in government departments was exceptional, and the early and mid-1970s saw an overall decline in the volumes of public sector work being offered to private contractors. The Heath Government's passion for consolidation reinforced trends toward the creation of big, centralised hospitals, which gradually eroded the market for those contractors who had been providing services to antiquated and rural hospitals. Of more immediate damage, however, was the 1974 reorganisation of the health service. In establishing new lines of 'functional management' within the NHS, the Conservative Government assured a strong voice in decision-making for managers of specialist departments at all levels of health administration. This they exercised to their advantage, particularly when it came to investment decisions, to ensure the viability and competitiveness of the in-house service. Thanks to these managers' investment in new equipment and training, work awarded to private contractors shrank significantly over the eight years in which functional management existed in the NHS. When the next reorganisation of the health service occurred in 1982, only four firms held contracts in either catering or cleaning sectors.

In 1978, the year before the Conservatives took power, the presence of contractors in both local government and the health service went virtually unnoticed. Very few contractors thought public sector work would grow significantly, and none would have predicted the explosion that was about to occur. But by the time of the General Election in May of 1979, the seeds of the present controversy had already been sown. The 'winter of discontent' had brought chaos to local authority and NHS services, and had convinced Conservative politicians at both local and national levels of the need to find ways to prevent such disruptions in the future. The birth of contracting out, or more specifically the first use of it as a party political weapon, was imminent.

Development of the NHS initiative

The Conservative Party was brought into government in 1979 on a wave of dissatisfaction with the Labour Government's handling of industrial action throughout the previous winter. Hospital strike action by ancillary workers featured prominently in the chaos – the first time since 1973 that major industrial action had been undertaken by this group. This strike action had two important effects. It hardened the new Government's resolve to limit trade union power and widened the public's support for such measures; secondly, it drew attention to the possibility of using private contractors, particularly in those hospitals that had been forced to rely on private firms as a stopgap measure for service delivery during the strike.

However, this was not the first time that the advantages of private contracting had been brought to the Conservatives' attention; the earliest lobbying efforts occurred well before the 1979 General Election. At the 1978 Conservative Party conference, the Conservative Medical Society presented a paper in favour of contracting out. Written by Stanley Balfour Lynn, Chairman of an American hospital management company, it argued that at least twenty-five services could be taken out of the NHS and carried out more efficiently by private enterprise. The same arguments were put forward by certain industry trade associations when they met with Gerard Vaughan, then Minister of Health, in October 1979. Laundry and linen service associations, the Association of British Launderers and Cleaners (ABLC) and the British Textile Rental Association (BTRA), were particularly active at this early stage.

The associations received encouragement from the Government early in 1980. In May of that year, Vaughan published the first in a series of circulars on the virtues of contracting out. Entitled *Revised Guidance on Contractual Arrangements and Cooperative Schemes*, it suggested that health authorities should consider ways of contracting out building maintenance, security, catering, computing, some types of transport, and laundry services. Authorities were encouraged to make contractual arrangements with private hospitals and nursing homes and to give financial help to capital projects outside the NHS. The circular noted that independent health facilities should be integrated within the NHS planning process, possibly by way of joint purchasing and training arrangements. Although this circular merely restated what had been suggested in government circulars as early as 1972, it revealed a newfound commitment.[2] It noted that, although details were out for consultation, the policy itself was firm and authorities should proceed with it immediately. Following publication of the document, Vaughan held meetings with representatives of the contract cleaning industry at which he both inquired whether any progress had been made by the companies as a result of direct commercial marketing and asked how prepared they were for wide-scale contracting out of domestic services. The Government's keen interest in competitive tendering, even at this early stage, was obvious.

In August of 1981, Vaughan wrote again to regional and area health authorities in an attempt to review what progress had been made in this area. His letter indicated that he was unhappy with the rebuffs accorded to commercial contractors by health authorities and noted that cleaning companies had received particularly hostile receptions. Other services singled out for attention included laundry, building and vehicle maintenance, and transport. The months following circulation of this letter saw increased lobbying activity on the part of contractors. Major service firms and their trade associations made use of the health service press to increase visibility among authorities and continued to push the DHSS for a formal commitment to contracting out in at least part of the NHS.

The contractors' campaign was considerably strengthened by the publication of *Reservicing Health* by the Adam Smith Institute in 1982. Written by Michael Forsyth, then a Conservative member of Westminster City Council, the pamphlet argued strongly in favour of using private contractors to provide 'hotel services' to the NHS.[3] It argued that the wide variations in the cost of in-house services across the country indicated inefficiencies in many areas, and that a reduction in the costs of these services would free funds for patient care. Forsyth noted that even relatively small savings in this sector (10 per cent) would allow major increases in capital expenditure (50 per cent). He argued further that ancillary or 'hotel' services were not related to the main purpose of the NHS and that private contractors could undertake these services more cheaply due to more efficient and less restrictive work practices. In support of his arguments, he cited numerous overseas examples of contracting out for ancillary services.

By this point, the DHSS had begun its own study of the feasibility of contracting out cleaning services. Interest in this particular service grew out of discussions between Lord Trenchard, then defence minister responsible for support services, and Geoffrey Finsberg, his counterpart in the DHSS, about the Ministry of Defence's recent experience of contracting out cleaning at its establishments. Motivated by a Rayner Scrutiny (a high-level investigation into the efficiency of the department), the MOD had undertaken an ambitious programme of contracting out domestic services at all of its sites including nine hospitals. In 1980, cleaning at 75 large sites had been 'privatised'; another 125 sites followed in 1981. Despite a concerted attempt to divide up the work between large and small contractors, the lion's share of the work was awarded to the four major firms in the field. They received contracts valued well in excess of £1 million; in return the MOD achieved savings ranging from 16 to 67 per cent.

Contact between Trenchard and Finsberg led to the launching of a study to determine the relevance of the MOD experience to the NHS. Staffed by DHSS administrators and external economic advisers, the study team's brief was to assess the costs and benefits of external provision of cleaning services in hospitals. The group's findings were not particularly encouraging for ministers: they suggested that the MOD experience was not directly relevant to the DHSS, partly due to the cultural differences between civilian and military hospitals but also because the centralisation of the MOD hospital network had simplified implementation of the contracting out policy. It questioned the savings that contracting out would bring to the DHSS, by noting that no adequate cost base for assessing current efficiency levels existed and that the cost of redundancy payments in the NHS would seriously reduce the percentage savings suggested by the MOD experience. The study report also highlighted the dangers associated with using private contractors on a large scale, suggesting that inexperienced staff could increase the risk of cross-infection and that the new staff's lack of institutional loyalty would result in reduced service standards. It cautioned that loss-leaders could be used to get rid of the in-house force, thus establishing a monopoly position for the contractor, and that the profit motive would require adoption of lowest-cost methods. To complicate matters, the report suggested, the tendering process itself was costly and no one really knew if the contract cleaning industry had the capacity to handle significant amounts of NHS work.[4]

The serious doubts raised by this study did not dissuade the Government from pushing ahead with its initiative, nor did the warnings from contractors that small scale mandatory contracting out at pilot hospitals would be less risky than a large scale tendering exercise. By the early summer of 1982, a draft circular had been prepared asking authorities to compare external to in-house prices and to write tender documents on a pilot basis. Regional authorities were to ensure that districts received tenders from at least three private companies; to facilitate this, the department included a list of potential bidders. Value Added Tax (VAT) was to be omitted from cost calculations because 'it was not a proper cost to the Exchequer'.[5]

This first draft circular was never published, and the details of its handling remain something of a mystery. Leaked to the *Health and Social Service Journal*, its contents aroused strong opposition from regional administrators. Soon after this, Norman Fowler (Secretary of State for Social Services) denied the circular's existence and administrators assumed it had been withdrawn. However, in July, the DHSS denied having withdrawn it and stated that administrators would be consulted before its scheduled publication in September. This incident aroused the antagonism of personnel throughout the health service as neither the members nor the administrators of regional or district health authorities had been consulted prior to the leak of the draft circular. Their anger was expressed clearly in the health service press, which criticised the Government for listening only to the needs of the contractors. But the circular did not appear as expected in September. No definite reasons for its delay were given, but it is likely that the DHSS did not consider the middle of a major pay dispute a suitable time to bring out such a controversial document and hoped that an additional period would allow the strong feelings expressed in the health service press to die down.

The draft circular was finally issued on 17 February 1983. It asked all health authorities to go out to tender for certain ancillary services, noting that this measure was a response to the lack of effort made by authorities to test private sector offerings, and announced the Government's plans to refund VAT paid by authorities on private sector contracts. In introducing the circular,

Norman Fowler emphasised the savings which competitive tendering would allow and gave assurances that contractors had the capacity to handle NHS work on a large scale. Other DHSS ministers highlighted the additional benefits contracting out would bring, such as the use of local firms and the creation of better community relationships for the hospital.

The measure evoked such strong feelings from health authorities that the DHSS granted a two-week extension of the six-week consultation period specified in the circular. The response from the health service during, and indeed after, this period was unequivocal. One *Health and Social Service Journal* editorial noted:

> a blind prejudice against the health unions and a somewhat ill-defined desire to increase managerial efficiency are the motivating forces behind this piece of lunacy ... At a time when the health services are already stretched to the limit, it is unreasonable to expect health managers to receive with equanimity the gross burden which this circular confers.[6]

Although the content of the circular itself clearly annoyed administrators, it was the lack of serious consultation undertaken by the DHSS that concerned them most. Many felt that the two-month consultation period had been designed to allow minimum consideration of alternatives and prevent any real amendments to the draft circular. They recognised that the Government, confident of the capacity of contractors to undertake the work, had made up its mind to require services to be put to tender. This commitment was clearly articulated in the manifesto upon which the Conservatives successfully fought the General Election in June 1983. It stated that, 'to release more money for looking after patients, we will reduce the costs of administering the Health Service. We are asking health authorities to make the maximum possible savings by putting services like laundry, catering and hospital cleaning out to competitive tender.'[7]

Though it is likely that the Government had indeed made up its mind about the need for competitive tendering prior to issuing the draft circular, the statutory consultation period was of some value. According to one commentator, 'it taught ministers that health authorities were highly sceptical of the value of contracting out, and that if the policy was to make headway, exhortation would have to be replaced by coercion.'[8] As a result of this consultation period, the final directive emerged as a much stronger and specific document than that published in February. Three major changes were made to take account of likely resistance:

1   Efficiency savings would accumulate directly to individual authorities instead of going towards general 'patient care'. This would provide the financial incentive needed to motivate authorities to approach the tendering exercise seriously.
2   Authorities were asked to ensure that 'staff interests are kept informed'. The earlier document had suggested that staff should 'be fully consulted before a decision to [write] tenders is taken'. This change was probably a reaction to the intensity of trade union opposition.
3   Regional authorities were told to prepare timetables for the districts and services under their control and to submit them to the DHSS. This requirement, an attempt to prevent undue delays by recalcitrant authorities, replaced the Department's original suggestion that regional authorities should monitor progress and report to ministers during periodic regional reviews.

The outcome of these and other minor changes was Circular HC (83) 18, *Competitive Tendering in The Provision of Domestic, Catering and Laundry Services*, issued on 8 September 1983.[9] Districts were asked to test the cost effectiveness of cleaning, laundry and catering services by going out to tender for each of them within the next three years. Acceptance of the lowest tender was required, unless authorities were not satisfied as to the ability of the contractor to honour the terms of the contract. The circular was clear about the speed with which the process should be undertaken. District health authorities were told to submit timetables to regional offices by February 1984; regional authorities, in turn, were to submit their aggregate timetables to the DHSS two months later. The entire process was to be completed by the end of 1986.

The document threw in certain extra benefits for contractors. VAT was to be refunded on all ancillary service contracts with the private sector from 1 September 1983. Authorities were required to seek tenders for laundry services prior to investing more than £0.5

million to upgrade facilities. Additional services such as housekeeping, ward supervision, and linen rental were cited as 'optional areas' where substantial savings might also be made. In addition, the final government circular warned against prejudicing the outcome of the tendering process in favour of the in-house staff. It suggested that the costs of making the existing staff redundant be amortised over the lifetime of the contract (usually three to five years) and cautioned that contractors' prices should not be used as a baseline for amending the value of the in-house bid after tenders have been received. It also asked authorities not to stipulate detailed staffing requirements or make other arrangements which might inhibit the competitive freedom of the contractor.

This final directive met with no greater enthusiasm than the previous draft circular had seven months earlier. Authority members and administrators were reluctant to undertake further change and hasten further confrontation. Even those who agreed with the principles behind it felt that the timing of the circular – coming as it did on the back of reorganisation and a major industrial dispute – was appalling. Scepticism about the policy was widespread and many predicted that its implementation would be both complex and controversial, as indeed it has been (see Chapter 6).

Development of the local authority initiative

Like their NHS counterparts, local authority services had been contracted out for many years before private provision became a controversial issue. In both sectors, industrial action during the winter of 1978–9 stimulated interest in alternative methods of service provision and highlighted the benefits of private delivery systems. Whereas in the NHS this interest was translated into central government action, the earliest contracting out initiatives in the local authority sector were made by a small number of Conservative-controlled local authorities. The following section examines first the events occurring at local and national levels between 1979 and 1983, and then the interplay between central and local activity in late 1983 and 1984 which led to the publication of a consultative document on compulsory tendering by the Department of Environment in February 1985.

Local activity

The origins of the present competitive tendering debate in local authorities can be traced back to the 'winter of discontent' in 1978–9. Local authority manual workers were at the forefront of industrial action and, for many, the sights and smells of the refuse collection strike are among the clearest memories of that winter. Prolonged action by refuse collectors and street cleaners brought home to many authorities the power that manual workers wielded over delivery of key services. Some councils were forced to employ private contractors during the strike to clear away the growing mountains of household and commercial refuse. Together with a growing realisation of the inflexibility of internal service provision, this experience led to widespread interest in both contracting out and competitive tendering.

The first to express more than academic interest in contracting out was Conservative-controlled Southend District Council. Members of the Council had for some time felt hampered by restrictive practices in both refuse and street cleaning services. The 'task and finish' scheme in operation, which allowed workers to go home whenever the job was finished, was considered outdated and expensive but despite repeated attempts the Council had not been able to remove it. The events of 1978–9 brought to a boil the simmering frustration of Council members. Like workers in other areas, Southend's manual employees took strike action in accordance with national policy. But they ignored the general 'return to work' advice from the unions and stayed out on strike until a wage settlement had been agreed. Their defiance of the general union approach moved the Council to take action.

Southend's decision to investigate competitive tendering may have been influenced by nearby Maldon District, which had previously used private contractors in certain parts of its refuse collection area. In any case, the Council proceeded cautiously, aware of the implications of any decision for industrial relations. It devoted four months to a detailed study of its needs, during which time negotiations with the unions continued. But negotiations did not prevent the unions expressing their opposition to such a move. The Transport and General Workers Union (T&GWU) took the lead with a series of demonstrations and marches aimed at preventing the Council from going ahead with the tendering process.

Prominent figures in the Labour Party came out to Southend to support the union cause and media coverage was extensive.

Union action did little to dissuade the Council, however. Ten firms were chosen from the many that had responded to the Council's advertisement in the *Southend Echo*; four were ultimately shortlisted. The in-house tender, which made capital but no staffing cuts, was also shortlisted. Exclusive Cleaning was eventually awarded the contract on the basis of a bid which offered projected annual savings of £492 920. Although this figure was later shown to be wrong, due to a miscalculation of the costs of servicing new property, Exclusive began the Southend refuse and street cleaning contract – very much in the public eye – in April 1981.[10]

The Southend contract caused reverberations throughout the local authority world. Other councils, concerned about the efficiency of their refuse services followed the progress of Southend's contract closely. Some were not satisfied that the potential savings would be achieved and suggested that Southend's claims were grossly exaggerated; others were more readily convinced.[11] One of the authorities which was particularly impressed by Southend's achievement was the London Borough of Wandsworth. Like Southend, Wandsworth had a history of poor industrial relations with its manual workers and a council determined to do something about it. Less than a year after Southend's contract began, in 1982, Wandsworth went out to tender for its street cleaning service and awarded it to Pritchard Services. This incident aroused minimal union protest and Wandsworth Council proceeded to go out to tender three months later for its refuse collection service. The unions soon realised what they were up against and organised a major campaign of industrial action which virtually brought a halt to all council activities in April of 1982. The confrontation in Wandsworth, documented in detail in Chapter 7, received significant coverage in the national and local media.

While the events in Wandsworth frightened some councils away from competitive tendering, they convinced others of the need to weaken the unions' hold over local government services. Throughout 1982, spokesmen from Southend and Wandsworth were invited to address a variety of professional meetings and the topic of contracting out received increasing attention in the local government press. It was not long before other authorities followed in

Southend's footsteps and put one or both of their major cleansing services out to competitive tender. All councils which undertook tendering exercises at this early stage were Conservative-controlled. Some were staunch ideological supporters of contracting out; others were looking for financial savings and, receiving no concessions from their in-house labour force, felt forced to go to tender. Nearly all had a history of industrial relations problems, which helps to explain why every one of these early exercises resulted in victory for the contractors and defeat for the direct labour force.

National activity

While Southend was soldiering through the tendering process, the Conservative Government was putting through its first competitive tendering legislation. The Local Government Planning and Land Act (1980) began life as a consultative paper which was issued in 1979. Suggestions contained in this document affected a wide range of local government activities, and included one set of proposals concerning increased efficiency of councils' direct labour organisations. These proposals suggested that efficiency improvements could be achieved by two methods: targets for the rate of return on capital and mandatory competitive tendering. An overall rate of return on capital of 5 per cent would be required for each category of work; failure to achieve this for three successive years could result in the withdrawal of the authority's power to undertake such work and closure of the direct labour organisation (DLO). In addition, competitive tendering would be required for a certain percentage of work above a given volume. Threshold values and tendering percentages varied according to the category of building work.[12]

Opposition to these proposals was strong, though it was confined to local government circles. The unions argued that these measures would lead to a decline in standards, as delays and defects would be more likely to occur, and that awarding contracts to the private sector increased the possibility of corruption among local officials. The requirement for a return on capital, they noted, would demand closure of depots and lead to a less responsive service. Local authority associations supported this view and argued that higher costs would result from the need for additional surveyors, technical officers and maintenance inspectors. However, little heed was paid to most of the concerns raised by local government interests and in November 1980 these measures came into force under the Local Government Planning and Land Act (1980).

Local authorities were reluctant to embrace the spirit of this portion of the Act, and several councils devised ways to avoid awarding contracts to the private sector. Work was arranged so that no contractor could realistically tender for it; in a few cases all work was put out simultaneously as a package. There is some evidence that certain authorities adjusted their in-house tender prices according to those submitted by contractors, and that other authorities were prone to ignoring outside tenders altogether. Although such recalcitrant behaviour was the exception rather than the rule, it did not go unnoticed. The building industry's trade association, the National Federation of Building Trades Employers, complained to the Government about the number of councils who were clearly manipulating the tendering process to achieve political objectives, and argued that it was the Government's duty to prevent this. In general, however, pressure from the Department of the Environment (DOE) did force most councils to take the new legislation seriously. Within three years the Act had led to widespread reductions in direct labour workforces, improved efficiency among many DLOs, and the total closure of others.[13]

The Government's commitment to the principles of competitive tendering was strengthened by the publication of *Reservicing Britain* by the Adam Smith Institute in 1980. Like its sister document published two years later, *Reservicing Health*, it was written by Michael Forsyth and extolled the virtues of contracting out. However this pamphlet was specifically directed at local authority services. It suggested that Britain was somewhat backward in its heavy reliance on publicly-provided services and drew heavily on US examples, quantifying and describing the savings which various American cities had made through contracting out refuse collection. It also listed a variety of continental and UK municipalities in which private contractors had been used successfully in place of direct labour.

Reservicing Britain contained three separate arguments. The first concerned the lack of accountability which then existed in local authority services. Forsyth argued that the public sector bureaucracy operated in its own interest and that private contractors, contrary to popular belief, were likely to be more accountable to the general public than an in-house service. A second argument contained in the pamphlet, one which was later repeated in *Reservicing Health,* focused on the fact that there was no need for most locally-based services to be run publicly. The third and final argument in favour of contracting out concerned the superior efficiency of private contractors. According to the pamphlet, the public sector was uneconomic because 'the combination of a protected monopoly position with a claim on tax revenues removes all incentive for efficiency of operation and quality of service.'[14] Only the private sector, Forsyth concluded, provided public accountability and control combined with efficiency and responsiveness to consumer needs.

Reservicing Britain was mailed to every local councillor in the country and circulated within the Conservative Party. Regardless of its obvious biases, it immediately became an authoritative source for proponents of contracting out at both national and local authority levels and secured much of the intellectual foundation for the re-evaluation of local authority services that was about to occur. While the Adam Smith Institute's pamphlet offered public evidence of the direction of Conservative thinking, the DOE was quietly continuing its own research into the efficiency of local government services. Not long after the introduction of the Local Government Planning and Land Act Act (1980), the Department commissioned management consultants Coopers and Lybrand to undertake a comprehensive examination of local authority service provision. The firm's findings, published in September 1981 in a document entitled *Service Provision and Pricing in Local Government,* furnished the Government with the evidence it needed to justify stronger control over service provision at local level.

Service Provision and Pricing noted that local authority politics frequently interfered with appropriate solutions to service problems. It suggested that authorities were isolated from good advice and ideas and, as a result, often relied on unsatisfactory approaches to costs and pricing. They also employed unimaginative and deficient tendering methods, and were generally sceptical of the virtues of contracting out. The report recommended a general improvement in the processes surrounding service provision. It highlighted the need for better identification of costs and for reviews of existing bonus schemes, and suggested that authorities might increase flexibility by introducing competitive tendering into a wide variety of functions.[15] But the Coopers and Lybrand report did *not* wholeheartedly endorse private contracting as an alternative to in-house provision. It examined both councils that had contracted out as well as those that had rejected private contractors and chosen to retain an in-house capability. In finding that local needs were best met in a variety of ways, Coopers and Lybrand cast a vote for both flexibility in approach and the retention of local discretion.[16]

By the time the Coopers and Lybrand report was made public, the Government (or more specifically, parts of it) was actively encouraging local authorities to contract out. Treasury ministers were particularly enthusiastic, with Leon Brittan (Chief Secretary to the Treasury) acting as his department's main protagonist. In 1982, he wrote to all departments concerned with local authorities asking what progress had been or could be made in contracting out local services. Other departments, clearly less enthusiastic than the Treasury, responded that the matter should be left to local authorities. Despite this advice, the drive towards competitive tendering for local services continued to gather momentum among senior Conservative politicians.

Local and national activities merge

It was not until late 1983, after the re-election of the Conservative Government, that developments at local authority and national levels began to affect one another significantly. The Conservative election manifesto itself noted that many authorities had saved money by going to tender and stated, 'we shall encourage every possible saving by this policy.' Although there was no evidence at that time of the exact form this encouragement would take (indeed a Government spokesman confirmed in July 1983 that no legislation was planned), the election itself indirectly provided the necessary stimulus for action. It brought into Parliament two of the chief protagonists in the debate – Michael Forsyth and Christopher Chope. Their presence in the House of Commons helped to transform what had been a piecemeal assault on the power of local authority manual workers into a Government commitment to enforce mandatory competitive tendering.

Michael Forsyth had already been instrumental in eliciting a Government commitment to competitive tendering in the NHS through his pamphlet *Reservicing Health*. Both this and *Reservicing Britain* were produced for the Adam Smith Institute while Forsyth was a Westminster City Councillor. During this same period Forsyth set up his own public relations firm, Michael Forsyth Associates, which was active in lobbying for increased acceptance of contracting out. The Pritchard Services Group was among the earliest clients of Forsyth Associates; later the major textile maintenance trade associations – the ABLC and BTRA – also became clients.

Christopher Chope came to Parliament through a different route. During his time as leader of Wandsworth Borough Council, the Council privatised refuse collection, street cleaning and gardening. Chope survived both media and trade union onslaughts to emerge with an even greater commitment to contracting out, and it did not take long for him to become one of the chief proponents of contracting out in Parliament. Although he was not retained as a consultant by a particular company, his determination and persistence were considerably greater than those of many MPs who established formal relationships with contracting firms. His questions on the floor of the House monitored the Government's progress in encouraging contracting out, beginning late in 1983 and continuing at frequent intervals until a tentative commitment to legislation was made.

Early in its second term, the Government was not particularly eager to embrace mandatory competitive tendering in local authorities. Throughout the first few months of 1984, ministers evaded Chope's questions and stated that they were considering what measures might be taken in this direction. In March, the Prime Minister confirmed her reluctance to legislate because 'it would be a very technical measure to put through the House.'[17] The Government's reluctance probably stemmed from several factors. Relationships between central and local government were already at an all-time low due to ratecapping and other restrictions. Patrick Jenkin, Secretary of State for the Environment, appeared to be less enthusiastic about such drastic measures than Norman Fowler had been at the DHSS. Furthermore, preliminary evidence had begun to show that the NHS tendering initiative was running into substantial problems.

But the spring of 1984 saw increased pressure put upon the Government by its own backbenchers. In April, Christopher Chope introduced a Ten-Minute Rule Bill which stated 'that this House believes that in the interest of obtaining better value for money, local authorities should be required by law to submit to competitive tendering a wider range of their functions and services.'[18] Ten-minute rule bills, devices used to publicise an issue on the floor of the House, are not debated formally and ministers and their parliamentary private secretaries traditionally refrain from voting. But support for Chope's bill was such that eighteen parliamentary private secretaries broke with tradition and voted in favour of it. Reports at the time suggested that ministers themselves had to be restrained from walking into the lobbies. Although the bill lost on a two-line whip by a margin of three (Ayes 167, Nays 170), Chope had succeeded in demonstrating to the Government the overwhelming support given to compulsory tendering by Conservative backbenchers.

In October 1984, Chope and others were rewarded with a commitment from the Government that formal action to encourage contracting out would be taken. It was not until February 1985, however, that the intentions of the Government were finally made clear with the publication of *Competition in the Provision of Local Authority Services* by the Department of the Environment, the Scottish Office, and the Welsh Office. This consultative document outlined the Government's plans to make competitive tendering mandatory from 1987 for a variety of local authority services including refuse collection and street cleaning, internal building cleaning, ground and vehicle maintenance, and catering. The approach taken by the DOE very closely resembled that of the Local Government Planning and Land Act (1980). Authorities would be required to keep separate accounts for each type of work and to achieve a financial target to be specified by the Secretary of State, who would also be given the power to select appropriate areas for tendering.

This DOE document was much stronger than that issued by the DHSS in February 1983 and indicated that the Government had learned numerous lessons from the mistakes made in formulating both the 1980 local authority DLO legislation and the final NHS tendering circular. It recognised that there are significant differences in the needs and requirements of individual services (something it failed to recognise in the case of NHS ancillary services) and suggested that phasing-in periods, contract length, and exemptions should vary from area to area. It allowed for a longer consultation period (ten weeks) than on either previous occasion and asked for advice on nearly all of the practical issues involved. While local government officials took this as a sign that 'the DOE has little practical ideal of how to proceed', such broad requests for advice could alternatively be construed as an attempt to avoid the criticism heaped on the DHSS for failing to give public sector administrators any real chance to air their viewpoints two years earlier.[19]

Implementation is another area in which important lessons appear to have been learned. The circular itself stated that the measures which were open to the Secretary of State to punish recalcitrant authorities under the 1980 Act (for example, closure of the in-house labour force) were too draconian and that a more flexible approach was required. Significant space was devoted to outlining the new powers which would fall to the Secretary of State. In addition to selecting services for tender and financial targets, he or she would have significant scope to take action against authorities who 'negate or limit' the results of competition and would have the power to nullify any term or condition not directly related to performance. Where suspicions of an unfair in-house win existed, the Secretary of State could direct the relevant authority to repeat the entire tendering process and, in cases of extreme 'disobedience', could close the authority's direct labour organisation.

Reaction to the consultative paper within the local authority community has been predictably hostile. Local administrators feel at a serious disadvantage in competing with the private sector. They cannot compete on pay, due to nationally agreed pay scales, and they cannot compete on 'profit' margins, due to the Secretary of State's return on capital targets. Most discriminatory, they say, is the fact that they are out of business after losing just one tender. But it is not just the competitive position that bothers these officials. Most feel that a specified rate of return on capital is 'a completely artificial proposition', as organisations have different requirements for capital.[20] All are afraid that too many restrictions will be placed upon them, and that the Secretary of State's powerful role as witness, judge and jury will allow for subjective definitions of unreasonable behaviour.

Criticism of the competitive tendering circular has not, however, been confined to the local authority press. *The Financial Times*, generally sympathetic to government policy if not to the details of its implementation, published a strongly worded editorial immediately following the circular's publication. In it, the paper argued that central government had gone beyond the bounds of its authority by proposing to set financial targets for local authority services. Authorities had too many financial targets as it was and the Government's emphasis on the lowest tender was likely to be counterproductive, just as it had been in the NHS. The editorial noted that

> the role of central government ought to be to set out rational arguments and make recommendations to local authorities. Most authorities . . . already have an incentive to achieve greater value for money but they deserve some flexibility in how they achieve it. The idea of the Secretary of State setting an ever greater number of financial targets for authorities – such as the current cost rate of return – is unappealing. Councils should be left more autonomy at this micro level.[21]

During the ten-week consultative period, the Department of Environment received approximately 450 deputations from interested parties. As expected, the trade unions and local authority associations came out strongly against the new measures; so too did the Labour Party, whose Opposition Environment Spokesman called the DOE circular 'a charter for rip-off merchants to make a killing out of the ratepayers'.[22] On the other side, contractors unanimously threw their support behind the proposed measures. Their only reservations concerned the scope of the initiative: most stated that there should be no exemptions from the tendering process and that a greater number of services, including laundry and linen rental, should be added to the DOE's list. It appears that the only unanticipated responses came from local Conservative politicians and councils, several of whom submitted strongly worded responses condemning the unprecedented level of interference in their affairs. It is as yet unclear what impact their misgivings will have upon the fate of mandatory tendering, still scheduled to appear on the 1986–7 legislative agenda.

Development of the central department initiative

The Government's enthusiasm for competitive tendering has not been limited to locally-based agencies. Since 1980, it has encouraged contracting out and competitive tendering in central government, most specifically in nationalised industries and central departments. Nationalised industries have contracted out many services for years; British Rail experimented with contract catering, the National Coal Board awarded a major workwear rental contract to a private firm, and many others have developed considerable experience with contract cleaning. The Government appears satisfied that these organisations will continue to employ private contractors where it is deemed to be cost-effective. As a result, central departments – operating in a less commercial environment than nationalised industries – have become the sole focus of what can be considered a third competitive tendering initiative. Although this initiative is more limited in its scope and has received less media attention than those in the NHS and local authorities, it is interesting insofar as it confirms the Government's wholehearted commitment to contracting out.

When the Conservative Government arrived in Whitehall in 1979, it found numerous departmental services already contracted out. Cleaning and maintenance were primarily undertaken by outside contractors, a legacy of the Wilson initiative in the late 1960s. In addition, each department had contracted out numerous specialist services – some unique to its area of operation. These varied from computer and management consultancy to more obscure areas, such as road design and seed testing. As with local and health authorities, Government departments found it easier in certain areas to tap private sector expertise than to develop their own. The first evidence of any desire to increase the amount of contracting out within departments appeared in 1980, when the Prime Minister announced in Parliament that it was the Government's policy to transfer work out of departments where this was 'commensurate with sound management and good value for money for the taxpayer'. At a meeting in December 1982, the Cabinet agreed that departments should aim to contract out much more of their work. Areas specified as potential targets included cleaning, building and ground maintenance, typing and reprographic work, vehicle maintenance and operation, debt collection, conveyance and training.

Throughout 1983 and 1984, the Treasury continued to publicise the advantages of contracting out departmental services. In mid-1984, the Chief Secretary highlighted the need to increase the scope of contracting out and was given approval to develop plans for a central department tendering initiative. His suggestions, put forward early the following year, received Cabinet approval and were made public in March 1985. Departments were to maximise opportunities for competitive tendering and contracting out, and top management systems (designed to highlight the relationship between departmental objectives and resources) were to be used to identify suitable areas. The Treasury accorded greatest potential to cleaning, laundry, catering, security guarding, and maintenance work, but noted that other areas which might be considered included messenger, library, postal and press-cutting services. These proposals requested that the original round of tendering be completed by April 1987, and that re-tendering occur on a regular basis.[23]

Following the announcement of this initiative, guidance on tendering and contracting out was sent to all Government departments. They were asked to prepare a summary of progress to date on contracting out and to suggest additional areas where contracting out might be undertaken. Because few departments keep a central record of service provision – indeed responsibility for contracting out is usually assumed locally – the task of preparing accurate and useful reports is expected to take some time. In the meantime, the Treasury has received estimates from most departments as to the percentage of services contracted out. These figures, shown in Table 2.1, indicate that central departments are well ahead of their local authority or NHS counterparts in terms of use of contractors.[24] Nearly half of all expenditure on five major ancillary services goes to private firms. Just under 85 per cent of all cleaning is done privately; similarly large percentages of maintenance, laundry and non-specialised catering work are contracted out.

Although contracting out has become the norm in many central department services, it does not appear that the switch from internal to external service provision has achieved more than a modest level of savings. Treasury officials estimate that the last five

TABLE 2.1 Contracting out in central departments (estimates for 1984–85)

Services	Total cost of services (£000's)	Cost of services contracted out (£000's)	%
Maintenance	116 000	95 000	83
Catering	115 000	9 100	8
Cleaning	69 200	58 400	84
Security guarding	66 500	5 000	8
Laundry	11 300	8 300	73
Total	378 000	175 800	46

Source: HM Treasury.

years of contracting out have seen aggregate departmental savings of approximately £100 million; although this figure appears large, it is actually a small proportion of the amount spent on departmental services over that time. An average savings figure of £20 million per year would constitute just over 5 per cent of this year's spending on these services.[25] Although these savings figures are no doubt acceptable to the Government, they pale in comparison with the percentage savings reported by health and local authorities.

However, contracting out of departmental services has been and continues to be linked closely to the Government's desire to reduce civil service manpower. In 1980, the Government announced an ambitious target for civil service manpower of 630 000 employees (a reduction of 10 per cent); this was achieved early in 1984 and new manpower targets were established. At regular intervals since the original announcement, the Treasury has written to departments asking for plans to reduce staff by up to 10 per cent before 1988. As early as December 1982, contracting out was suggested as one means of reducing staff and it appears that it has been fairly effective in doing so. Government estimates suggest that some 20 000 civil service jobs have been 'saved' over a five year period through contracting out; in 1984–5, 2 500 jobs disappeared through this process.[26] Further evidence of the close connection between contracting out and the Government's manpower objectives can be found in the structure of the new departmental tendering initiative. It is being directed and monitored by the manpower control division within the Treasury, much to the dismay of the officials involved. They suggest, and many other civil servants agree, that 'testing the market' should be seen as an efficiency exercise, not as a means to replace public sector labour with its private sector counterpart.

The staffing implications associated with competitive tendering in central departments have resulted in widespread opposition to contracting out from civil service unions. In some cases, the unions have mounted successful campaigns to delay or obstruct the privatisation process. In the case of the Heavy Goods Vehicle Testing Stations (HGVTS), for example, the unions' successful campaign to win generous transfer payments for HGVTS employees helped convince the Government to drop plans to turn the stations over to Lloyds' Register of Shipping. But victories have been few and far between and to date union opposition has had a very limited impact upon central government action. Although the civil service unions' campaign may become more vocal and more visible as a result of the Government's new departmental tendering policy, most union representatives recognise that the commitment behind the policy is overwhelming and are therefore likely to adopt a pragmatic attitude when it comes to cooperating in future tendering exercises.[27]

Analysing the tendering 'boom'

> Legislation [in the local authority sector] would never happen. It wouldn't be effective because the industry couldn't bid for it.

This comment was made in March 1984 by a senior Pritchard Services executive, and it was echoed by senior managers and directors of other major companies active in the local authority cleansing market. It illustrates nicely that the speed with which the Government has embraced this policy, first for the NHS and then for local government, has been remarkable and has astonished even the most optimistic of contractors. The rapid rise of competitive tendering is by no means unique among political phenomena; numerous initiatives have, at one time or another, gripped the imagination of policy-makers in such a way that the traditional 'agenda-building' process was bypassed. But the rise of competitive tendering can and should be distinguished from other 'policy booms'. The policy involved no new concepts or ideas; competitive tendering is a fairly routine process and one which had already been used by the public sector for many years. It is curious that such a widely-accepted procedure should so rapidly have become the focus of one minor and two major political initiatives.

Three specific aspects of the policy-making process are examined below. The first is the political environment, in particular the suitability of the policy for Conservative goals and objectives. The second aspect is the influence of political lobbyists and their proximity to the policy-making process. The third and final aspect considered is the weakness of those opposed to the tendering policy and their failure to present a realistic alternative. Though not the only factors which contributed to the rapid development of this issue, these topics provide a good introduction to the roles and motives of key political actors which are examined more closely in later chapters.

The ideological environment

> The real purpose of contracting out, as with state industry privatisation, is as much to weaken the unions' monopoly as to save money.[28]

This comment, made in *The Economist* in September 1983, aptly summarises the main attractions of competitive tendering to the Conservative Party. The numerous objectives that have been attributed to the policy generally fall into one of two categories: loosening the control of public sector unions or increasing competition and efficiency in the economy. The former is a covert set of objectives whilst the latter is overt. Competitive tendering is ideally suited to achieve *both* of these objectives simultaneously, and it is this simple fact which explains its widespread appeal to members of the Conservative Party.

Competitive tendering and contracting out fit into the Conservative Government's comprehensive and sustained attack upon trade union power. In particular, they offer scope for reducing the 'stranglehold' that the Party attributes to public sector unions. Competitive tendering alone, even when it does not lead to contracting out, serves to undermine the unions' position within authorities in two ways. First, it puts downward pressure on take-home pay, often through revisions of bonus schemes, thus under-mining the unions' credibility as 'protectors' of the worker. Secondly, because conditions of service are determined nationally, authorities are forced to make competitive savings through reductions in full-time numbers; this generally results in a decline in local union membership.

Contracting out intensifies these credibility and membership problems and has correspondingly more serious implications for the longer-term bargaining power of trade unions. It is extremely difficult for the trade unions to establish a solid presence within a contractor's workforce. Active union members are often reluctant to apply for jobs with a private firm; those that do apply stand a good chance of being turned down. The majority of workers hired by the contractor, either from the previous in-house workforce or from outside, are part-timers who tend to show less interest in union benefits than full-time workers. Perhaps the most substantial barrier to union activity comes from the contracting organisation itself; many contractors have refused union recognition unless one union can prove membership amongst a very high percentage of the workforce.

There are other factors which have contributed to Conservative support for competitive tendering as a means to weaken the public-sector unions. One has been its suitability as a method by which to undermine the position of 'ancillary' workers in the NHS and manual workers in local government. Both groups of workers are highly unionised and have historically led the union movement within their respective sectors. Many government supporters believe that silencing their voices, often thought of as disproportionately loud to their numbers, will serve to minimise the likelihood of further industrial action in each of these areas.

The second reason why competitive tendering has proved so popular within the Conservative Party has to do with its purported contribution toward economic efficiency. According to government supporters, the key objectives of the Conservative campaign – a reduction in the size of the state, increased competition to foster the operation of a free market, and tighter control over inflation – can all be furthered by the adoption of a mandatory tendering policy. Compulsory tendering introduces competition to government and thus helps to identify and reduce waste and inefficiency in the public sector. It is also a step forward toward contracting out –

the replacement of direct labour by external provision. Contracting out is desirable due to the natural superiority which laissez-faire proponents ascribe to the commercial sector. It also helps to increase the flexibility of the labour force and is seen as a useful tool in controlling inflation, one of the Government's primary concerns. Wage demands are lowered in the short term due to the poor remuneration offered by contractors, and in the longer term by the contractors' reluctance to pay above the minimum necessary to sustain their public image. The Public Sector Borrowing Requirement (PSBR), another potential source of inflationary pressure, is also brought under greater control as state agencies save money by putting contracts out to tender.

The strength of political lobbying

Although the speed with which competitive tendering developed as a political issue defies traditional coalition or agenda-building theory, a focus on lobbying is useful in highlighting the role of key supporters of the policy. Three sets of actors warrant particular attention – the contractors, the 'new right' ideologists and organisations, and Conservative Party members.

Private sector contractors and their trade associations played the foremost role in the lobbying campaign. At least three separate industries – catering, cleaning and textile maintenance – were involved in lobbying efforts in the early 1980s. Contracting firms fought their war on a number of separate battlefields. Party conferences and meetings with ministers were favoured, but they also used local authority and NHS exhibitions and seminars. Informal lobbying through Conservative Party channels helped secure some parliamentary support, but the most visible means by which contractors furthered their cause was through paid lobbyists. A few hired Michael Forsyth Associates to do their public relations work for them, while others went directly to the House of Commons to find suitable 'lobbyists' among the swollen back-benches of the Conservative Party. Some looked to civil servants to help them make inroads into the public sector. The Contract Cleaning and Maintenance Association (CCMA), for example, recruited John Hall from the Ministry of Defence; formerly in charge of monitoring the contracting out of cleaning in MOD buildings, Hall became the CCMA's Secretary-General. Another example involves Hospital Hygiene Services (HHS), a cleaning firm based in Yorkshire, which hired one of the DHSS administrators responsible for putting together the Department's competitive tendering circular.

The contracting out lobby received significant moral support from new right authors and institutions. The role of the Adam Smith Institute (ASI) was particularly significant. Its regular, radical publications on the virtues of free enterprise gave the contractors' campaign intellectual credentials. The Institute's contributions to the contracting out campaign were not limited to *Reservicing Britain* and *Reservicing Health*, though these were clearly the most important. On the eve of the Conservative Party conference in 1983, ASI published its Omega Project's report on local government. Among its numerous radical recommendations, the report proposed that *all* local authority services should be put out to contract and that even the monitoring of these services should be privatised. It suggested that trading services which were not profitable should be subsidised, but should still be carried out by private contractors.[29]

The Institute's arguments did much to engage the interest of a third set of protagonists – Conservative Party members. By the time the Government formally committed itself to competitive tendering in the NHS, it was receiving pressure from all walks of party life. Local councillors emphasised the virtues of contracting out at party conferences. Splinter groups within the party, such as the Tory Reform Group and the Bow Group, went on record demanding mandatory contracting out. The Tory Reform Group went so far as to publish a pamphlet entitled *High Noon in the National Health Service*, which powerfully documented the reasons why competitive tendering would prove 'too soft' a policy.[30] Significant pressure was also exerted by an assortment of individual backbench MPs. Some had been hired as paid consultants to lobby for the contractors' cause, and it is likely that they pursued the subject informally with senior members of the government. More visible were the efforts of those MPs who succeeded in raising the issue on the floor of the House of Commons. Together, these individuals and party factions provided the government with the internal support it needed to proceed with the relevant initiatives.

A weakened opposition

A third factor which contributed significantly to the development of the competitive tendering policy was the absence of a strong campaign against it. The ease with which the Government was able to force the policy upon the NHS reflected the high degree of fragmentation and demoralisation among those affected and the absence of any viable parliamentary opposition. The NHS initiative was launched fairly soon after the 1982 reorganisation. Morale was at an all-time low, particularly among functional managers whose professional role had been downgraded. The combination of reorganisation, industrial action, financial constraints and the continued growth of private medicine left a large body of NHS administrators disillusioned about their future job prospects and unwilling to fight yet another losing battle. Little support came from the clinical sector; the Royal College of Nursing adopted a policy of 'benevolent neutrality' which was sharply criticised by the major public sector trade unions. To complicate matters, the Government appeared to have covert support for its policy among some of the more commercially-minded hospital administrators. This gave rise to conflicts within the ranks of hospital management in many locations, further preventing the formation of any unified opposition to the Government's policy.

Demoralised and fragmented opposition also characterised the unions' campaign against the government initiative. Public sector trade unions found it difficult to combat the tendering policy. The 1982 disputes left their membership demoralised, so much so that any call to national action against contracting out stood little chance of success. This forced the unions to adopt a strategy in which local activists were to take the lead in opposing the policy and resulted in an episodic and scattered opposition. The unions' position was further undermined by the lack of cohesion and cooperation within the trade union movement; this was particularly pronounced in the health service sector where NUPE and COHSE found it difficult to establish a concerted and joint campaign against the tendering initiative (see Chapter 4).

A lack of coherent opposition to the Government's policy also characterised the Labour Party's role in the present debate. Confirmation of its disapproval of competitive tendering is not easy to find, and is usually relegated to local anti-privatisation pamphlets or to occasional parliamentary questions. This makes it marginally more visible than the Liberal–SDP Alliance's policy of supporting privatisation 'where it is believed to both maintain standards and make savings', but hardly enough to have any impact upon the wider public.[31] The Government, with an explicit ideological framework, has been able to rely on the right-wing think tanks for both legitimation of its more radical policies and research on their applicability in new contexts. The Opposition, in the absence of both a unifying ideological framework and the institutional resources to develop one, has failed manifestly to devise an alternative approach to improving service provision in local agencies. Together with the difficulties which would characterise a mandatory return of privatised services to direct provision, this lack of a credible alternative has placed substantial obstacles in the way of an effective opposition policy.

Conclusion

Contracting out is by no means a new phenomenon. For many years, it was seen as a convenient device to compensate for shortages in manpower; only recently has it been imbued with party political connotations. Ironically, it was Harold Wilson who first saw the scope which contracting out offered as a means to achieve political ends. Far from compensating for shortages of manpower, his move to install contract cleaners throughout government departments was an attempt to create just such shortages. His objective at the time of the 1968 contracting out exercise, to cut civil service numbers, bears a striking resemblance to Margaret Thatcher's objectives in embracing the very same policy. However, the scope of the present initiative is much broader than that undertaken by Wilson in the late 1960s: competitive tendering has continued to be encouraged in government departments, a massive programme of mandatory tendering for three ancillary services in the NHS has been added, and a similar programme for local authority services has been tentatively scheduled to begin in 1987.

Although the initiatives outlined in this chapter should be viewed as component parts of one larger Conservative policy, their origins and patterns of political development have varied considerably. Competitive tendering in the NHS developed in what might be termed a 'top-down' fashion. Contracting out in the NHS declined steadily throughout the 1970s and, by 1979, few people in the health service saw it as a fruitful or interesting exercise. Inspiration for the introduction of competitive tendering and the re-introduction of contracting out came exclusively from central sources. Local authority tendering has followed a significantly different route. Until recently, its growth as a salient political issue has been a 'bottom-up' affair – somewhat divorced from central intervention, with inspiration coming primarily from a handful of Conservative-controlled local councils. The differences in the way that NHS and local authority policies have developed are significant and help to explain why competitive tendering has been considerably less successful in the former sector than it has been in the latter.

3 The Contract Service Industries

The rise of competitive tendering as a political phenomenon was forecast to have a dramatic and immediate impact upon those industries capable of providing one or more of the relevant public sector services. It opened up the vast public sector market virtually overnight, providing an obvious answer to the problem of stable and declining markets in the manufacturing sector. This new market was expected to fuel consistent and rapid growth for these service industries during a rather lacklustre period for British industry as a whole. Stock market activity became strong, with acquisitions and takeovers almost too frequent to monitor effectively, and diversification was common. Industry analysts' predictions of high levels of growth for the major service companies were based partly on expectations of future public sector market penetration.

But the opening of the public sector market has proved something of a disappointment to date, particularly for some of the older companies involved. It has led to the entrance of new competitors on an unprecedented scale, and has ushered in an era of fierce competition. Profit margins, which have traditionally been small but secure, have been slashed. Both old and new firms have been the targets of a vigorous 'smear' campaign by public sector trade unions. So strong has this campaign been that several of the largest and most respected firms in service industries have withdrawn from public sector tendering exercises in certain areas. Nearly all of the major contractors have become publicity-shy and highly selective about which contracts they are willing to undertake.

This behaviour is best understood in the context of the industries in which these contractors operate. This chapter examines the three service industries which have been at the centre of the debate over tendering in the NHS: contract cleaning, laundry and contract catering. The structure, size and competitive characteristics of each industry are described and the impact of the opening of the public sector market is examined. This is followed by a brief portrait of five of the major contracting firms, drawn from recent data on their respective commercial activities and financial performances.

The contract cleaning industry

The contract cleaning industry supplies a wide range of public sector services including hospital and school cleaning, building maintenance, street cleaning and refuse collection. For this reason, it has received a proportionately larger share of political and media attention than any other industry and has made significant inroads into a variety of government markets: local authorities, government departments, nationalised industries and the NHS. So significant has the presence of the contract cleaner been that for many he has come to typify contractors in general. The difficulties which the cleaning industry experienced during its formative stages gave rise to the image of the 'cowboy' contractor, a stereotype which the unions have employed indiscriminately against contracting firms in other industries. Brief though it may be, the history of the contract cleaning industry is thus central to an understanding of the tenor of the wider debate.

History

The origins of the contract cleaning industry can be traced back into the nineteenth century, when very basic cleaning methods were employed by a wide variety of individuals and small business operations. However, the modern cleaning industry did not really begin to develop in Britain until after the Second World War. Throughout the 1940s and 1950s it remained small in scale, highly fragmented and locally-based. Private companies remained reluctant to employ outside labour to clean their premises, partly for security reasons and partly out of loyalty to existing staff. Cost-savings offered by outside contractors were negligible or non-existent.

Contract cleaning grew more rapidly in the 1960s. The normal inconvenience of recruiting and supervising staff was exacerbated by conditions of full employment; this meant that organisations had general difficulties in obtaining labour and specific problems in recruiting the right sort of supervisory talent. Contract cleaners relieved them of both of these 'headaches'. These private firms did not claim to provide a more economical or better service, but emphasised the convenience associated with contract cleaning. Records from the period indicate that contractors rarely quoted prices cheaper than that which could be achieved by in-house labour; even those in the industry accepted that the savings issue was irrelevant. One industry spokesman noted,

> From time to time we hear reference to the use of scientific applications to cleaning; that contract cleaners for this reason or that can do the work cheaper and that they are able to do it better. I wonder whether we in the industry are misleading ourselves. Can contract cleaners do a better job? I cannot see why we should unless we have some closely guarded secret process. Can we do it cheaper? I see no reason why we can unless the firm employing our labour is extremely inefficient .... We have to pay labour; we have overheads and we have to make a profit. In many cases, I suggest we are unlikely to be cheaper.[1]

Pricing was a problem for the industry throughout the 1960s. Spokesmen for the industry warned customers against accepting the lowest tender and advised companies against engaging in price-cutting practices. Pricing difficulties manifested themselves clearly in two distinct forms towards the end of the decade. The first was the formation of what trade journals termed a 'pseudo-trade association' by half a dozen small firms outside London. Spokesmen for the larger companies accused them of engaging in price-fixing activities, designed specifically to win contracts from the older, established firms. The second event which caused concern within the trade, and which played a key part in the development of the cowboy image, was the emergence of 'contract selling' on a fairly wide scale. Contract selling, a peculiar version of subcontracting, involved an established firm 'selling' a contract it had won to a less experienced firm for a specific sum of money; the smaller firm then assumed total responsibility for carrying out the contract. Problems arose due to the highly competitive but unrealistic prices tendered by the larger firms to win the contracts. Many 'subcontractors' found it impossible to carry out the specified work at the quoted price; as a result, they provided an inadequate level of service, lost money, and often went bankrupt during the course of the contract.

Documents dating back to the late 1960s link the problems the industry was having with the formation in 1967 of its trade association, the Contract Cleaning and Maintenance Association (CCMA). Its formal aims were threefold: to promote a greater awareness of the need for training, to raise standards throughout the industry, and to promote good relationships between clients and member companies. In 1971, the Secretary of the CCMA gave an indication of its informal aims: 'Unfortunately, the industry has had its share of "get-rich-quick" operators; the CCMA hopes that in time, by insistence by member firms on good service to the client and a fair standard of practice, much of the old memory will be eradicated.'[2] The CCMA established a Code of Good Practice to help formalise relationships between its members and their clients. It also set up rules to help define the relationship between one member firm and another, which touched on issues such as head-hunting, unethical promotional activities and judicial action.

By the early 1970s, contract cleaning had clearly become more acceptable. A 1971 survey showed that the UK cleaning industry had a turnover of approximately £60 million and consisted of upwards of 800 firms. Of the 721 firms contacted by the Prices & Incomes Board, 325 (45 per cent) employed more than ten people and 262 (36 per cent) were specialist cleaners. Surveys conducted in the US and UK at that time both indicated that administrative convenience remained the primary reason for using contract cleaners. Few claimed that it improved cleaning or saved significant amounts of money. It is interesting that the US study cited the elimination of union problems as one of the foremost advantages of contracting out – an early warning of what was to follow in Britain.[3]

Contract cleaning in Britain maintained a steady pace of growth throughout the 1970s. The widespread move to offices entailed the cleaning of more sophisticated floor surfaces and required a level of expertise that many firms could not provide internally. Rising employment costs began to figure in the economics of contracting, which themselves became more important as the economic situation deteriorated and cost-cutting exercises became common. Customers began to demand multiple services and the larger firms diversified to meet their needs. As a result of these changes, cleaning companies grew rapidly and by the time the first substantial local authority contract was put out to tender in 1980, there were a number of firms capable of taking on public sector contracts.

The contract cleaning market

The contract cleaning market is vast, encompassing a variety of business and institutional premises in both private and public sectors. In the private sector, major areas of interest include industrial, retail and commercial sites including office blocks, hotels and leisure facilities. In the public sector, major firms have already made inroads into airport, transport terminal and nationalised industry work and are hoping to increase their penetration in hospital and school cleaning markets. Other areas of potential include the cleaning of central and local government buildings, street cleaning, refuse collection and public parks maintenance.

Accurate estimates of the size of the potential market for contract cleaning services are hard to find. Most cleaning of industrial and commercial premises continues to be done in-house and the cost of this work is unknown. Estimates of the total cleaning market vary widely between £3000 million and £5000 million per annum, with the public sector acknowledged to account for somewhere between half and two-thirds of all cleaning work. The industry's own conservative estimates, shown in Table 3.1, suggest that the major growth area for the industry is the public sector: penetration is low, on the order of 2½ per cent, and the market is large. In contract, contractors' share of the smaller, private sector market is estimated to be 50 per cent.

The latest recession has had a dramatic effect on the market for contract cleaning. The declining number of jobs, and indeed businesses, in the manufacturing sector has not been offset by growth in the service sector. Though office cleaning work as a percentage of all cleaning has grown, a downturn in building occupancy rates has meant little if any real growth in cleaning industry volumes. Recent studies have shown that the industry has experienced an overall decline in sales volume over the past five years if inflation is taken into account. While sales rose 23 per cent

TABLE 3.1   Cleaning: estimated market size – 1984 (£m)

	Contracted	In-house	Total
Private sector	500	500	1 000
Public sector	50	1 950	2 000
Total cleaning market	**550**	**2 450**	**3 000**

Source: Contract Cleaning and Maintenance Association.

between 1980 and 1984, inflation caused prices to rise 36 per cent. The weighted figure for 1984 sales is thus 91 per cent of the corresponding sales figure for 1980. Although the industry's trade association indicates that the market is now growing rapidly, investment analysts are unsure and suggest that the market could still be shrinking.[4] Given such uncertain prospects, it was predictable that the industry would put tremendous effort into establishing a foothold in what appeared to be the one guaranteed growth area – the public sector.

Contract cleaning firms

The contract cleaning industry is highly fragmented with six or seven relatively large companies and hundreds of small companies, many aimed at satisfying specialist or local needs. The major contract cleaning companies, shown in Table 3.2, accounted for approximately one-third of the total industry turnover in 1984. The two largest, Pritchard Services and Office Cleaning Services (OCS), are among the oldest companies in the business and together account for about 15 per cent of all sales. Five of the major contract cleaning firms are British-owned; Servisystem is the UK cleaning subsidiary of a Danish multinational.

The larger companies active in the cleaning field loosely fall into one of two categories. The first grouping consists of firms whose origins lie within the cleaning sector, such as Brengreen, OCS and Pritchard. Although these firms have diversified into other fields that require 'man-management' expertise, such as security and portering services, they have retained strong foundations in cleaning. The remaining large firms within the cleaning sector have

TABLE 3.2   Contract cleaning: market share – 1984

Company or division	%
Office Cleaning Services (OCS)	10
Pritchard Services	6
Brengreen	5
Initial Cleaning Services	4
Reckitt Cleaning Services	4
Servisystem	2
Home Counties	2
Subtotal	**33**
Other firms	67
Total	**100**

Source: Calculated from figures provided in *Contract Cleaning: Keynote Report* (London: Keynote Publications, 1985).

moved into cleaning from a variety of other businesses. Textile maintenance and rental companies, such as Initial and Sunlight, have now established contract cleaning divisions. Among their top competitors are the cleaning subsidiaries of firms as diverse as Reckitt & Colman, Grand Metropolitan and Securicor.

Although most of these firms claim to have a national presence, the great bulk of their work is in the South-east and coverage in other areas is often patchy.[5] As a result, a large percentage of work falls to a variety of medium and small firms who operate on a regional or local basis. Barriers to entry in the cleaning industry are extremely low and, in some areas (such as office cleaning), virtually non-existent. Advertising spending is limited; sales activity generally consists of personal visits or mail shots. Economies of scale are minimal and small local contractors can compete successfully against the major national firms. Although it is perhaps no longer as easy as it once was, industry managers admit that it is still possible to 'get rich quick' in cleaning.

It is hardly surprising, therefore, that the past few years have seen a tremendous growth in the number of companies competing for cleaning contracts. Entry into the industry has intensified competition and put severe downward pressure on prices. Though it might be argued that the lowering of prices has contributed to the increased demand for cleaning services in the market place, it is clear that it has also put a squeeze on the profitability of cleaning firms right across the industry. Those who have been in the business for some time complain about the intensity of competition, but appear quietly confident that competitors will soon begin dropping out and that normal margins will return. One lobbyist for the industry noted: 'if they thought in 50 years' time they'd be making the same profits, they wouldn't be in it. It's a commercial decision.'

The financial performance of contract cleaning firms over the past few years, discussed in more detail later in this chapter, has been mixed. The year 1984 saw a general decline in profit growth, although reported annual profit increases of between 25 per cent and 45 per cent for the major cleaners are clearly very solid. Return on capital has consistently been high, particularly among firms whose primary business lies outside the cleaning market. Profit margins have hovered between 4 per cent and 7 per cent for the more successful major firms, though the 'second division' majors have seen their margins cut to between 1 per cent and 3 per cent. Rapid growth and competitive pressures have led to an ongoing programme of acquisitions by the major contract cleaning companies. While some of the firms are cautious in their purchases, others are buying up small cleaning companies at a phenomenal rate. Many of these smaller acquisitions are aimed at extending the geographical reach of the parent companies from headquarters in the South-east. Often they are orchestrated on an informal basis; as the Chairman of one of the fastest growing firms noted, 'cleaning companies aren't for sale. We just make deals if it's convenient.'

The speed at which the larger companies are expanding has led to a shortage of managerial talent. Those managers who have established solid reputations within the industry command a salary premium, and head-hunting is commonplace. Some of the newer companies have successfully recruited top names from competitors. The Hawley Group, for example, succeeded in hiring Jim Derham from Crothall and Mike Davies from RCO to fill the Chairman and Managing Director slots in its new hospital cleaning company, Mediclean. It also lured Graeme Crothall away from his family's company to help in developing its hospital services business in America (although this relationship was terminated in 1984). The largest company in the sector, Pritchard, appears to provide the bulk of the industry talent. As one Pritchard manager stated, 'there's a one-way flow of people from us to other contractors. None of them ever come here.'[6]

The laundry (textile maintenance) industry

History

Although laundry companies proudly trace their roots back as far as the Egyptian civilisation of 4500 years ago, the first real evidence of a 'laundry industry' does not appear until Medieval times. Beginning in 1297, several guilds were formed in different parts of England in an attempt to both ensure standards of quality in laundry work and deter people from patronising non-guild members. These guilds were the direct ancestors of today's sophisticated and well developed trade network. The first formal trade association, the National Laundry Association, was formed in 1886. Its primary objective was to protect its members and in 1897 its name was changed to the National Trade Protection Association. During this period, trade associations were also springing up in provincial areas and by 1900 the 'West of Scotland', 'Northern Counties' and 'Western District' laundry associations, among others, were reasonably well respected and proved a counterbalance to the London-based 'National' association. The individual associations did not work together until 1901, when the Federation of Laundry Associations was formed to deal with major issues. The Federation achieved several political successes in the first two decades of the twentieth century and the desire for a more unified grouping grew. In 1920, the organisation's name was changed to the National Federation of Launderers, and the regional 'associations' become regional groupings. This was the forerunner of today's Association of British Cleaning Laundry and Rental Services (ABCLRS).[7]

It was during this period that several of the largest companies in the industry today were founded. Most began as small networks of receiving shops, which acted as collection and delivery points for customer's goods. As new techniques reduced the cost of their operations and widened the appeal of the service, these firms grew rapidly. Several began experimenting with new fields: linen supply and workwear cleaning, for example, became popular services due to continued growth in the hotel and industrial sectors respectively. Success in these new areas contributed to rapid and consistent industry growth throughout the 1920s and 1930s.[8] But this growth was halted by World War II, which caused a shift to armed forces work and a near disastrous shortage of staff and materials. The industry was forced to recruit inexperienced labour, which led to a serious deterioration in standards. This hurt the industry's reputation and, soon after the war, a public relations department was set up within the trade association to restore the pre-war image of the industry. By this time, however, a range of threats to traditional laundry work – including textile rental and dry cleaning services, drip-dry clothes, and domestic washing machines – had arisen. As a result, most laundry firms intensified their diversification into a range of complimentary services. Today, nearly all of the major laundry companies are engaged in a variety of other textile rental or textile maintenance activities.

The textile maintenance market

Although it is possible to estimate the amount and value of laundry processed each year in the UK, a single 'laundry industry' does not really exist. Laundry and linen rental are generally considered two of many 'textile maintenance' services provided by a range of both large and small companies. The textile maintenance market can be broken into two analytically distinct areas: textile rental and textile cleaning. Textile rental involves the supply and maintenance of workwear, cabinet towels, dust mats, industrial wiping cloths and linen to a variety of commercial, industrial and public sector clients. Textile cleaning primarily involves the maintenance of textiles owned by clients, specifically laundry and dry cleaning. While certain companies may concentrate on one or two services within this market, the major companies maintain a wide presence in several rental and cleaning activities. The most significant areas of the market are shown in Table 3.3.

The major textile rental service provided by these companies is rental of commercial or industrial garments. Although the workwear rental market grew rapidly between 1977 and 1981, primarily as a result of the National Coal Board's decision to rent garments for its 225 000 workers, it has been hit hard by the decline in the heavy industrial sector and turnover in this market has dropped

TABLE 3.3   Textile maintenance market: turnover by segment – 1983

Area	Turnover (£ million)	%
TEXTILE RENTAL		
Workwear rental	128	25
Cabinet towel rental	62	12
Linen rental	50	10
Ancillary rental	30	6
Dust mat rental	20	4
Industrial wiping cloth rental	20	4
Subtotal	*310*	*61*
TEXTILE CLEANING		
Dry cleaning	150	29
Laundry	50	10
Subtotal	*200*	*39*
Total	**510**	**100**

Source: Monopolies and Mergers Commission, *The British Electric Traction Company PLC and Initial PLC: A Report on the Proposed Merger*, Cmnd 9444 (London: HMSO, 1985).

from £131 million in 1981 to £128 million in 1984. Competition is intense due to widespread excess capacity, and prices have fallen significantly. Other rental markets have pulled through the recession in better shape. Dust mat rental services are expanding; linen rental has grown steadily as a result of increased occupancy rates at hotels. Cabinet towel rental, really a subset of the hand drying market, is perhaps the most competitive area due to the existing high penetration in the UK market. Rental of industrial wiping cloths is a specialist activity dominated almost exclusively by Initial Services.[9]

Prospects in the textile cleaning sector are not particularly encouraging. Dry cleaning work, which experienced a drop in turnover of 20 per cent between 1977 and 1981, has recovered and has expanded in both volume and value terms since 1981. The laundry sector also experienced a drop in turnover during the late 1970s (falling by one-third from 1978 to 1981), from which it has yet to recover: total turnover fell by 10 per cent in absolute terms between 1981 and 1983 and by approximately 20 per cent if the figures are adjusted for inflation. Much of this decline was due to competition from textile rental and in-house laundry services, and from the growth in household ownership of washing machines.

The textile maintenance market, as a whole, is relatively mature and growth in one area tends to be offset by losses in another. The emphasis is very much on finding new markets offering solid growth potential and a number of firms are diversifying into fields wholly unrelated to textile maintenance, such as contract cleaning or personal security services. Many have looked eagerly to the public sector. Although laundry companies have been doing 'overflow' work for a variety of health authorities for years, the rise of competitive tendering offered the first substantial opportunity to expand in this sector. The appeal of NHS work is best understood by comparing the existing market with the potential NHS market. Whereas in 1984 private laundry firms conducted £50m worth of business in laundry and a similar amount in linen services, the NHS markets for these services were estimated to be worth £60m and £109m respectively. Tendering in the NHS thus offered the possibility of doubling and tripling the market for contract laundry and linen services respectively – a good prospect by any standards, but one made even more attractive by the likelihood of declining markets elsewhere.

Textile maintenance firms

The textile maintenance industry is highly concentrated, with six large firms accounting for over 50 per cent of the total industry turnover. Five of these six sizeable firms owe their origins to textile maintenance activities; only Pritchard Services, whose core business lies in the contract cleaning field, has diversified into textile services through a concerted programme of sizeable acquisitions. Although most major firms concentrate on specific sectors of the overall market, nearly all maintain a smaller presence in related maintenance activities. The dominance of the major firms across the range of services can be seen in Table 3.4.

Initial Services is clearly the market leader, with a dominant position in all but one of the rental markets. Its market position was recently strengthened when BET (formerly known as British

TABLE 3.4 Textile maintenance: market share – 1983

	Workwear rental £m	%	Cabinet towel rental £m	%	Dust mat rental £m	%	Industrial wiping cloth rental £m	%	Linen rental £m	%	Laundry £m	%	Dry cleaning £m	%	Ancillary rental* £m	TOTAL £m	%
Initial	29.4	23	23.4	38	7.8	39	15.3	76	0.6	1	1.9	4	—	—	14.6	93.0	18
Sketchley	21.9	17	1.4	2	0.6	3	0.1	—	—	—	—	—	31.0	21	—	55.0	11
Johnson	6.9	5	3.5	6	1.0	5	—	—	2.8	6	1.1	2	34.9	23	0.3	50.6	10
Advance	6.6	5	15.3	25	2.7	13	—	—	3.3	7	4.7	9	0.2	—	4.5	37.3	7
Pritchard	15.8	12	7.1	11	1.7	8	1.2	6	3.1	6	1.0	2	0.1	—	1.4	31.4	6
Sunlight	6.4	5	1.0	2	—	—	—	—	11.8	24	6.7	13	0.8	1	0.3	27.0	5
Sub-total	*87.0*	*68*	*51.7*	*83*	*13.9*	*70*	*16.6*	*83*	*21.8*	*44*	*15.5*	*31*	*66.9*	*45*	*21.2*	*294.4*	*58*
Other companies	41.0	32	10.3	17	6.1	30	3.4	17	28.2	56	34.5	69	83.1	55	8.8	215.6	42
Total	**128.0**	**100**	**62.0**	**100**	**20.0**	**100**	**20.0**	**100**	**50.0**	**100**	**50.0**	**100**	**150.0**	**100**	**30.0**	**510.0**	**100**

* Ancillary rental would include the rental of soap dispensers and flat towels. Percentages are omitted for this category, as it represents residual turnover.
Source: Monopolies and Mergers Commission, *The British Electric Traction Company PLC and Initial PLC*, Cmnd 9444 (London: HMSO, 1985).

Electric Traction), which had owned 41 per cent of the firm, bought out the remaining 59 per cent. BET also owns Advance Services and plans to integrate the activities of the two companies; this will give it direct control over 25 per cent of the entire textile mainten-ance market. Neither Initial nor Advance, however, maintains as dominant a position in the cleaning sectors as they do in the rental areas. Dry cleaning is something of a specialist field with two of the majors, Sketchley and Johnson, accounting for 45 per cent of all turnover; the remainder of the market is highly fragmented and falls to a variety of smaller regional or local firms. Laundry is similar in that numerous small firms offer competition at a local level, although there are signs that the market share of the major firms, who currently account for only one-third of the total laundry turnover, is growing.

The competitive environment in the textile maintenance industry generally, and in the laundry sector specifically, is significantly different from that of the contract cleaning industry discussed earlier. Textile maintenance is a well-established industry with a handful of dominant suppliers, many of whom have been in the business since the turn of the century. Barriers to entry are comparatively high, as a result of the capital-intensive nature of both rental and cleaning work. Excess capacity in the laundry sector and increasing concentration among customers has meant highly competitive pricing and lower profit margins – a combi-nation unlikely to attract new entrants. Economies of scale are such that the larger firms are pushing many of the smaller firms out of the market, as they attempt to expand from their bases in London and the South-east.

The textile maintenance industry does display one striking similarity to the contract cleaning industry: acquisition activity has been extensive and frenzied over the past few years. While the majority of these acquisitions have involved the purchase of smaller, regionally-based companies by major firms, a number of the proposed acquisitions have concerned sizeable targets. Within the past two years, three major acquisition proposals within the textile maintenance industry have been referred to the Monopolies and Mergers Commission (MMC). In 1982, Sunlight and Initial attempted separate takeovers of the Johnson Group; both saw the Group as providing a foundation for a move into the dry cleaning sector. The MMC handled the two proposals simultaneously, and ruled against both of them. In 1985, BET successfully acquired the 59 per cent share of Initial that it did not already own, despite vigorous protests to the MMC from the two firms' chief competitors.

The acquisition activity in the textile maintenance field has not been instigated exclusively by the industry leaders. As noted earlier, Pritchard Services moved into the textile maintenance field by purchasing a number of sizeable textile cleaning and rental firms; in 1983, it purchased Spring Grove, a workwear rental and washroom equipment firm, for the sum of £15 million. Brengreen Holdings, another company firmly based in the contract cleaning field, set similar sights on the textile industry and attempted a takeover of the Sunlight Service Group in 1983. Although the bid failed, at a cost of some £600 000 to the firm, it is possible that Brengreen will try again to enter this market in the future.[10]

The contract catering industry

History

The origins of the contract catering industry date back centuries, to catering specifically organised for particular cultural or sporting events. Small catering companies developed as the number of household servants among middle- and upper-class households declined. However, real growth in contract catering did not occur until the twentieth century. Industrial catering became popular with the development of manufacturing industry and the proliferation of factory canteens. Increases in leisure time and the development of the automobile led to an unprecedented level of mobility, resulting in increased demand for roadside catering and lodging services. More recently, demand for catering services has come from institutional sources such as schools and hospitals.

Catering companies today provide a variety of contract services to their customers. Many commercial contracts involve the catering company purchasing the right to supply catering services at a particular location for a specified period of time; in these cases the contractor is free to charge whatever price the market will bear. Other catering contracts involve agreements to supply a given level of service, the cost of which will be reimbursed by the owner. These management fee contracts, which may or may not involve charging subsidised prices to the consumer, are typical of most forms of institutional catering. Other forms of contract catering constitute a relatively small share of catering turnover. These would include temporary catering for sporting or social events and catering consultancy, a new form of catering service which involves giving advice on planning, design, stock control and hygiene standards.

The contract catering market

The market for contract catering is best seen as a subset of the catering market as a whole, which can be broken down into two areas: commercial and non-commercial catering. Commercial catering accounts for over 80 per cent of all catering expenditure in the UK. There are approximately 235 000 commercial outlets – including restaurants and pubs – providing food to the general public; some of these outlets will be owned and operated by contract caterers (for example, Kardomah coffee shops owned by Trusthouse Forte and Truman pubs owned by Grand Metropolitan). Non-commercial catering generally refers to services provided by institutions (primarily schools and hospitals), businesses and government departments for their own staff and for their direct clients. In 1984 non-commercial outlets were responsible for only about 17 per cent of the expenditure on catering, but accounted for 40 per cent of the total number of meals served annually.[11]

As shown in Table 3.5, the non-commercial segment of the catering industry experienced a marked decline during the year 1984. This was caused by the decline in manufacturing industry and the corresponding increase in employment in companies where meals are not offered to staff. The 7 per cent decline in the institutional sector was primarily due to a decrease in the number of schools providing a meal service. Overall, however, the contract catering industry does not appear to have been affected dramatically by the recent recession. Although comprehensive figures on total turnover are not available due to the number of small firms in the industry, analysts highlight recent increases in the number of businesses reporting results between 1980 and 1983 (from 1196 to 1500) and substantial increases in their turnover (from £575 million to £850 million) as signs of healthy growth.

TABLE 3.5   Catering: market size – 1983 and 1984

Area	1983 (£m)	1984 (£m)	% change
Commercial	239 440	235 745	−1.5
Non-commercial:	78 750	72 470	−8.0
institutional	52 700	48 920	−7.2
staff catering	26 050	23 550	−9.6
Total	**318 190**	**308 215**	−3.1

Source: *Contract Catering: Keynote Report* (London: Keynote Publications, 1985).

Contract catering firms

The contract catering industry consists of a small number of large companies and a large number of small ones. The industry is dominated by two of the biggest and most successful British companies, Trusthouse Forte (THF) and Grand Metropolitan. Both firms operate a number of businesses in the commercial catering sector, including a range of hotel and restaurant chains which bear such familiar names as Little Chef, Berni Inns and Quality Inns. Their respective contract catering subsidiaries together account for about one-third of the industry's total turn-over; this figure rises to about 50 per cent if specialist subsidiaries (such as THF's airport and motorway catering divisions) are included.

Grand Metropolitan's activities in the contract catering sector are channelled through its Compass Services subsidiary, which has approximately 2000 clients and maintains particular strength in the industrial catering sector. Although Compass operates through a number of regional divisions, its business is very much dominated by contracts in the South-east. Trusthouse Forte has a number of subsidiaries in the field, as shown in Table 3.6. Its general contract catering work is undertaken by Gardner Merchant, the largest company operating in this sphere. Gardner Merchant has upwards of 2800 clients, to whom it serves an estimated million meals each day. It trades on a broad geographic scale, with 17 offices in Britain and others throughout Europe.

Compass and Gardner Merchant do not operate in a total vacuum. Sutcliffe Catering has a turnover in the region of £85 million and has proved a formidable competitor for work in the expanding public sector market; ARA Services reported a turnover of £50 million in 1983–4. However, unlike laundry and cleaning sectors, the industry has witnessed little entry from large firms with core businesses in other areas. This is primarily due to the presence of significant economies of scale (particularly in regard to food purchasing power), the need for substantial investment in both capital and management talent, and the level of expertise required to cater for institutional clients. It may also reflect the dominance of the two major companies, whose technical and managerial resources are enormous and whose professionalism is taken for granted. Both companies put tremendous emphasis upon training and management; Trusthouse Forte spends upwards of £5 million each year on training and education and both it and Grand Metropolitan run residential training colleges for their employees.[12]

Profit margins in contract catering are not particularly high, often between 2 per cent and 4 per cent, and most firms rely on a high turnover of stock to meet their financial targets. To compensate for the general decline in industrial and institutional catering, the industry is now looking to a number of new specialist markets. Catering consultancy, a comparatively profitable area, is likely to grow; a number of the larger firms have also moved into the provision of automatic vending machines. Another area of specialist catering in which the medium and large contractors have shown interest is the hospital sector. As noted in Chapter 2, the industry's respectable share of NHS work during the 1960s was lost following

TABLE 3.6   Contract catering: sales performance (1983–4)*

Company	Turnover (£m)
Gardner Merchant (THF)	185.9
Airport Catering Services (THF)	102.7
Sutcliffe Catering Group	83.4
ARA Services	49.6
Forte's Service Areas (THF)	45.0

*This table excludes Compass Services, whose accounts are unavailable.
Source: *Contact Catering: Keynote Report* (London: Keynote Publications, 1985).

the introduction of functional management in 1974 and, by 1982, contract caterers serviced only 3 of the 2000 NHS hospitals.[13]

The new public sector market

The industries examined on the preceding pages differ dramatically from one another. Catering and textile maintenance are older, relatively mature industries with a high degree of concentration. Contract cleaning, in contrast, is a relatively new and rapidly growing industry with a high level of fragmentation among firms. Despite these significant differences, all three industries have shared one important feature – static or declining markets for their services. The lack of opportunities for organic growth has pushed major competitors in all three industries toward acquisition and diversification; it has also generated a great deal of interest in the new public sector markets. The following section examines how these competitors reacted to these new markets. It looks first at the influence that the companies have had on the development of government policy and then, conversely, at the influence that the NHS initiative has had on the competitive environment within these three industries.

Influencing the Government

The strategy employed by the major contractors to gain a foothold in the public sector markets has been both simple and successful. Unlike the unions, who have devoted tremendous effort to mobilising public opinion, the contractors have directed their lobbying efforts almost exclusively at the political decision-makers, particularly those at national level. Their campaign has been low-key, often operating behind closed ministerial doors, and virtually invisible to those outside mainstream Conservative Party politics. Four aspects of this lobbying campaign are of particular interest: trade association activity, Conservative activists in service industries, direct lobbying of Parliament, and corporate links with the Conservative Party.

All three of the industries examined on the preceding pages have one or more active trade associations. The major associations for

the contract cleaning, laundry and catering industries respectively
are the CCMA (Contract Cleaning and Maintenance Association),
the ABLCRS (Association of British Laundry, Cleaning and
Rental Services) and the BHRCA (British Hotel, Restaurant, and
Caterers Association). Each of these organisations has played a
role in the development of the contracting out debate. As noted in
Chapter 2, all three associations began meetings with government
ministers and civil servants early on in the first Thatcher Government, and these meetings have continued at regular intervals. The
associations have also been active in promoting their members'
interests in the relevant trade and professional press.

Some of the most effective, and by far the cheapest, weapons in
the contractors' arsenal were those individuals who were involved in
both a contract industry and in Conservative Party politics. David
Evans, Chairman and founder of Brengreen Holdings, served as a
Conservative Councillor on St Albans Council up until May 1984.
At the Tory Party conference in 1981, his speech in favour of
contracting out won great applause and helped to establish the
relationship he now enjoys with senior party officials. Michael
Forsyth is another example. His connections with the cleaning and
laundry industries were channelled through his public relations
firm while he was a Conservative councillor on Westminster City
Council; at the same time, he wrote pamphlets for the Adam Smith
Institute. Although his firm is still active in this field, since 1983
most of Forsyth's time has been spent in Parliament, as Conservative Member for Stirling.

As noted in Chapter 2, much of the public relations lobbying by
contract service industries has been undertaken by Michael Forsyth Associates. Pritchard Services, the largest and most diversified
firm in the field, has been a client since January 1982. Before the
merger of the Association of British Launderers and Cleaners and
British Textile Rental Association in 1984, a 'Common Interest
Committee' formed by the two associations retained the same
public relations firm to lobby on their behalf and the relationship
continued with the ABLCRS. The strategy of Forsyth Associates is
straightforward: it exerts political pressure both nationally
through parliamentary public relations and locally through coverage in the media. However, not all contract service companies
favour the use of external lobbyists and some have looked to
Parliament for their 'public relations' advisors. A list of MPs who

were affiliated with one or another service companies in early 1986 is shown in Table 3.7.

A final method which many trade unionists believe has been used by the companies to influence the government is direct contributions to Conservative Party funds. Company donors, of course, are quick to disclaim any political motives and suggest that contributions should be seen only as a vague endorsement of Conservative values. Although the real purpose behind these contributions cannot easily be determined, it is simply worth noting that the relationship between individual companies and the Conservative Party as a whole exists. Table 3.8 offers a selection of donations by the major firms between 1982 and 1984.

Overall, the contractors' campaign to convince the Government of the merits of private provision of public services appears to have been highly successful. But it would be wrong to assign too much

TABLE 3.7   **Parliamentary connections***

Name of MP	Organisation	Relationship
Michael Forsyth	Pritchard	Consultant
	Public and Local Service Efficiency Campaign	Consultant
Marcus Fox	Care Services	Director
Geoffrey Finsberg	OCS	Consultant
Anthony Grant	Pritchard	Consultant
Dr Brian Mawhinney	Servicemaster	Director

* as at 1/86
Source: *Register of Members' Interests* (House of Commons, January 1986).

TABLE 3.8   **Selected donations to the Conservative Party: 1982–4**

Company	1982 (£)	1983 (£)	1984 (£)	Total (£)
BET	10 000	10 000	20 000	40 000
Pritchard	10 000	21 000	12 000	43 000
Brengreen	—	5 164	21 480	26 644

Source: BET, Pritchard, and Brengreen Annual Reports for the years 1982, 1983 and 1984.

weight to the tactics employed by the firms and their trade associations. Their lobbying campaign was fairly typical of those commonly mounted by a variety of commercial concerns and, in other circumstances, might well have led nowhere. But the contractors were preaching to the converted, telling the Government something it wanted to hear. The impact of these words, as one contractor put it, 'far exceeded our wildest expectations'.

The impact of new markets

By 1985, the Government had committed itself to compulsory tendering in 2000 NHS hospitals and had indicated that another 522 local authorities might begin the same exercise for a range of services as early as 1987. The volume of work involved in tendering on this sort of scale is substantially greater than that which most firms can handle. Although contractors predicted this problem and urged the Government to 'go slow' in implementing the tendering initiative, their warnings were ignored. As a result, major contractors have been inundated with invitations to tender and have been forced to become selective about which they will accept. The cleaning industry has been most dramatically affected by the sudden opening of the NHS market, but both laundry and contract catering industries have been affected as well and it is useful to look at them first.

The laundry industry, prior to competitive tendering, suffered from declining demand and severe overcapacity. Health service contracts quickly soaked up much of this excess capacity, particularly in the South-east where the volume of work being put out to tender was greatest. Many of the major firms, operating at or near capacity in this region, have had to consider sizeable investment in new plant in order to continue to compete for NHS work. The opening of this market has also intensified existing pressure on both prices and margins. Many laundry companies have priced their tenders on a marginal cost basis, in an effort to minimise excess capacity and gain a foothold in the NHS. As a result, costs per laundered item quoted by these companies have been significantly lower for NHS work than for their existing clients in the private sector. However this marginal costing approach can only be successful in the short term: although it can help the major companies to win contracts, it will not provide them with the revenue needed to invest in new equipment and plant. It will be interesting to monitor competition in the laundry industry once excess capacity no longer exists.

Competitive tendering has not turned out to be of overwhelming interest to the catering industry for a number of reasons. Very few catering companies are capable of undertaking hospital catering, due to the significant expertise it requires. In addition, the larger catering companies regard NHS catering services as fairly efficient and see substantial competition from in-house tenders. But the most immediate reason for the 'arms-length' attitude of many catering companies has been the mandatory imposition of fixed price contracts for NHS catering work. Institutional catering contracts have traditionally been undertaken on a management fee basis, due to difficulties in both estimating food prices and predicting dietary needs over an extended period of time. Such contracts guarantee that the contractor will earn a certain amount of profit; fixed price contracts do not. The Government's choice of the latter has caused many firms to steer clear of NHS work and has precipitated the withdrawal of several of the older catering firms from the market. This has allowed new entrants to the UK market to secure the new NHS catering contracts that have not been awarded in-house. But the number of catering awards that have witnessed real competition is small and the DHSS is itself concerned about the lack of headway being made in the catering sector.

The biggest impact of the opening of the public sector market has occurred in the contract cleaning field. Cleaners, unlike their catering colleagues, have been very successful in competing against in-house labour forces. Much of this is due to the peculiar economics of contract cleaning, a more labour-intensive industry than either catering or laundry. Contract cleaning managers estimate that about 90 per cent of the cost of any contract is labour-related. Success in the contract cleaning field is largely dependent upon keeping labour costs as low as possible through high productivity, good management and low wage/benefit packages. It is for this reason that contract cleaning displays such a high proportion of part-time workers. By employing workers for less than the statutory number of hours, the cleaning company is not required to provide either employee benefits or national insurance payments.[14]

The CCMA estimates that approximately two-thirds of all contract cleaning workers are employed on a part-time basis.

The ability to make savings on labour, either by reducing numbers and benefits or by increasing the proportion of part-time workers, puts the contract cleaner in an advantageous position when competing against public sector workforces. Both the NHS and local authorities are required to provide a minimum wage and a certain package of benefits. They too can make savings by reducing numbers and shifting to part-time work, but this involves redundancies and losses in take-home pay to existing staff and is therefore an unacceptable option. As a result, contract cleaners have found it relatively easy to undercut in-house prices in competitive tendering situations. Their success, coupled with the extraordinarily low barriers to entry into the cleaning field, has stimulated widespread interest and led to numerous new entrants into the industry. This change has hurt the position of older contractors who refer cynically to the 'new broom enthusiasm' of recent entrants.

This enthusiasm has manifest itself in extremely competitive pricing strategies, which have squeezed profit margins throughout the industry and have led to the phenomenon known as 'loss leaders'. Although much has been made of these loss-leader bids, in straight commercial terms there is nothing unusual or particularly unscrupulous about them. By setting a low initial price, a firm can establish itself in the market, build a track record, and try to foster some sort of company loyalty. Once its reputation has been established, it will be able to command a 'premium' (in other words charge more profitable prices) – particularly if other competitors have been squeezed out of the market. This behaviour, sometimes referred to as 'penetration pricing', is a common commercial approach to a new product or market. Senior managers in the cleaning industry acknowledge that this loss-leader behaviour did occur in response to the opening of new public sector markets and explain it in terms of the need to gain early operating experience and justify investment in staff, publicity and tendering costs. The Managing Director of one of the most successful hospital cleaning firms in mid-1985: 'In the early days, prices were suicidal. People were quoting [operating] prices that weren't workable. Now they're putting in higher prices.'

Local administrators and trade unions, however, continue to be concerned about this form of commercial behaviour. They argue that unrealistic pricing by cleaning contractors could mean skimping and shortcuts and lead to a decline in standards of service; few believe that monitoring systems are sophisticated enough to prevent this. They also point out that because the most 'enthusiastic' companies are often unable to cross-subsidise contracts due to their poor financial positions, the threat of these contractors withdrawing from loss-making contracts is very real. Although withdrawal or termination has occurred in a number of cases, the issue of 'loss-leaders' may have been blown up out of proportion.[15] The quoting of low, and occasionally unworkable, contract prices has not always been intentional. Competitive tendering for local authority or NHS work is often as new to the contractor as it is to the authority, and many firms have underestimated the cost of providing the specified level of service. Most typically, contractors fail to consider the obstacles which could arise in the course of a cleaning routine (for example, parked cars mean that streets must be swept manually) or do not take into account the cost of non-cleaning tasks. These oversights have often turned what were intended to be profitable contracts into loss-makers.

Loss-leader behaviour, whether intentional or not, has clearly taken its toll on the cleaning industry and has particularly hurt those older contractors previously involved in public sector work. In order to safeguard their existing market share, the older firms have been forced to adopt an altogether different approach to pricing (and therefore to costs and labour deployment) than the one they had employed in the past. In practical terms, this has meant lower take-home pay, less convenient schedules, and poorer conditions of service for nearly all of their existing public sector contract staff and has led to serious industrial unrest in a number of hospitals. Despite the radical changes made in labour deployment by many of these firms, a number of their long-standing contracts have been lost to competitors.

The intensity of competition in the cleaning industry also manifests itself outside the pricing sphere. Reluctant to criticise each other in public, contractors are quick to do so on a private or personal level. And when it comes to winning important contracts, several companies appear to have adopted a 'no holds barred' attitude. One example of the behaviour which has characterised this competitive phase in the contract cleaning industry's history is a letter written by the Technical Director of one of the biggest cleaning firms to the Gloucester City Engineer during the period that Gloucester was accepting tenders for its refuse and street cleaning service in 1983. In it he stated,

Broadly speaking, there are two distinct types of approaches which are being made to the market. The first, which includes amongst its protagonists at least two of the major companies, involves using inadequate numbers of people, paying the lowest possible rates of pay, giving poor conditions of service (e.g. no pension benefits), using old vehicles maintained to minimum standards, and generally keeping costs at an absolute rock bottom level .... The residents of the relevant authorities, e.g. [names omitted] will, I believe, confirm the problems which arise when decisions are taken to use such contractors.

In conclusion, although the contract cleaning industry's reaction to the opening of the public sector market was very different to those of the laundry and catering industries, in historical terms it was not unusual. Contract cleaning has always been a 'cut-throat' business; the price-cutting and contract selling which occurred during the late 1960s and early 1970s suggest that the industry has reflected these competitive tendencies from its earliest days. The development of competitive tendering in local authorities and the NHS has simply provided a new showcase for an intensively competitive industry.

Company profiles

The preceding sections have demonstrated that the cleaning, textile maintenance, and catering industries have unique structural and competitive characteristics. Despite these variations across industries, there has been a significant amount of diversification from one industry into another, motivated primarily by the lack of growth in the firms' traditional markets. A number of firms have now consolidated their positions and maintain a substantial presence in several of the areas under examination. The remainder of this chapter outlines the commercial positions of five of the largest 'diversified' firms, shown in Table 3.9, and summarises the recent financial performance of these five as a group.[16] Although particular mention is made of each company's public sector presence, it should be emphasised that in all but one case, public sector work constitutes an extremely small proportion of their annual turnover. A more detailed and comprehensive picture of each firm's commercial activities is given in Tables 3.10–3.14.

TABLE 3.9   Major contractors: relevant areas of expertise

	Pritchard	Brengreen	Hawley	BET (Initial)	Sunlight
Hospital cleaning	X	X	X	X	X
School cleaning			X	X	X
Public cleansing*	X	X	X		
Laundry	X			X	X
Catering	X				

* Public cleansing activities include refuse collection, street cleaning, and maintenance of public conveniences.

Pritchard Services

The Pritchard Services Group is the most diversified company in the contract service sector, both in geographical and functional terms. It operates throughout Europe, Australasia and North America. From its origins in building maintenance, it has moved into health care, catering, textile maintenance and security. Pritchard is also the largest of the contract service firms and its annual turnover of just under £446 million in 1984 puts it among the top 250 UK companies. Its success as a commercial enterprise was confirmed by references to it in Walter Goldsmith's and David Clutterbuck's book, *The Winning Streak*, which documented the formulas behind success in British industry. Pritchard spokesmen ascribed the company's growth to its fast decisions on acquisitions, devolved responsibility and the willingness to undertake small contracts as a training ground for new managers.[17]

Pritchard has more experience of public sector work than any of the other major contractors. As noted in Chapter 2, its health care

TABLE 3.10   Pritchard Services Group
The Pritchard Services Group is based in Britain and operates across a broad geographical base. The company began as a building maintenance firm, but has diversified rapidly and now operates in all major service sectors: health care, catering, textile maintenance and security.

Pritchard Services: 1984 financial performance

Area	Turnover £000s	%	Operating profit £000s	%
USA	249 347	55.8	7 890	41.9
UK/Ireland	83 555	18.7	7 795	41.4
Australasia	59 038	13.2	1 988	10.5
Continental Europe	20 493	4.6	407	2.2
Canada	27 629	6.2	458	2.4
Other	6 529	1.5	311	1.6
Total	**446 591**	**100.0**	**18 849**	**100.0**

Source: *Report and Accounts 1984*, Pritchard Services Group.

Health care   Pritchard's growth in the health care sector has been rapid, and this area now accounts for the largest share of the firm's turnover. Activity in this market began in 1971 with the acquisition of Crothall and Company (UK), the leader in the small market for hospital services in the UK. The acquisition of the parent company, Crothall International, in 1980 enabled Pritchard to establish itself as a leading competitor in the American, New Zealand, and Australian markets. One year later it strengthened its position in North America with the acquisition of National Medical Consultants, an American group involved in the provision of hospital housekeeping and temporary nursing services.

Building maintenance   Pritchard's building maintenance activities include commercial and industrial cleaning, the provision of janitorial supplies and general maintenance services. The firm has a strong position in the UK contract cleaning market, where it focuses on smaller customers and specialist cleaning assignments. Its position in the municipal cleaning market, where it is represented by Pritchard Industrial Services, is somewhat less secure.

Linen rental   Textile rental is clearly the most profitable division within the Pritchard Group, accounting for only 7 per cent of total turnover but 22 per cent of all operating profit in 1984. Nearly all work in this sector is conducted in the UK and Ireland. The recent acquisition of Spring Grove and its integration with United Linen Services, Pritchard's existing subsidiary, has given the firm an estimated 11 per cent share of the UK textile rental market.

Catering   Catering and vending services accounted for just over 16 per cent of the group's turnover in 1984. In Australia and North America, its major markets, Pritchard has moved into specialist areas (such as vending machines and the design of food delivery systems) to compensate for the declining number of institutional clients. Two major new acquisitions, Food Concepts Inc. and Automatic Catering Inc., are seen as a foundation for continued expansion in the US market.

Security   Pritchard provides a variety of security services, ranging from cash-carrying to alarm monitoring and personal guarding. Although security services remain a relatively small and competitive area, accounting for 5.3 per cent of turnover and 4 per cent of profits in 1984, Pritchard recently acquired Zeus Security in an attempt to expand its share of the London guarding market.

subsidiary, Crothall, has operated in the NHS since 1961 and for years held about 90 per cent of all NHS cleaning work awarded to contractors. Although the amount of NHS work available to contractors dropped dramatically in the early 1970s, Crothall maintained a prominent position in the market right up until the present round of competitive tendering. However, the Government's initiative transformed Crothall's near-monopoly position entirely. New competitors, pricing aggressively in order to establish a foothold in the market, were awarded the majority of contracts that went out to tender, including many that Crothall had held for years. The company is only now beginning to find its feet again in this market.

Pritchard has also been active in the local authority market, providing street cleansing, refuse collection and pest control services to a number of authorities. Although Pritchard got into this market at an early stage, the explosion in local authority work that was expected never occurred and the company presently operates only three major public cleansing contracts. Because of its size and involvement in both local authority and NHS contracts, the firm has been the primary target of the anti-privatisation campaign mounted by trade unions. It has suffered through prolonged, disruptive and occasionally violent action on two separate occasions: in Wandsworth, where it won the refuse collection contract in 1982, and at Barking Hospital, where it was forced to make drastic cuts in labour costs in order to retain an existing contract when it came up for renewal in 1983. Both incidents have contributed to a more cautious and selective approach to public sector contracts on the part of the firm.

Brengreen

Brengreen Holdings, small in comparison to its major competitors, is often looked upon as the protagonist in the current debate over public sector contracting out. Brengreen's subsidiary, Exclusive, won the first controversial public sector contract in Southend in 1979 and Brengreen's Chairman, David Evans, played a pivotal role in convincing the Conservative Party of the merits of contract cleaning. Evans himself is a fascinating character, displaying much of the entrepreneurial spirit that has long been associated with contract cleaners. After playing football for Aston Villa, he accepted a job with a cleaning company in 1954. In 1960, he decided to strike out on his own and he and his wife began an office cleaning business. Twenty-four years and several takeovers later, in 1984, Evans' small empire had revenues in excess of £40 million and employed some 23 000 people.

TABLE 3.11 Brengreen Holdings
Brengreen has grown rapidly and is now considered a market leader alongside older and much larger competitors. Although its activities are mainly confined to the UK, the firm has established a number of partnership arrangements with cleaning firms in the Middle and Far East.

Brengreen Holdings: 1984 Financial Performance

Area	Turnover £000s	%	Profit before tax £000s	%
Commercial cleaning	27 713	68.2	1 460	59.7
Cleansing services	10 375	25.5	789	32.3
Other activities	2 556	6.3	195	8.0
Total	**40 644**	**100.0**	**4 444**	**100.0**

Source: *Annual Report and Accounts 1984*, Brengreen Group.

Commercial cleaning Exclusive Cleaning forms the backbone of the Brengreen group, and accounted for 68 per cent of total group turnover in 1984. Its primary business is the cleaning of buildings, from factories and hotels to supermarkets and shopping malls. A large share of the division's turnover is accounted for by public sector contracts, primarily with central government departments. Exclusive Health Care has recently been formed as a subsidiary of Exclusive Cleaning to provide domestic services to NHS hospitals.

Municipal cleansing The other major division within the Brengreen group is Exclusive Cleansing, which provides street cleaning, refuse collection and public convenience cleaning services to local authorities. Exclusive pioneered this market at Southend in 1981 and, having built upon its success there, now considers itself to be the market leader. In 1984, revenue from municipal cleansing activities stood at 25 per cent of the group's total turnover.

Other activities Brengreen engages in a number of other, unrelated services which account for a small percentage of the firm's turnover and profit. These include a leasing company and a travel agency. In 1984 Brengreen acquired the White Cross Group, a company which designs and assembles refuse compactors and provides waste disposal services, in the expectation of increased waste disposal work following the abolition of the metropolitan counties.

Brengreen, like Pritchard Services, has a comparatively long history of undertaking public sector work. It began cleaning government buildings in the 1960s, and was a major beneficiary of Harold Wilson's decision to contract out departmental cleaning on a wide scale. Ever since that time, public sector work has been an important component of Brengreen's business base. Brengreen's involvement with the public sector ranges from contracts with central departments and nationalised industries to more recent successes in local authorities and the health service. It has won nearly half of all municipal cleansing contracts awarded privately and, despite a slower start in the health service, had secured 11 hospital cleaning contracts by the end of 1985.

Hawley

The Hawley Group is the fastest growing of all contractors presently tendering for NHS and local authority contracts. In five years, its turnover has grown from £27 million (1980) to £298 million (1984); this places it among the 400 largest UK companies.[18] This rapid growth has primarily been fuelled by a substantial campaign of acquisitions in the United States and Britain. North America currently accounts for 53 per cent of total turnover and Britain is responsible for another 41 per cent. Hawley's primary interests, according to its 1984 annual report, lie in industries

TABLE 3.12 Hawley Group
The Hawley Group has developed as an Anglo-American company, with a strong presence in American, Canadian and British service markets. Cleaning and maintenance work are undertaken on both sides of the Atlantic; most other activities – including the provision of security, home-improvement and travel-related services – are specific to either the North American or UK market.

Hawley Group: 1984 financial performance

Area	Sales £000s	%	Profit £000s
Cleaning and maintenance	110 427	37.0	6 689
Home improvements	93 429	31.3	9 828
Security	62 397	20.9	6 616
Travel and leisure	28 974	9.7	3 280
Associated companies	—	—	7 812
Other*	2 901	1.0	(2 739)
Total	**298 128**	**100.0**	**31 485**

* Central costs, financial services and discontinued activities.
Source: *1984 Report and Accounts*, Hawley Group.

Cleaning and maintenance Hawley's turnover in the cleaning sector moved from £29 million in 1983 to £110 million in 1984, largely as a result of substantial acquisitions in the US market. It now operates through two major subsidiaries in the US, Omni Building Services and Oxford Services, and has a strong presence in the hospital cleaning sector through United Health Services. In the UK, Hawley's cleaning and maintenance work is channelled through Provincial Cleaning Services. Since it began trading in 1980, Provincial has acquired numerous smaller cleaning companies which have enabled it to service a variety of commercial and institutional clients.

Home improvements Hawley's home improvement services are conducted exclusively in the UK. Sales for this division rose an impressive 124 per cent in 1984 and accounted for 31 per cent of the firm's turnover. Activities in this field include design and installation of fitted bedrooms and kitchens, showers and windows.

Security Security activities are based in the US, and accounted for 21 per cent of turnover and 10.6 per cent of group profit in 1984. The major activity within this division is the provision of computerised alarm services based on a central monitoring network.

Travel and leisure Hawley's travel and leisure division operates in the UK through two tour operators and one travel agency. It accounted for 10 per cent of Hawley's turnover in 1984 and, like its sister divisions, reported extraordinary sales growth (up 150 per cent) over the previous year.

featuring strong cash flows and low capital requirements. Cleaning, maintenance and home improvements account for two-thirds of the group's turnover and just less than half of its profits. Other activities include the provision of security, home improvement, and travel-related services.

Hawley is one of the newest companies to establish a foothold in the public sector market. In 1982, Hawley established Mediclean, a specialist hospital cleaning company, with the express intention of tendering for NHS work. To compensate for the new company's lack of experience in the field, Hawley brought in experienced managers from competitor firms. This has helped Mediclean to become one of the fastest growing and most successful companies competing for NHS work. Like other major competitors, its success has made it a target of the unions' opposition campaign and disruptions at several of its earliest contract locations have caused it to become more selective in bidding for public sector work. Never-theless, Mediclean has been inundated with invitations to tender and looks set to obtain a significant volume of work in the NHS market. Hawley has also shown an interest in the local authority market, where its Provincial subsidiary has gained contracts to clean numer-ous schools throughout South-east England.

BET

BET is a huge conglomerate, with some 60 000 employees and a turnover of £1263 million in 1984. It operates in six major areas: transport, construction, publishing, leisure, electronics and indus-trial services. BET established itself as the major force in the textile maintenance market in 1985 with the acquisition of the remaining shares in Initial Services, the largest firm in the UK textile maintenance market. Its involvement with the laundry industry dates back to 1934, when it entered into a joint venture with Advance Laundries Ltd. After Advance Laundries became a subsidiary in 1955, BET continued to expand its interests in other laundry companies; by 1980, it had subsidiary holdings in both the Sunlight and Initial Service Groups. Its holding in Sunlight was reduced just prior to Initial's attempted takeover of the Johnson Group in 1983; as noted earlier, its acquisition of the outstanding 59 per cent of Initial shares was completed in 1985 after gaining the approval of the Monopolies and Mergers Commission.[19]

Initial Services is itself among the largest contracting companies in the UK and presently operates in both the textile maintenance and the office-cleaning markets. It is an old company, founded in 1903 to supply linen to a variety of commercial customers. Each item was marked with the customers 'initial' and returned to the same location after cleaning. It became a public company in 1928, and has since established a presence in all textile maintenance markets with the exception of dry cleaning. In 1984, Initial Services reported a turnover of £250 million. Nearly 60 per cent of this was accounted for by UK-based businesses; the remainder arose from rental or cleaning services offered in the US, Europe and a number of South-east Asian countries.[20]

TABLE 3.13   Initial

Initial PLC, now a subsidiary of BET, is the largest firm in the textile maintenance industry and maintains a commanding presence in work-wear, cabinet towel, dustmat and industrial wiping cloth rental markets. The absence of growth in these sectors has encouraged it to diversify and contract cleaning now accounts for over 15 per cent of its turnover.

Initial: 1984 financial performance

Area	Turnover £000s	%	Operating profit £000s	%
Hire and replacement	179 931	71.9	24 696	80.6
Office and general cleaning	38 653	15.4	1 779	5.8
Manufacturing	22 002	8.8	2 339	7.6
Other activities	9 884	3.9	1 812	5.9
Total	**250 470**	**100.0**	**30 626**	**100.0**

Source: *Annual Report 1984*, Initial PLC.

Rental services   Rental services accounted for 72 per cent of the Initial Group's turnover and 80 per cent of its profit in 1984. Initial Services, the largest division within the company, provides cabinet towel rental, linen hire, and laundry services to 250 000 small and medium-sized clients and operates through 64 branch locations in the UK alone. Initial Workwear Services, geared to larger customers primarily involved in manufacturing industry, provides a hiring and cleaning service for industrial workwear. A third division, Initial Industrial Services, is involved in the rental and cleaning of dustmats and industrial wiping cloths, fairly specialised markets in which it maintains a sizeable lead over competitors. Automatic Services, a fourth division, engages in the rental of warm air dryers.

Contract Cleaning   Initial operates in all of the major areas of the UK contract cleaning market through its Initial Service Cleaners division. With 640 full-time and 12 400 part-time workers, it holds approximately 4 per cent of the total UK contract cleaning market. Like many of its competitors, it established a health care services division to cater to the expanding NHS market, and has been quick to gain a foothold in the local authority market. Recently Initial acquired Descaling Contractors Ltd, a firm which provides specialist pipe surveying and cleaning services to local authorities.

Manufacturing   Initial's manufacturing subsidiaries exist primarily to support its rental service businesses: Initial Service Textiles manufactures cleaning cloths and cabinet towels and Initial Garment Manufacturing produces a range of industrial workwear. The Group's Engineering Products division consists of two subsidiaries engaged in the production of towel cabinets and bathroom textiles.

Other activities   Initial has moved into the growing market for security services, through the acquisition of 90 per cent of the share capital of Arrow Surveillance Systems. The firm has interests in leasing and film production and also maintains printing and drink-vending subsidiaries.

Advance Services is much smaller than Initial and its interests lie almost exclusively in the textile maintenance market. In 1983 its turnover was £40.5 million. It is the market leader in the cabinet towel rental area and has a sizeable presence in both dust mat and linen rental markets. It also has a good share of both contract and domestic laundry markets, and maintains other interests in workwear, dry cleaning and ancillary services. Advance operates through 24 branches across the UK and its fleet of 600 vehicles distributes workwear, cabinet towels and linen to a variety of customers.

Both Initial and Advance Services had limited experience of NHS laundry work prior to the introduction of mandatory competitive tendering in 1983. Although they have managed to win several NHS laundry contracts, BET's biggest inroads into the NHS have been in the cleaning sector where Initial Service Cleaners (through its recently established health care division) has secured an impressive share of the NHS market. By the end of 1985, it had won 18 health service contracts and was reasonably well placed to benefit from forthcoming tendering exercises. Initial Service Cleaners has also made inroads into the local authority market, winning school cleaning contracts in a number of counties.

Sunlight

The Sunlight Service Group, like the Initial Service Group, has diversified from its traditional base in the textile maintenance industry into contract cleaning and security. Founded at the turn of the century as a laundry company, it became a public company in 1928 and continued to grow rapidly, both organically and through acquisition.[21] It is now one of the largest firms in the textile maintenance industry, and the only one of the majors with a traditional base in the laundry sector. Sunlight's business is conducted almost exclusively in the UK; its operations in France and Holland accounted for only 3 per cent of the group's turnover in 1984 and are growing more slowly than its UK-based subsidiaries.

The decline in the laundry sector has not had as dramatic an impact upon Sunlight as one might expect. The firm's turnover grew from £39 million in 1983 to £58 million in 1984, an increase of 47 per cent. This display of strength resulted from a concerted programme of acquisitions in both textile maintenance and cleaning fields. Despite its aborted attempts to take over two of the largest firms in the industry, Johnson and Spring Grove, in 1983, Sunlight's acquisitions have continued to be both numerous and substantial. In 1984, the firm acquired 16 companies of assorted sizes and functions. Sunlight has a good record of returning loss-making companies to profitability, and looks primarily for companies which can expand its geographic and functional coverage.[22] Although the extent of the recent acquisition programme has caused serious disruptions to existing businesses, it is expected that the restructuring of the company will allow it to respond more flexibly to changes in the marketplace.

Sunlight's laundry division has undertaken 'overflow contracts' for the NHS for many years. Small in scale, these contracts have nevertheless served to establish the company's reputation within the NHS. It expects to benefit significantly from the current round

TABLE 3.14   Sunlight Service Group
Sunlight Service's traditional strength lies in the textile maintenance market, more specifically in linen rental and laundry services. Poor prospects in these sectors have encouraged the Group to undertake an ambitious programme of acquisition and to diversify into contract cleaning, security and computer services.

Sunlight Service Group: 1984 financial performance

Area	Turnover £000s	%	Profit £000s
Textile maintenance	41 088	70.8	5 188
Commercial cleaning	11 098	19.1	692
Security	4 918	8.5	348
Other	939	1.6	18
Central overheads and interest			(1 872)
Total	**58 043**	**100.0**	**4 374**

Textile maintenance   In 1984, textile maintenance work accounted for about 70 per cent of Sunlight's turnover and 83 per cent of its profit. The firm provides three types of services: linen hire, workwear and ancillary industrial rental, and laundry. Modeluxe Linen Services is the largest supplier to the UK hotel and restaurant trade, with an estimated 25 per cent of the total market. Sunlight Industrial Services provides workwear rental on a national basis, and holds approximately 5 per cent of this market. National Sunlight Laundries, the traditional core of Sunlight's business, maintains the largest share of the laundry market (13 per cent).

Contract cleaning   Numerous acquisitions in the office cleaning field have been integrated into Sunlight's cleaning subsidiary, the Pall Mall Cleaning Group, which accounted for just under 20 per cent of the group's 1984 turnover. Margins in the contract cleaning field have been low, however, and the division was responsible for only 11 per cent of group profits. Returns from the division's activities in the hospital sector have been particularly disappointing.

Security   Sunlight has established a significant presence in the 'guarding' market in Central London, and also offers alarm monitoring and keyholding services. Although this division accounted for less than 9 per cent of 1984 turnover, it is looking to expand its geographical base significantly over the next few years.

of tendering and has made sizeable investment in new facilities to meet the hygiene standards required to undertake specialised hospital work. Pall Mall, the group's cleaning arm, has been equally active in securing both NHS domestic and school cleaning contracts. Margins in both of these areas have proved disappointing, however, and the company has recently become extremely selective about its activities in the contract cleaning field.

Financial performance

The financial stability of the contracting companies has been an area of concern to both public sector unions and local and health authority administrators. Both groups realise that margins on public sector work have been slim, and are concerned that certain contractors may not be able to sustain low margin or loss-making contracts. But the five companies examined here are rarely the targets of such concern. Three of them – Initial, Pritchard, and Sunlight – are older companies, with histories of successful performance within their respective sectors. All five are among the 100 largest companies in Britain and are growing very rapidly. For example, the Hawley Group has increased its turnover ten-fold in just four years; Pritchard Services has increased its turnover by a factor of five over the same period. Both of these firms have engaged in acquisition behaviour on an unprecedented scale. This thirst for acquisitions can be attributed to the nature of their core business – contract cleaning. Its low capital demands ensure good cash-flow prospects, and pave the way for the continual purchase of smaller companies needed to round out geographical or functional portfolios.

It is interesting to compare the latest financial results from these five companies. Table 3.15 displays their 1984 results, as documented in their respective annual reports. Although this offers only a snapshot view of the positions of competitors, it provides a good illustration of some of the key features of the contract industries as a whole:

● *Turnover* Although Pritchard remains the largest company by a wide margin, most of its revenues arise from overseas trading. Initial maintains the largest turnover within the UK,

TABLE 3.15 Major contractors: 1984 financial performance

	Date of accounts	Turnover (£m)	Turnover in UK (%)	Profit before tax	Return (profit margin) (%)	Capital employed (£m)	Return on capital	Liquidity*	No. of employees	Average wage per employee
Pritchard	12/84	447	19.0	15.0	3.4	166.0	9.0	1.08	51 674	4 001
Brengreen	3/84	41	87.5	2.4	5.9	17.4	13.8	1.55	15 775	1 585
Hawley	12/84	298	41.0	31.5	10.6	189.3	16.6	1.01	32 439	3 252
Initial	3/84	229	59.3	28.7	12.5	144.6	19.8	1.30	29 991	3 056
Sunlight	3/84	58	96.7	4.4	7.5	35.7	12.3	1.28	9 606	2 779

* Current assets ÷ current liabilities.
Sources: 1984 Annual Reports from all companies.

reporting revenues of £135 million in this market in 1984. It is interesting to note that the two fastest growing companies – Pritchard and Hawley – are also the companies which have made the most significant investment in the American market.

● *Profitability* Profitability across the five companies varies widely. The slowest growing company, Initial, has consistently reported the highest profit margins and did so again in 1984 (12.5 per cent). The largest group, Pritchard Services, reported returns of only 3.4 per cent, similar to its performance in previous years.

● *Return on Capital* All companies appear to have earned satisfactory returns on capital in 1984, ranging from 9 per cent to 19 per cent. Initial reported a 20 per cent return on capital, in keeping with its good results in previous years. Pritchard reported the lowest figure at 9.8 per cent, a dramatic drop from its 15 per cent return in 1983.

● *Liquidity* Liquidity ratios, which compare current assets to current liabilities, are generally adequate. Not surprisingly, the fastest growing companies – Pritchard and Hawley – report ratios hovering around the 1.0 mark. Those companies who are in the process of consolidating past acquisitions are better placed with ratios between 1.3 and 1.5.

● *Employee remuneration* Average wage rates, calculated by dividing the aggregate wage bill of the company by the number of employees, are extremely low across these five companies. In 1984, they varied from £1500 to £4600, with those firms based primarily in the UK exhibiting the lowest average payment per employee. These unusually low rates reflect both the high percentage of part-time employees and the low hourly rates paid to operatives in the cleaning and textile maintenance industries.

The most commercially agressive company at the moment appears to be the Hawley Group, whose ten-fold expansion over a four-year period is clearly exceptional. The most stable company, judged by financial performance only, appears to be Initial Services. It is not growing as fast as the others, displaying less interest in acquisitions and new markets. Nevertheless, its profit margins and returns on capital have consistently been higher than those of its competitors, its expansion in the contract cleaning sector has been steady, and its leadership of the textile maintenance market is unlikely to be challenged. The other three companies fall somewhere between these two extremes. Brengreen continues to rely heavily on its cleaning base, seemingly intent upon expansion overseas, but has made overtures in the direction of the textile maintenance market. Sunlight has moved in the other direction – diversifying from laundry into security, cleaning and computer services. Pritchard Services, having extended itself through a worldwide programme of acquisitions, is looking to consolidate its interests and achieve higher levels of profitability in the numerous markets where it maintains a significant presence.

In summary, the commercial activities of the five companies examined here highlight several of the trends mentioned earlier in the chapter. Both older and newer companies are expanding rapidly despite the effects of the recession, diversifying from traditional markets through concerted programmes of acquisition and integration. Most have tended to concentrate on businesses with reliable cash flows; only Initial has moved into manufacturing, which requires much higher levels of investment. All five companies are likely to exhibit continued growth, as smaller competitors are pushed out of both textile maintenance and cleaning markets. Their financial strength allows them to cross-subsidise activities, sustaining temporary losses which smaller firms could not consider. Increasing concentration and rising barriers to entry can only mean a strengthening of their respective positions in the market.

The future

The individual contract industries examined in this chapter are all at different stages of development. The textile maintenance industry is the most mature, with a high level of concentration and very little new entry; major competitors are looking to maintain market share and diversify into both related and unrelated areas. The contract catering industry is less mature. Both the market and the number of competitors in the field are still expanding, despite the dominant position of the two major companies who are looking to move into specialist areas within the catering sphere. The contract cleaning market is clearly the youngest and thus the most competitive market of the three. The combination of a highly fragmented market and low entry barriers has resulted in an influx of new companies and very chaotic pricing behaviour. These trends have been exaggerated by the opening of new markets, most notably those within the public sector.

There are signs, however, that the contract cleaning industry is beginning to mature. Competitive pricing behaviour still exists, but it is somewhat less intense than it was in the early 1980s and many of the major firms are no longer willing to put in unrealistic bids for work. The combination of poor margins and sizeable acquisition programmes by the major companies has meant that the number of competitors in the cleaning field is no longer growing. It is likely that the remainder of the 1980s will witness continued takeover activity, which will no doubt result in a much slimmer and more concentrated industry. This transformation will not, of course, happen overnight and there is likely to be a temporary return to the rough and tumble days of 1983–4 if and when the local authority market opens up in 1987. The older cleaning firms are all too aware of this and are lobbying the Government to establish a list of 'approved contractors' for larger contracts, thus raising the entry barriers into this market.

Although public sector work will continue to play a part in the future strategies of contractors in all three industries, it is no longer the only, or even the major, prospect on the horizon. Their one-time enthusiasm for this market has been tempered by the sobering experiences of the early 1980s, including poor success ratios in winning contracts, an inability to hold on to older contracts, unworkable specifications, industrial action and universally disappointing margins. Those who thought rapid growth in the local authority market would compensate for declining markets elsewhere have been bitterly disappointed as interest in privatisation had faded. Those who expected that public sector contracts would bring prestige and have positive spin-off effects on other parts of their businesses have suffered nothing but negative publicity from the unions' campaign of opposition. Many of the larger companies have withdrawn from the market, some on a more permanent basis than others. Until activity in the public sector becomes less 'political' and less controversial, the primary strategic objective of most major contractors will remain the cultivation of private sector markets both in Britain and overseas. The contractors' experience is best summed up in a paragraph from Sunlight's 1984 Annual Report:

> As a matter of policy, our exposure to work arising from the DHSS and the local authorities has been limited until the commercial and operating parameters become clearer. The margins presently available in these areas are in general not adequate. When taken with the support costs necessary to obtain and maintain the work, this means this area of activity has yet to see benefit from its presence in this sector.

4 The Trade Union Response

Contract service firms played an important role in bringing competitive tendering to the political agenda, but no more significant than that played by the trade unions. Without the industrial action of the 1970s and early 1980s, the policy of compulsory tendering would not have become nearly so popular within the Conservative Party; without the sustained campaign of union opposition to the policy, the entire exercise would not have received nearly so much media attention or aroused quite so much controversy as it has over the past two years. Far from being seen as one of many cost-saving management initiatives put forward by the Government, the tendering policy has come to be viewed as a direct attack upon trade union power.

This perception is clearly justified. The tendering process itself very clearly pits the Government against the public sector unions. The Government is looking for efficiency improvements in the service sector; in most authorities, this can only be achieved by reducing staff, lowering conditions of service, and instituting more flexible working arrangements. All three actions clearly undermine the position of both locally-based public service workers and their trade unions. Competitive tendering can be thought of as a zero-sum game, in which the Government and the public sector trade unions are the players: the greater the efficiency savings, the more dramatic the effect upon union members.

This chapter considers the position and role of the trade unions in greater depth. It examines the trends in public sector unionism which set the context for contracting out, the general effects of tendering and contracting out upon unions and their members, the specific techniques which the unions have used to combat government policy, and the strengths and weaknesses of the unions' current strategies.

Background

In the years following World War II, trade unions were accepted as a necessary counterbalance to the power of capital in the economic system; both Labour and Conservative governments did their best to avoid confrontation with the union movement in order to keep industrial relations out of politics.[1] By 1980, the atmosphere had changed dramatically. Fundamental questions were being asked about the power of trade unions in many sectors of the economy and industrial relations issues had risen to the top of the political agenda. As David Heald and Gillian Morris noted in 1984, the change has been both dramatic and comprehensive:

> The transformation of the agenda seems virtually complete. The 'good employer' tradition has died and the official promotion of public sector trade unionism as one of the bases for sound industrial relations abruptly reversed; such is the change in the political climate that the hitherto unthinkable can not only be thought, but might be implemented as well.[2]

To understand the forces behind this change, it is necessary to go back to the post-war period, which saw relatively quiet but continuous growth in the strength of the trade union movement. The scarcity of labour which resulted from the full employment policies of successive governments gave the trade unions a strong hand in collective bargaining decisions. Steady growth in the economy allowed wage demands to be met by both Conservative and Labour governments. Although the number of small strikes grew as the control exerted by trade union leaders over their membership began to decline, the commitment to keep industrial relations out of politics was strong and the unions entered the 1960s in a more powerful position than ever before.

Economic crises, however, radically altered the relationship between the trade unions and the major political parties. The first dramatic changes occurred in the mid-1960s when the Wilson Government was forced to look to an incomes policy to remedy a sterling crisis and balance of payments problems. Although the trade union movement initially went along with this policy, in hopes of a return to free collective bargaining when the crises had past, support began to wane as the 1960s drew to a close and it became clear that public sector pay settlements were out of line with those in the private sector.[3] Devaluation of the pound in 1967 exacerbated existing tensions, and by late 1969 the policy of statutory incomes control had been discredited. These last years of the 1966 Wilson Government produced a notable spread of militant behaviour to both white-collar workers and public sector employees. Although many union leaders were themselves willing to offer continued support to the Government, rank and file members resented the control over their incomes and put pressure on their leaders to take a more militant stand. The number of strikes, most of them unofficial, grew dramatically from 1968. Of particular note is the unofficial, localised action taken by refuse collectors in 1969 which turned into a long, official strike and resulted in a substantial pay settlement. In many ways, this action marked the beginning of a new era in the history of local government manual workers.

Public sector employees and unions took centre stage in the confrontation between Edward Heath's Government and the trade union movement. Abandoning the Churchillian prescription of conflict avoidance, the Heath Government undertook legal measures to restore order to what it viewed as industrial chaos. It also stood fast against pay claims in the public sector, on the grounds that central government had to set an example for private sector employers; this stance further disrupted the relationship between private and public sector pay and resulted in a series of damaging disputes in key sectors of the economy. Action by ancillary workers in hospitals added to the chaos in nearly all of the major nationalised industries. In March 1973, some 25 000 ancillary workers went on strike over the issue of pay parity with local authority workers, causing widespread disruption in laundry, catering and domestic services and forcing the closure of several hospital wards. Although the outcome of the month-long action – equal pay instalments and earlier rises – was less than a spectacular victory for the unions, the strike marked the first significant signs of militancy among hospital ancillaries and sowed the seeds for action later in the 1970s.

This period saw rapid growth in the size of public sector unions. Between 1970 and 1975, NUPE membership increased from 305 000 to 508 000 and COHSE membership grew from 78 000 to 143 000.[4] Although this growth was partly a reflection of increasing levels of public expenditure and a larger state bureaucracy, it can also be attributed to the growing status and appeal of the trade union movement. Many public sector workers realised that their 'guinea pig' role in the Government's attempts at income restraint had led to a marked deterioration in their relative financial well-being and saw that union action had been instrumental in achieving settlements beneficial to members. In contrast to the situation today, the public sector unions were increasingly viewed as highly effective instruments in protecting public sector employees from political manipulation by the state.

The return of a Labour government in 1974 ushered in a brief period of relative quiet in industrial relations, usually attributed to Labour's 'Social Contract' which gave the unions' national leadership a significant and unprecedented role in the determination of economic policy. Economic problems intervened once more, however, and the sterling crisis of 1976 put great pressure on the Government to strengthen the policy of 'income restraint' in an attempt to control inflation. As a result of the imposition of cash limits, the number of strikes began to increase. By late 1978, little remained of the Social Contract. The 'winter of discontent' of 1978–9 saw action intensify as many of those who had been active in 1973 – teachers, hospital workers, railwaymen, postmen and power workers – staged a repeat performance. Ancillary workers once again laid siege to the NHS, blocking vital supplies and forcing closure of hospital wards; refuse workers allowed huge rubbish tips to accumulate in the streets while their demands for a 40 per cent pay rise went unmet.

Although the defeat of the Labour Party in the 1979 General Election confirmed the public's view that the breakdown of industrial authority had gone too far, the election of the Conservatives did not soften the public sector unions' newfound militancy. On the contrary, it strengthened the determination of those in the more militant areas of the trade union movement (including both local authority manual and NHS ancillary workers) and the first two years of the new administration saw a series of isolated strikes. Several early confrontations occurred between the Government and the health service unions. COHSE and NUPE threatened to boycott private patients in NHS pay beds; this was followed by local action in the form of an overtime ban by catering workers and a strike by porters over bonus payments in 1980 and 1981, respectively. The most serious recent dispute in the health service occurred in 1982. Like previous disputes, this one concerned wages and the broader issue of wage restraint. But unlike its predecessors, the 1982 dispute received the support of a wide cross-section of the health service community and dragged on for months. Ancillary workers were once again at the forefront of action, a fact that did not go unnoticed by the Government. As the *Health and Social Service Journal* reported in June of 1982, 'ministers are understood to be annoyed by the attitude of the unions in the present pay dispute and particularly the activities of ancillary staff in certain hospitals.'⁵

This strike helped to convince Conservative supporters of the need to take action against public sector unions. One example of the pressure placed upon the government by its supporters can be found in a paper published by the Institute of Directors in 1982. It noted: 'The key industrial relations problem for the future as we emerge from the recession is the ability (and threat) of some public sector unions to inhibit recovery. Their strength enables them to pursue claims for unearned wage increases to obstruct necessary productivity improvements. If nothing is done to contain public sector unions, they will be able to undermine the effectiveness of all the employment legislation so far introduced by the present government.'⁶ In response to both internal pressure and changes in attitudes among the public, the Conservative Government has pushed through a concerted programme of labour legislation, attacking the closed shop (by requiring frequent membership ballots and by extending the number of situations where a closed shop is illegal) and placing severe limits on industrial action (through a narrowing of immunity rights and restrictions on secondary action and picketing). The Government has also called into question the political role of unions by requiring regular referendums on the issue of political funds. The weight of this comprehensive programme has fallen equally on both public and private sector unions.

Public sector unions have simultaneously come under attack from the Government's privatisation initiative. Each of the major forms of privatisation has had a profound impact upon the trade unions' status, decreasing the potential membership market and increasing the downward pressure upon existing wage and benefit packages. Denationalisation, for example, has removed access to public sector funding and has often resulted in a shift from one to numerous 'employer units'. Deregulation has frequently ensured a wider role for non-unionised labour. Contracting out has had a significant and direct impact upon both individual unions and their members and, for reasons documented in the following section, is arguably the most serious threat to the unions of all current privatisation initiatives.

The effects of contracting out

The impact of competitive tendering and contracting out upon unions is difficult to quantify, as the policy in its present state has only recently been implemented and the full effects of the change will not become obvious for some time. But the new policy has serious implications for trade unions even in the short term, foremost of which is the negative effect that manpower reductions will have on membership totals. As shown in Figure 4.1, membership of public sector unions has fallen gradually since 1981–2 after increasing dramatically during the 1960s and 1970s. COHSE witnessed a decline of 3.4 per cent between 1982 and 1984; over this same period NUPE and NALGO membership totals declined by 2.1 per cent and 2 per cent respectively.[7] Although these changes are small when compared with the decline in membership of the largest private sector unions, they are one important factor behind the public sector unions' recent financial problems.

The Government's policy of mandatory tendering affects membership totals in several ways. Competitive tendering generally results in a smaller number of staff being proposed to undertake the contract by both in-house and external bidders. Regardless of whether the contract is awarded in-house or to a contractor, less jobs result from the exercise and the unions must increase their penetration among re-employed workers to sustain membership totals. If the contract is awarded externally, the effect upon membership is likely to be more dramatic as a high percentage of union members will not apply for jobs with contractors. Those who do and are hired privately are not always interested in renewing their subscriptions, especially if the fight to save the in-house service has been a particularly bitter one. New workers hired externally by the contractor, particularly part-timers, are usually

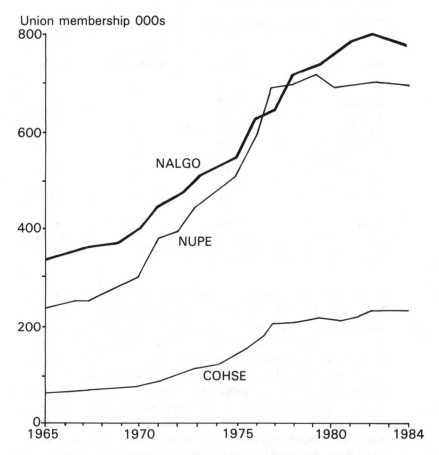

Figure 4.1   Trends in public sector union membership: 1965–84
Source: Annual Reports. Trade Union Congress 1965–84.

reluctant to enter into any formal association with a trade union. Retention of both old and new members is difficult as staff turnover within contractors' organisations is high.

The problem of limited membership within contracting firms is serious and highlights a second problem facing the trade unions. Without significant penetration among the contractor's employees, unions are unlikely to be granted recognition rights by the company, and without full recognition rights the union has little power to negotiate for its members. Several contractors originally agreed

TABLE 4.1   Selected job losses: local authority cleansing

Area	Previous number of jobs	Jobs after privatisation	% loss
Wirral	456	254	44
Southend	297	213	28
Merton	176	95	46
Eastbourne	140	90	36
Milton Keynes	104	74	29
S. Oxfordshire	59	43	27
Tandridge	58	37	36
Taunton Deane	43	22	49
Mendip	35	24	31
Total	1 368	852	38

Source: *Privatisation: Who Loses? Who Profits?* (London: Labour Research Department, 1983); *Public Service Action*, 1, 2, 4 (1983).

to recognise unions who recruited more than half of their work-force, but this target demanded an organising ability which few unions could sustain during the transition from public to private sector. Although the criteria for recognition have generally become looser and agreements with contractors are now being reached on a site by site basis, establishing a permanent union presence within a private firm remains a difficult task. Those who were once responsible for recruitment, particularly former shop stewards, are rarely interested in jobs with private sector contractors. Activists who do apply for available posts are unlikely to be accepted in any case, as contractors are keen to avoid future industrial relations problems.

Competitive tendering has other deleterious effects upon trade unions. It undermines the credibility of the public sector union movement. While in theory public sector workers should look to their union to shield them from the vagaries of the tendering process, in practice there is little the unions can do to honour their commitment to protect members from 'exploitation' by employers. Although they can oppose the tendering process, on a number of occasions union action has only served to aggravate the adverse effects of the tendering process (see Chapters 6 and 7). The uncertainty surrounding the tendering process has a damaging effect upon the morale of the existing staff. Not all understand the mechanics of the tendering process; most are extremely concerned that they will lose their job. The operating environment becomes much less secure and working conditions deteriorate in three main ways: job losses, pay reductions and changes to conditions of service.

Job losses

Because many ancillary services are highly labour-intensive, the savings demanded by competitive tendering in the NHS are usually made by reducing labour costs. Both competitive tendering and contracting out have led to a significant decline in the numbers of people employed and the hours which individuals work. It is difficult to quantify the number of staff who have lost their jobs as a result of the NHS tendering initiative because the only redundancy figures collected centrally by the DHSS refer to employees who receive premature superannuation payments; those collected locally by health authorities are equally misleading because many redundant individuals start work immediately for the private contractor.[8] (One survey, conducted in June of 1985, reported that there had been 3000 redundancies in the first 100 contracts awarded to the private sector.)[9] However, it is clear that domestic services have seen the largest number of job losses; the less labour-intensive areas of laundry and catering have seen in-house, and occasionally external, awards with comparatively minor adjustments to staffing levels.

The situation in local authorities is similar to that in the NHS. Cleaning staff have been hardest hit by the tendering process, with job losses averaging just under 40 per cent. Estimates of these losses or 'savings', as the contractors call them, are widely publicised and the staffing changes associated with ten recent cleansing contracts are shown in Table 4.1. These figures should be taken as indicative only, as several contractors have found it impossible to operate at proposed staffing levels and have had to recruit additional external employees.

Numbers of redundancies do not adequately portray the dynamics of the job loss process. Certain employees do very well as a result of tendering and contracting out arrangements. Competitive tendering has offered older workers the chance to retire early at enhanced payment levels; many employees in the 50–60 age range have been particularly keen to do so and have welcomed the tendering process with open arms. Local authority and health service administrators confirm that the older the workforce, the less chance there is of serious resistance to tendering exercises. Some younger workers also do well as a result of the tendering process. Those who are immediately taken on by the contractor receive a redundancy payment without ever losing a day's wages. Many are happy to work longer hours in return for larger weekly pay packets.

But there is another side to the 'wastage' process. Although the CCMA estimates that between 60 per cent and 80 per cent of an in-house cleaning force will generally apply to continue working under the contractor, there is overwhelming evidence that contractors select only the youngest and strongest applicants from the former in-house staff and that any shortages in staffing totals are generally filled by the recruitment of outsiders. Many contractors and indeed some administrators believe that the 'less able' individuals would not be able to handle the increased workload which is an inevitable result of the tendering process. Whether or not this is true, the fact that the tendering process results in 'survival of the fittest' has caused general concern both within the trade union movement and within specific authorities. One incident which was publicised widely by the unions saw a manager from a contracting firm reject two mentally-handicapped men who had been sweeping the streets of one local authority for 20 years. The company's spokesman reportedly told the press, 'We don't have any room for the "John Dawsons" and "Peter Smiths" of this world.'

Such an incident highlights the fact that there are important differences for employees between an in-house win and a private contractor's victory. Both will demand reductions in staffing levels, but the methods used to decide who will remain in employment and the environment in which these decisions are made can differ dramatically. Implementation of an in-house contract is character-ised by greater elements of choice for the employee and emphasis is generally put on natural wastage as a means to reduce the work-force. Implementation of an external contract creates choice for the employer only, often at the expense of the less able employees.

Pay

The issue of pay has probably caused more concern among a wider audience than any other single issue raised by the competitive tendering process. It has brought the Government into conflict with both contractors and administrators, and has served to deepen the antipathy between unions and contractors. In such an environment, it is easy to forget that it is only recently that rates of pay have become a controversial aspect of contracting out, and that for many years contractors' wage rates were equal to or above those of the public sector. Quite aside from the historical footnote, however, there are two distinct issues to consider when examining the effects of contracting out upon levels of payment to union members and their non-unionised colleagues. The first is the question of pay scales and rates, the main area of controversy. The second is the question of take-home pay, an equally relevant measure for workers whose pay packets consist of substantial bonus or overtime payments.

For years, pay rates in the public sector have been based on notions of a 'fair wage'. The concept dates back to 1891, though it was not formalised into legislation until the Fair Wages Resolution became law in 1946. This law asked contractors undertaking work for government departments to observe the terms and conditions of employment established by representative joint negotiating machinery or arbitration. In the NHS, contractors' remuneration packages had to compare favourably with the Ancillary Staffs Council settlements under the Whitley system. Until recently this meant that contractors would match rates of pay, as well as matching fairly generous holiday, sick leave and compassionate leave entitlements. Although local authorities did not come under the auspices of the Fair Wages Resolution, the vast majority of authorities have for many years included their own version of a fair wages clause in outside contracts.

The question of a fair or minimum wage came into sharp political focus in 1983, when the Government announced its intention to rescind the Fair Wages Resolution which had stood as law for 37 years. As one DHSS administrator noted, 'the government wants to keep pay as an issue between the contractor and his staff, related to local conditions; it should not be determined by nationally negotiated public sector wage settlements.' The rescindment came into force in September 1983, the same month that the Government issued its final directive on competitive tendering in the NHS. At this time, the Government issued guidance suggesting that health authorities should henceforth omit the clause from their contracts, and wrote to all central government contractors asking if they could reduce the price of the contracts presently underway. Contractors responded that they could not cut wages in the middle of a contract but agreed to enter lower wage rates into future contracts.

A government committed to slowing the public sector pay spiral and increasing flexibility in the labour force could be expected to endorse the removal of minimum wage rates in order to increase competition and enhance the operation of the 'free market'. What is surprising, however, is that the Conservative Government undertook abolition of this clause against the express desire of the contract industries to retain it. For months preceding announcement of the resolution's rescindment, the contract service trade associations had lobbied against the proposed measure. The advantages of maintaining the Fair Wages Resolution were articulated in repeated meetings with ministers and civil servants: the resolution made it easier to deal with trade unions, it simplified evaluation of the in-house tender, and it maintained standards in the relevant industries by discouraging the entry of 'cowboy' operators. In fact, the Fair Wages Resolution had acted as an insulation device, protecting contractors from entry by 'low-cost' firms and at the same time shielding them from accusations of exploitation of unskilled labour. As the Managing Director of one of the largest cleaning firms said in 1984: 'now we're being forced to do the things the unions said we did. I think it gives a bigger stick for the "antis" than had they left it alone. You cannot blame the trade unions if the basics are taken away.'

Feeling on this issue was particularly strong among cleaning contractors, who had only recently begun to shed the 'cowboy' image that had plagued them for so long. Within nine months of the withdrawal of the Fair Wages Resolution, in May of 1984, Contract Cleaning and Maintenance Association Health Service Section members agreed among themselves to respect the existing Whitley rates of pay. This formal, though not contractual, agreement has been adhered to diligently since that time and the companies involved have made savings exclusively through reductions in conditions of service and numbers of full-time employees. Many health authority administrators and members expressed equally strong views on the issue of fair wages. Several district health authorities ignored the Government's exhortations and included fair wages clauses in their tender documents; in most cases, this action resulted in continued ministerial pressure to have the clauses removed.

To understand the major changes in financial status that have resulted from the tendering process, it is necessary to consider the two effects that the process has had upon workers' take-home pay. The first involves alteration to, or abolition of, existing bonus schemes; the second concerns the reorientation of the hours which individual employees work. Originally an attempt by local authorities to attract qualified labour, public sector bonus schemes were later used to satisfy union demands for increased pay during a period of stringent wage restraint. Although bonus schemes have outlived their political usefulness in the eyes of many public sector officials and have been proven to bear little relation to either motivation or performance, they have nevertheless become an entrenched fact of industrial relations life in many authorities.[10] In general, these schemes guarantee workers bonuses of anywhere from 10 per cent to 80 per cent on top of their basic wage in return for a specified level of performance. Average bonuses for cleaners in the NHS generally fall between 10 per cent and 25 per cent of basic salary; refuse collectors in local authorities earn considerably higher bonuses. Before the introduction of competitive tendering and contracting out, authorities were reluctant to attempt adjustments to these bonus systems; now such adjustments are often taken for granted in an attempt to develop a competitive in-house bid. The impact of revised work schedules and bonus schemes upon employees is straightforward: less pay for the same work or more work for the same pay.

A second way in which competitive tendering has reduced levels of take-home pay concerns a reorientation of the hours worked by individual employees. This trend has manifested itself both in a reduction in the amount of holiday, overtime or weekend work available and in a decrease in the number of full-time workers. On average, more than two-thirds of a contracting company's employees are part-timers and this, combined with skilful scheduling of full and part-time workers' hours, has allowed contractors to make dramatic savings over what might be considered 'normal' labour costs. Similar cost-saving techniques are now being used by public administrators, many of whom have found that the only way to remain competitive without making employees redundant is to shift the general emphasis from full-time to part-time labour. It is for this reason that unions can correctly claim that the tendering process means a deterioration in the workers' financial position, regardless of which side is awarded the contract.

Conditions of service

Redundancy and pay issues are important, but by far the most obvious effects of the tendering process can be seen in changes in workers' conditions of service. Unlike the first two issues, changes in conditions and benefits occur only where a contract is awarded externally; in-house conditions of employment remain protected by nationally negotiated agreements. However, the changes which do occur when a service is contracted out are significant. Public sector arrangements for holiday and sickness pay, disciplinary procedures and pensions are better than those offered by many of the major contractors. Annual leave entitlements in the health service vary from four weeks after one year of service to five weeks after ten years of service for an employee working a five-day week. Those working six days per week are entitled to five weeks after the first year and earn an additional week after ten years.[11] This contrasts with the arrangements set up by major contractors, who generally provide two weeks after the first year of service, three weeks after the second, and four weeks after four or five years. Public and private sick leave arrangements also vary dramatically. A worker falling ill after one year of service would receive two months full-pay and two months half-pay under the NHS scheme; this same worker would probably receive either one or two *weeks'* worth of pay under a private contractor. This disparity becomes even more pronounced among workers with longer records of service. Pension arrangements are rare in the private sector; those that do exist often apply exclusively to supervisory or managerial staff.

Summary

It is a Hobson's choice for workers in the NHS. Either they accept the in-house tender which probably will be on NHS wages and conditions but certainly will mean much lower staffing levels, more difficult hours of work and generally inferior working conditions, or they can go out to a private cleaning company where they will get what the government euphemistically calls 'the going rate' for cleaning work.[12]

As Jeremy Corbyn noted on the floor of the House of Commons in December 1984, competitive tendering will inevitably have a negative effect upon the trade union members. Job losses, reductions in pay, and deteriorating conditions of service are the most visible outcomes of the tendering process. However, as noted earlier, these are by no means the only changes that the process has wrought and less quantifiable changes in the employee's working environment are equally important. The tendering process has served to remove the job security which service workers enjoyed as public sector employees. Those who are now employed by a private contractor as a result of competitive tendering have less security than most other private sector workers, as their livelihood depends on continual renewals of the company's contract. Those who have remained public sector employees as the result of an in-house win have similar problems: if the in-house team does not win the contract when it comes up for re-tendering, they too may be made redundant.

From the unions' point of view, the tendering process is effectively telling ancillary and other service workers that they are dispensable. It asks that workers be looked upon as a commodity, with no premium paid for experience or skill, creating a situation where the only important difference between the experienced team and the contractor's newly hired workers is their cost. Consequently both union and non-union members are demoralised. Not only have the material trappings of their job been reduced, but any sense of security, importance or belonging has been undermined. On top of this, they have watched their only real advocates – the trade unions – lose the power which once served to protect them. It is hard to dispute union claims that the Government is achieving its savings at the expense of those least able to defend themselves.

The union campaign

Having outlined the reasons why the unions have reacted so

sharply to the Government's tendering policy, it is useful to describe the scope and characteristics of their opposition campaign. The unions' campaign against contracting out should be seen as one component of their larger fight against privatisation in general. It has drawn on many of the same techniques and arguments used to fight denationalisation and deregulation initiatives and, like other campaigns, has been directed primarily at the public rather than at the policy-makers themselves. However, there are two particular features which distinguish opposition to the tendering initiative from other anti-privatisation campaigns. First, the fight against contracting out has been unusually long: it began in local authorities in 1980, spread to the health service three years later, and, in response to DOE compulsory tendering proposals, looks set to focus once again on local authorities. A second distinctive feature of the campaign against contracting out is its scope. Some 200 health authorities have gone or will be going through the tendering process at least half a dozen times each in the near future; this has paved the way for union activity on an unprecedented scale. Both of these features should be kept in mind when reading the following section. It takes a closer look at the unions' campaign of opposition to the Government's policy, describing both the rationale behind it and the major strategies upon which it has been built. The section also considers some of the problems which have plagued the union campaign, and comments on the achievements of union opposition to date.

As a result of the Government's portrayal of competitive tendering as an 'objective' check upon the efficiency of in-house labour forces, there is little political capital to be gained by publicly opposing the tendering process itself. Instead the unions have chosen to focus on two sets of dangers associated with contracting out: those concerning the affected employees and those concerning the ultimate consumers of the service. The direct and measurable effects of contracting out upon employees include those documented on the previous pages: redundancies, decreases in take-home pay, and a significant deterioration in conditions of service. Alone, these are neither an unusual nor an altogether convincing legitimation of opposition to contracting out, particularly as such changes should in theory lead to lower public spending and thus lower taxes (depending on the amount of tax foregone and the size of the increases in transfer payments resulting from redundancies).

However in the context of NHS ancillary workers or local authority street sweepers, whom the general public recognises as poorly paid and often unskilled, these arguments take on more powerful and emotional connotations and have been used skilfully by the unions to sway administrators and authority members to support in-house tenders.

A second set of issues concerns the impact of contracting out upon the service itself. Unions argue that the quality of service will deteriorate for three specific reasons. First, contractors will employ unexperienced and uncommitted workers who will not understand how the service operates, nor will they particularly care. Secondly, contractors will employ low-cost methods of operation in an attempt to safeguard what are generally acknowledged to be slim profit margins. Thirdly, authorities will lose direct control of the service as well as any flexibility they previously enjoyed; according to the unions, contractors are unlikely to be as responsive to the wider organisation's needs as the in-house force and may act in a monopolistic fashion when the time comes to relet the contract.

The twin issues of effects upon employees and upon the quality of service have served as a foundation upon which the unions' campaign against contracting out has been built. This campaign itself has taken numerous forms, varying from authority to authority and from union to union, and it is impossible to identify a single union approach to the fight against contracting out. However, some of the techniques common to a majority of individual union approaches can be isolated. The following section looks at two sets of these techniques. The first set is 'organisational' in nature and includes techniques used to structure the union campaign and mobilise internal support. The second set can be considered more 'strategic' and incorporates the methods used to convince public opinion of the dangers of contracting out.

Internal organisation

Trade unions have employed a number of methods to organise their campaigns of resistance to contracting out. To a great extent, their choice of methods has been influenced by poor financial situations and near-universal problems of morale. Three aspects of what might be considered an 'internal' campaign to mobilise and sustain support are analysed below: national policy lines, educational initiatives and communication networks.

Policy lines   As a result of widespread apathy among their respective memberships, most trade unions decided to allow local branches to take the initiative in opposing contracting out. The general arrangement was that the national organisations would give official backing to any local action which fell within the scope of their guidelines for opposing privatisation; they would not, however, orchestrate a 'national' campaign of industrial action. Although it was never stated publicly, union leaders clearly believed that the support needed for a national strike was absent. 'Weaknesses in branch organisation or enthusiasm' were quoted by NALGO as a reason to avoid specific forms of action against privatisation; one NUPE official, referring to the national membership, noted: 'They're just not prepared to fight'.[13]

Although the initiative was placed clearly with local branches, union headquarters continued to hand down 'policy' lines. One particular line recommended by all of the major public sector unions was concerted opposition to the tendering process. It was believed that opposition would help influence the outcome of the process by convincing authority members of the strong feeling among staff and by persuading administrators to develop a workable and conservative in-house tender. It could also serve to delay the process, delays being useful insofar as they allow the union time to mount a public campaign to save the in-house service. In practice, however, local opposition has not always had the intended effect upon tendering processes and has occasionally forced sympathetic authorities to contract out a service they would have liked to retain.

Educational initiatives   In the absence of national union initiatives, union officials recognised the need for improved training and education of their local officials and shop stewards. One aspect of the unions' educational efforts has involved sending shop stewards and local officials on formal training courses, designed to teach campaign organisers the methods which can be employed to influence the outcome of the tendering process. The TUC Health Service Committee has run a series of two-day workshops designed to train full-time officers and union representatives; these workshops deal with campaigning at local level and developing appropriate responses to the tendering process. Other seminars and courses have been organised on a regional basis by both the unions themselves and by other organisations committed to fighting privatisation. Several of these seminars have been designed specifically to familiarise trade unionists with the operations of the large contractors.

The unions' educational effort has also involved the publication and circulation of large quantities of educational material, much of it designed to explain how the tendering process works. This material is interesting in that most of it is directed at showing members how they can influence the outcome of the process, which seems to conflict with local policies of non-cooperation with tendering exercises. Suggested methods of influencing the outcome tend to fall into two categories: influencing the contract and participating in the adjudication process. Tremendous emphasis has been placed on influencing the content of the contract documents, as experience has shown that carefully drafted documents can alienate contractors and offer a significant advantage to the in-house team. The range of contract provisions which unions have asked their members to promote is wide, as shown in Table 4.2, and reflects the optimistic views about the bargaining power of unions which union leaders have publicly expressed since the start of the campaign. In practice, however, union organisers realise that inclusion of more than a few of these contract provisions in any one authority is unlikely.

The unions have also attempted to teach members how to act as an outside 'jury' in the adjudication process. Union members have been asked to scrutinise the financial and commercial positions of all shortlisted contractors and to examine the tender prices submitted by these companies with an eye to uncovering 'unrealistic' bids. COHSE, for example, asks its members to ensure that:

- all hidden costs are identified (e.g. fuel, water, telephone, parking, canteen facilities, security, etc.).
- all redundancy and early retirement costs are included.
- the contractor will purchase supplies through the District Supplies Department *without* benefit of any NHS discounts.
- the loss in revenue from equipment or facilities made redundant by contracting out is included.

In addition, the union asks its members to undertake a rough calculation of contractors' margins, based on operatives' wages as a

TABLE 4.2   Selected trade union education material ('How to influence the contract')

Area	Union demand
Employment and trade union rights	Fair Wages Clause Protection of bonus schemes Protection of existing staff levels Written undertaking on trade union recognition and negotiating rights Agreement to employ existing staff Minimum 16 hours per week for part-time staff
Health and safety	Evidence of detailed training programmes Submission of an annual report to authority on health and safety Provision of safety equipment and protective clothing Evidence of 'safe' levels of supervision
Standards and specifications	Requirement for quality control system to be run by contractor Undertaking of 24 hour and emergency care Shift rotas to suit other authority staff New equipment to be purchased by NHS and leased to contractors
Contract documents	Strong penalty clauses Delete arbitration clauses Termination clauses to include all relevant costs Strict variation clauses

Source: COHSE, 'Privatisation: A Negotiator's Guide to Specifications and Tenders', 1985.

known percentage of contract cost. In the case of NHS domestics, for example, members would 'multiply the NHS cleaners' hourly rate by the number of cleaning hours per day offered by the contractor then divide this by seven and multiply by ten (as cleaners wages are roughly 70 per cent of the total cost of the contract)'.[14] According to COHSE, if the quoted price is more than 5 per cent under the calculated figure, then the contractor in question is almost certainly cutting services.

Communication networks   One of the most important elements of each union's strategy to fight privatisation has been a strong network of internal communication. Union campaigns against contracting out have been fragmented due to the local nature of the tendering process and the prolonged period over which tendering has taken place. However, this fragmentation has offered the unions a chance to develop more effective techniques of opposition by studying local experiences in the early days of tendering. A primary objective of the communication network has therefore been to increase individual branches' chances of success in combatting contracting out by circulating 'lessons' learned in previous campaigns. Other objectives include the dissemination of information about contractors' performance in the public sector and about authorities' tendering timetables. Some of the types of information which have provided the basis for communication between national officers and local branches are shown in Table 4.3.

Research departments within the trade unions have generally acted as central information terminals, collecting information from

TABLE 4.3 Internal union communication

Item	Purpose
Authority timetables	Allow local members to prepare for tendering; secure support from neighbouring branches
Contract award summaries	Demonstrate in-house performance against contractors; highlight major competitors
Contract performance data	Highlight contractors' failures to provide appropriate levels of service and savings
Procedural techniques	Ensure widespread adoption of successful techniques and strategies
Legal issues	Help identify areas of local discretion; demonstrate legality of opposition techniques
Company information	Display financial and commercial problems of contractors; identify key personnel
Internal authority documents	Promote further understanding of authorities' intentions and methodologies

individual branches and passing it on to the wider union membership. The sophistication of this network varies from union to union
due to the reluctance of some unions' branches to channel information to head office and to the absence of a communal approach to
data among the major public sector unions. NUPE appears to
operate the most advanced internal communication network. Regular reports submitted by local officials and union representatives
have allowed for the creation and maintenance of an up-to-date
database covering contracting out activity across the country;
updates and summary lists, covering developments in both the NHS
and local authorities, are sent regularly to the key NUPE personnel.
So sophisticated is the NUPE system that DHSS administrators
have suggested that it provides the only comprehensive monitoring
of the Government's NHS initiative.

External strategies

Running parallel to the unions' internal education and mobili-
sation activities has been a major campaign to convince the external
world of the dangers of contracting out. This public campaign has
been prolonged and expensive, but it has succeeded in bringing the
issue of contracting out to the forefront of the political agenda in
many local communities. The campaign itself has been undertaken
on several levels. Individual unions have funded and developed
their own initiatives, based upon the position and outlook of their
own membership; simultaneously, the TUC has waged a coordi-
nated campaign designed to act as a focal point for all trade union
opposition. Both individual and TUC campaigns share the same
objectives and approach: they aim to 're-educate' public opinion
which has, in recent years, become sceptical about the role and
contribution of public sector trade unions. These campaigns are
designed to increase the understanding and appreciation of public
services, primarily by contrasting the present situation with that
which could occur if private contractors took control over local
services.

Although a variety of techniques have been employed in the 're-
education' process, four particular methods have been at the
forefront of the respective union campaigns. The most visible and
arguably the most effective technique has been the so-called 'smear
campaign' aimed at highlighting the poor performance of contrac-

tors. Other common techniques include industrial action, the formation of linkages with other community-based groups, and the use of legal rulings.

The 'smear campaign'

The smear campaign comes in many forms: the first concerns ownership. Allegations that foreigners are taking over the health service or profiting out of local waste disposal are common ... The second smear is that the industry is nothing more nor less than 'cowboys', 'get rich quick' merchants, 'in for a fast buck', 'here today gone tomorrow' types ... The next attack made against the industry is that it does not care about service, only about profit. This attack comes in a dozen different ways ... most of these concern contractors not performing up to standard and of incurring frequent customer dissatisfaction with the way they do the job.[15]

This quote was taken from *The Truth on the Smear Campaign Against Contract Cleaning*, a pamphlet published by the Aims of Industry organisation in 1985. It highlights the fact that the central plank of the unions' public campaign concerns the inability of contractors to provide an adequate standard of service to public agencies. Unions attribute this situation to two causes: the lack of experience in public sector work and the commercial pressures which demand a significant return on investment. The unions have tried to support these arguments with practical evidence of contractors' failures. Most have chosen a wide definition of 'failures', using it to refer to incidents where expected savings have not been achieved, where complaints about the standard of service have been registered, and where contractors have withdrawn from their contractual obligations. Capitalising on the media's fondness for public sector scandals, the unions have gained significant coverage of these 'failures' in newspapers and on television. Several pamphlets documenting contractors' problems have been published by the unions and circulated widely, to the consternation of both the Government and the affected companies.

The most widely circulated of these reports has also come in for the greatest criticism. In November 1984, the TUC published *Contractors' Failures* and sent copies to all health authorities. This document claimed to identify problems in 67 separate cases involving contracting out; with approximately 100 contracts out to the private sector at that time, this suggested that contractors had failed to meet authority needs in two out of every three cases. Given the apparently damning nature of its findings, it was predictable that the document would be attacked almost as soon as it was made public. Criticism came not from the contractors, who have consistently tried to avoid publicity of any sort, but from members of the Conservative Party. One typical attack appeared in the Winter 1984–5 issue of *Crossbow*, a Conservative Party journal. This article attempted to demonstrate that only a small minority of the specified cases could be considered failures, by noting that nearly half of the supposed failures were still in private hands and that 9 of the 69 cases considered by the TUC never involved a contract. It suggested that 'The overwhelming, if unintentional impression given by the TUC booklet supports the view that the contractors are, by and large, doing a good job under often difficult conditions.'[16]

The DHSS agreed with the view that the booklet greatly overstated any problems that contractors were having. DHSS spokesmen denied that all but two cases could be considered failures, and suggested that the TUC was trying to capitalise on the 'teething pains' which were an inevitable and temporary result of the shift from an in-house to an externally provided service. Despite these questions over the accuracy of the TUC document, it appears to have succeeded in awakening a number of authorities to the possibilities of contractor failure. Along with the other publications documenting sub-standard performance by contractors, it helped convince health authorities across the country of the need to build adequate safeguards into the contract documents; these safeguards generally put additional costs upon contractors and thus provided a significant boost to the union's campaign.

Highlighting contract 'failures' has been only one arm of the unions' prolonged and intense 'smear campaign'. A second tactic designed to sway administrative opinion has involved a concerted attack upon the financial stability of the contracting companies. Significant efforts have been undertaken to show that these firms have not performed satisfactorily in recent years and that they do not maintain adequate financial reserves, facts which would increase the likelihood of cuts in service and bankruptcy during the course of the contract. Analyses of financial performance have been as comprehensive in scope as the TUC's document describing performance failures. One such analysis, entitled *Would You 'Approve' This Lot?* and published by the West Midlands Regional TUC Health Service Coordinating Committee, examined the 47 companies on the West Midland RHA's 'approved contractor' list. It found that only 8 of the 47 companies on the list had relevant NHS experience and that 27 of the 47 companies did not show proper accounts.[17]

Two other aspects of the unions' 'smear campaign' should be mentioned. One involves the use of testimony from former employees of contracting firms. Such testimony has come both from legitimate long-serving employees, who have either resigned or been made redundant, and from anti-privatisation activists, who have gone undercover to secure brief employment with one of the major companies. Individuals in both groups have attested to the lack of training, the failure to observe health and safety regulations, and the totalitarian approach to personnel and industrial relations issues which they found characterised life under a contractor; these experiences have predictably been publicised widely both within and outside of the trade union movement.[18] Another aspect of the unions' campaign has involved highlighting the complex network of linkages between contractors and the Conservative Party. The unions have given wide publicity to the contributions made by the contracting firms to the Conservative Party. They have also publicised several incidents whereby public sector officials have been given jobs by contracting firms, in an attempt to suggest that contractors may have 'bought' work in the public sector.

Industrial action　Industrial action is a second weapon used by the unions to bring the dangers of contracting out to public attention. Although the initiative for such action has had to come from local areas, union headquarters have been quick to support any dispute that they feel has the potential to capture significant media attention. The result of this relationship has been a series of locally-based strikes, several of which have developed rapidly into platforms upon which the wider union movement has expressed its opposition to contracting out.

The first concerted attempts by the unions to capitalise on local disputes occurred early in 1984 and involved two well respected London hospitals, Hammersmith and Barking. These two disputes overlapped chronologically, and there was some cross-fertilisation of union activity and personnel. Although both disputes received considerable publicity because of the regular appearance of union leaders and politicians on the picket lines, neither resulted in a 'victory' for the unions. Later in 1984, union attention moved to Addenbrooke's Hospital in Cambridge where the transition from one contractor (Crothall) to another (OCS) had caused complaints about the standard of service and precipitated a strike by domestic staff. Although this and several other disputes in the South-east continued throughout 1985, the focus of industrial action gradually moved to the North. Union officials publicly attributed this geographical shift to the fact that Northern authorities began to implement the Government's tendering policy rather late in the day, but privately recognised that support for industrial action in the South-east had faded in the face of overwhelming evidence of defeat. Most remained optimistic that industrial action would be more successful in the North, thanks to a higher degree of grassroots support and more sympathetic attitudes on the part of health authorities.

Links with other organisations   The unions have tried to increase public support and visibility by working with organisations and community groups likely to share the unions' interest in retaining in-house services. Branches have been encouraged to establish both formal and informal links with both political and pressure groups at local level. Typical of this sort of link was the 'Campaign Against Privatisation: Resistance '83' organised in Basingstoke in 1983; initiated by the local trades councils, it drew in public sector unions, local Labour Party delegates, tenant groups and representatives from Labour groups on both Basingstoke Council and Hampshire County Council. A different type of linkage was set up in Coventry, where 15 unions in local government, the NHS, the civil service, education and the nationalised industries came together to form the 'Coventry Public Sector Alliance'. The objective of both local campaigns was to inform and educate public opinion about the dangers of privatisation.[19]

Legal rulings   Efforts to change public opinion have also involved use of the courts and legal rulings. Three types of issues have been the subject of these rulings, each geared to fighting privatisation on a different front. The first issue upon which the unions sought legal advice was the concept of fair wages and its application to local authorities. In 1983, the Central Arbitration Committee ruled that Grand Metropolitan must raise the wages and cut the hours of the workers on its Wandsworth refuse collection contract in order to comply with the fair wages clause specified in the Borough's Standing Orders. Although this represented a clear victory for the unions in Wandsworth, it was a short-lived one due to the Borough's immediate removal of the fair wages clause from all of its contracts. A similar case was brought and won against Exclusive Cleansing in Milton Keynes in 1984, but again there was little compulsion to implement the CAC ruling and the victory was more symbolic than it was substantial.

A second issue which has been a focus of the unions' legal attention has been the changing of conditions of service for school meals staff in continuous employment, a tactic used by several county councils to increase the efficiency of their services. In many cases these changes have occurred alongside threats of contracting out, thus forcing employees to accept the new package. In November 1983, NUPE successfully challenged the right of Hert-fordshire County Council to alter unilaterally the conditions of service for those on the school meals staff. (The council later found that it could avert legal problems by sacking the staff and then re-employing them on the new terms.) In Birmingham, NUPE won an injunction against a similar sacking and re-employing exercise on the grounds that the decision to carry out this action was not taken by the proper council committee.

A third legal issue addressed by the unions has been the legal standing of the Government's circular on competitive tendering in the NHS. In early 1984, COHSE and other unions commissioned a legal opinion which stated that the circular did not have the standing of an instruction and that therefore health authorities were not obliged to accept the lowest bid. This also meant that they had the right to specify conditions of service (including wage rates), some-thing that the Government has persistently argued that they cannot in any circumstances do. Although this legal opinion was widely publicised both within the trade union movement and in the House of Commons, it had little if any effect upon the plans of health authorities to complete the present round of tendering.

A critical assessment

These four techniques – a 'smear campaign', industrial action, local linkages and legal rulings – have all contributed to the union's campaign to win public opinion, although some have been more successful than others. Efforts to discredit contractors by revealing contract failures, financial instability, inadequate personnel policies and linkages with the Conservative Party have been particularly visible and have put sustained pressure upon the most successful contracting firms. The Managing Director of one of these firms commented in 1985 that he spent one-quarter of his time dealing with media queries based on union accusations. Although his company's experience has been more unpleasant than most, it is safe to say that few companies have been left unscathed by this powerful and vituperative 'revelation' campaign.

Industrial action has been somewhat less successful than the unions had hoped, and has generally failed to protect individual local services. Nevertheless, it has provided the unions with a channel through which they can publicise the deterioration in pay and conditions associated with the tendering process. It has also led to disruptions in ancillary services after tendering exercises have taken place, which have furnished the unions with evidence of a decline in service standards that they can quickly attribute to the introduction of a new contractor. In addition, industrial action has served to frighten many authorities away from employing contractors that have been involved in well-publicised disputes; authorities which have never contracted out are particularly keen to minimise the risks of future disruptions in key services.

The impact of links with community-based organisations is difficult to measure, as the creation of such support networks is primarily a defensive measure designed to achieve subtle changes in public awareness prior to the start of any tendering activity. Although these local networks have yet to prevent a determined authority from undertaking the tendering process, or indeed from contracting out, the unions remain convinced of the importance of building grassroots support and highlight numerous examples in which they believe linkages like those in Coventry or Basingstoke have been central to an authority's decision to remain with direct labour. Legal rulings have also played a limited but valuable role in the unions' opposition campaign. Although they have rarely contributed to the material well-being of union members, they have provided important victories at times when morale within the unions has been extremely low. These legal victories have also provided an additional source of media coverage, thus contributing to increased public awareness of the contracting out issue. Unions view this media coverage as a valuable weapon against publicity-shy contractors, few of whom want their name associated with legal 'trouble'.

Overall, the unions' campaign has been successful on a number of fronts. It has helped to push the issues surrounding competitive tendering to the forefront of many local political agendas; this has generally meant that the process itself is undertaken more slowly and more carefully than might otherwise be the case. The unions' campaign has also had a recognisable impact upon the thinking of both authority members and officers. The dramatic portrayal of potential changes in the individual workers' environment has inspired many authorities to include fair wages clauses in their tendering documents; likewise, the detailed descriptions of contractors 'failures' have prompted many to include 'protective' clauses which place extra costs on the outside tenderers. Both developments have helped to improve the competitive position of in-house labour forces.

But beyond these 'procedural' victories, it is clear that the opposition campaign has not been as successful as many within the trade union movement had hoped it might be. To a certain extent, the lack of success can be attributed to local officials' refusals to cooperate with the tendering process – a strategy that, in practice, has often removed any chance that an in-house force once had of retaining the service. But this behaviour itself is not fully to blame for the unions' rather lacklustre performance. Equally significant have been the internal problems within and between unions which have served to limit the effectiveness of the union campaign.

Intra-union problems

Many of the problems that have plagued individual unions throughout the contracting out debate are common to the trade union movement as a whole. Morale within public sector unions is at an all-time low, due to the Conservative Government's determination to neutralise the trade union movement and reduce the size of the state sector. The economic situation has aggravated the morale problem: the majority of union members are concerned primarily with holding on to a job and are no longer willing to fight for a bigger share of the pie. The lack of success in previous campaigns to protect public services has also contributed to widespread apathy at local level. This is particularly true in the health service, where the lessons of the 1982 strike did not rapidly disappear from memory. As one official noted in mid-1984: 'We are still suffering from the effects of the 1982 pay dispute. That knocked the stuffing out of us for the moment.'[20]

Financial problems have compounded the problems of morale and have placed serious constraints on the tactics employed by public sector unions. Declining membership and a series of costly campaigns to protect public services have left union coffers low. New activities, such as the referendum on political funds, have proved an added drain on resources. The scope of the Government's privatisation plans for 1985–6 and 1986–7 are likely to lead to further reductions in membership and additional costly campaigns, both of which will prolong and exacerbate this unsatisfactory financial situation.

Political problems in formulating strategies to oppose privatisation have also affected individual unions' campaign activities. The great majority of privatisation issues, including contracting out, have witnessed a clash between proponents of 'high-principled' and 'pragmatic' views within trade unions. 'High-principled' strategists have encouraged non-cooperation with, and indeed obstruction of, any government attempt to weaken the public sector. 'Pragmatic' strategists have been equally opposed to government policy, but have adopted a more realistic attitude which recognises the inevitability of the tendering process. As a result, their primary concern has been to minimise the damage likely to arise from it, even if this involves cooperating with the development of an in-house tender. This difference in views and strategic approaches within individual unions has frequently had a considerable impact upon the techniques employed during local tendering exercises. Some national officials have been forced to articulate policies with which they do not agree and conflicting signals have occasionally been sent to local representatives or union officials. This has tended to increase the discretion enjoyed by these locally-based individuals, who on occasion have used local situations to further their own political objectives to the detriment of the unions' local membership.

The lack of leadership which has characterised individual union campaigns against contracting out is a by-product of both the conflicting strategic approaches noted above and the unions' decision to devolve responsibility for action to the local areas. The leader of one NUPE branch argued: 'The trouble is that trade union leaders are not leading. All they say is "you take action; we'll support you".' Although this absence of leadership has not been the result of an oversight on the part of senior union officials but has reflected a recognition of their own inability to motivate action in the face of widespread apathy, such a realistic approach has led to a 'catch-22' situation with many local areas waiting for inspiration that is not forthcoming. This situation has given rise to sharp criticism among some union officers, one of whom stated, 'we'll have to recognise that an official policy is nonsense policy. We need a policy to identify and fund winners, instead of funding all "official" action. The tail is wagging the dog.'

A divergence of the unions' organisational needs from the needs of its local membership is another problem which has plagued individual union campaigns. In order to meet the organisational needs of the unions, including protecting membership levels and maintaining credibility as a shield against the vagaries of the marketplace, both national and local union officers have had to adopt an aggressive and hard-line stance against the tendering process and have encouraged their members to do the same. But the consequences of the hard-line approach have rarely been beneficial for individual union members. It has frequently transformed the relationship between an authority's management team and the in-house workforce, erecting a wall between the two groups and encouraging the authority to adopt uncharacteristically harsh attitudes toward the local union movement. Occasionally it has led to industrial action, which in nearly all cases has left union members worse off than they previously were and has further alienated public administrators. Although early on in the tendering initiative few local members questioned the need for strong and determined opposition, successive failures in key campaigns such as at Hammersmith and Barking have sparked a growing recognition of the likely impact of industrial action and union members have become increasingly reluctant to follow their local leaders into battle. The combination of this reluctance with the financial, morale and leadership problems noted above has placed significant obstacles in the path of those unions which have tried to maintain an effective campaign against contracting out.

Inter-union friction

The ability of the trade union movement to mount an effective campaign against contracting out has been further hampered by the lack of coordination between individual trade unions. Tension between unions is partially a result of occupational antagonism; for example, the formation of a joint ad-hoc committee to fight privatisation in Westminster by NALGO and NUPE was characterised by mistrust on the part of both unions. One of the major problems, according to participants, was the 'them and us' attitudes based on the fact that 'NALGO members have "careers" and NUPE members have "jobs"'.[21] Differences in political complexion and fierce competition for members have provided additional and potent sources of inter-union friction.

Public sector unions have compounded these structural problems by disagreeing on the precise strategy that should be adopted to counter the contracting out threat. Some unions have leant towards the 'high-principled' view while others have favoured the more 'pragmatic' approach, reflecting a similar tension to that which has emerged within individual unions. These strategic differences appear to have three proximate causes. First, the political allegiances of those in senior policy-making decisions within the respective unions vary from the radical left to the moderate right. Secondly, each union has felt it important to uphold its own historical traditions in fighting for concessions from the government and has avoided methods of 'battle' that might violate these traditions. Thirdly, because the profiles of union membership and penetration in each sector vary from union to union, so too does the relative importance of the contracting out debate and the methods deemed most appropriate to fight it.

The present relationship between COHSE and NUPE offers a good example of the tensions which have existed below the surface of the union movement. Delicate at the best of times, the relationship between the two unions has been put under additional strain as a result of the NHS tendering initiative. Because both unions maintain a significant presence in the NHS, contracting out represents a significant threat to both of their futures. However, cooperation between the two unions in opposing the policy has not been as great as one might expect. Formal cooperation has consisted of a Joint Liaison Arrangement between the respective National Executive Committees; informal cooperation at branch level has been sporadic and localised. The failure to provide a recognisable, united front can be partially explained by the unions' antagonistic attitude towards one another. NUPE, generally recognised as the most aggressive of the NHS unions, claims that COHSE's approach to contracting out is weak and unprincipled. COHSE, in turn, claims that NUPE's words are not backed up by action. One COHSE official noted, 'NUPE may seem more principled, but underneath they're pragmatic; COHSE stands firm. I never believe one word that NUPE says because they always do the opposite.'

Although little love appears to be lost between these two unions at national level, the relationship between them at local level has varied from authority to authority. In some areas, the unions' area officers and shop stewards have cooperated only under pressure from the authority; in others the unions have worked well together to delay or defeat local moves towards contracting out. In any case, the relationship between COHSE and NUPE is probably an extreme example of the tensions which exist among unions. The other unions affected by the health service initiative, GMBATU and the T&GWU for instance, have much broader based memberships and comparatively lower penetration in the health service. For these reasons they have assumed a subordinate and somewhat less controversial role in the opposition campaign.

It is difficult to assess the impact that coordination problems within the union movement have had upon the fight against competitive tendering and contracting out. Tensions have manifested themselves regularly in relatively minor ways, such as the reluctance to share information or the failure to establish a joint information bank, and only occasionally in more significant ways, such as the inability of local unions to agree upon an approach to the submission of an in-house tender. Overall, it appears that the measurable impact of 'suboptimal cooperation' has been limited. It has not really affected the unions' public campaign, which is based solidly on a well-rehearsed and well-researched war of words. The only significant impact has been at local level, where a number of union campaigns were not as comprehensive as they might have been. Whether earlier and more extensive cooperation from the relevant trade unions would have staved off privatisation in these areas is by no means clear.

On the positive side, there have indeed been attempts to address the issue of inter-union cooperation. In 1985, the General Secretaries of the four unions affected by the NHS initiative together instructed their offices to cooperate in opposing privatisation. Simultaneously, the TUC, whose job it is to foster cooperation throughout the trade union movement, specifically asked unions to establish joint regional coordinating committees to monitor and organise local privatisation initiatives. Throughout the campaign, the TUC has acted as a central clearing house for information needed to monitor and oppose the tendering process and has, as noted earlier, sponsored a number of training courses for local union officials. Beyond this, however, its coordinating role has been limited and most of its efforts have been directed at organising the all-important public and media campaigns. The most serious attempts to foster cooperation between unions have usually occurred at local or regional, rather than national, levels. Reference has already been made to the Coventry Public Sector Alliance which involved 15 public sector unions; a similar campaign was recently launched in Newcastle. There, a Joint Union Committee was formed from representatives of all the unions either directly or indirectly affected by contracting out; this included NUPE, COHSE, GMBATU, EETPU, UCATT, NALGO, RCN, RCM and the Society of Radiographers. The Committee's objective has been to disrupt and obstruct the tendering process as a whole, rather than fight battles on individual services.

Both intra-union and inter-union problems have limited the effectiveness of the campaign of opposition to the government's tendering policy. But even at the best of times, there would be little the unions could do to soften the impact of the policy significantly. Additional resources might help to extend the intensity and frequency of industrial action, but industrial action has been singularly unsuccessful as a technique to influence the tendering process and it is unlikely that even national strike action would do much to achieve the unions' objectives. Each and every show of strength by the unions has been met tit-for-tat by the Government.

The timetabling of the exercise has itself been a very divisive mechanism, undermining several unions' policies of joint action. In many ways, competitive tendering has presented the unions and their members with a no-win situation.

In spite of the seemingly insurmountable obstacles, the unions have maintained determined and highly visible opposition to the Government's policy, and, in doing so, have won an unusual sort of respect from public administrators and contractors. Both groups admit that the unions have skilfully employed a variety of techniques to draw attention to their cause and have frequently woven these techniques into fairly sophisticated and coherent opposition strategies. NUPE, for example, looks upon its struggle against contracting out as a type of 'trench warfare' which consists of three separate stages or levels:

1   The first stage of opposition is directed at preventing contractors from getting a foot in the local or health authority's door. Emphasis is put on awareness of the potential threat of contracting out, and attempts will be made to dissuade the authority from undertaking the tendering process. It is during this first stage that linkages within the local community, particularly with local Labour Party councillors, assume critical importance.

2   Action moves to the second 'trench' once the authority has decided to begin the tendering process. This next phase of the struggle involves three separate activities: public campaigning, industrial action and detailed negotiations on the content of the contract documents themselves. Any in-house tender drawn up by the authority will not be endorsed.

3   If (as is more than likely given a policy of non-cooperation), contractors are awarded the contract, the struggle then moves to a third level. Union organisers will attempt to mobilise both authority staff and client groups so that any contractual failure to provide the specified level of service will be reported. They will also aim to organise and recruit the contractor's staff; key issues upon which the recruitment campaigns are based include wages and conditions of service. Finally, the union will use a variety of methods to begin lobbying for a return of the service to the public sector.

NUPE's strategy represents the 'hard line' among unions and is not always adhered to, even by its own officials. Nevertheless, it highlights the flexibility of approach which characterises nearly all of the union campaigns. As David Williams, General Secretary of COHSE, noted in 1984:

> The important lessons to be learned are that branches must have a policy to combat privatisation and be prepared to adopt different tactics at different stages of the policy. A failure to persuade the DHA not to privatise should not be regarded as a defeat, but as a signal that the next stage of the campaign may require a totally different approach.[22]

Concluding comments

The flexibility of these campaign strategies has proved a great asset to the trade unions. It has permitted them to uphold the 'principled' stance of non-cooperation with tendering while adopting a more practical approach to influencing the outcome of the process; it has also allowed them to maintain a significant presence at every stage of the tendering process. But the sophistication inherent in such a 'flexible' approach has made it difficult for union members to understand their own campaign of opposition; many have been unsure about whether or not they should be cooperating with the authority's management team. Along with numerous other factors, this indecisiveness has served to weaken the unions' respective bases of support and has undermined their bargaining power against both authorities and contractors.

The intensity of the unions' campaign, like its flexibility, has proved a source of both strength and weakness. As noted earlier, it has prejudiced some authorities, particularly risk-averse ones, toward retaining an in-house force and has led to the construction of extensive 'safety nets' around the tendering process. These safety nets, consisting of tighter specifications, greater insurance precautions and restrictions on conditions of service, have clearly hurt the contractors. But industrial action and refusals to cooperate have simultaneously alienated a large number of health and local administrators who were once sympathetic to the unions' cause. Industrial action has also had negative consequences for industrial relations and employee welfare in a number of services presently run by contractors and has strengthened the Government's determination to enforce its own rigorous approach to the tendering process.

It is too early to predict how successful the unions' present strategy will be. Only about half of all NHS services had been put out to tender by the end of 1985 and local authority services are unlikely to go out in significant volume until 1987 at the earliest. Furthermore, it is not easy to identify the impact of union action in those areas that have gone out to tender, as the numerous other factors that influence an authority's provision decision make correlations between the level of union activity and the tendering outcome impossible to establish. It is also too early to predict what effects competitive tendering and contracting out will have upon public sector unions in the long run. If the tendering process outlasts the present government and becomes institutionalised within local and health authorities, then traditional methods of advocating employees' interests will probably give way to different and more effective strategies. However if competitive tendering proves to be just another public sector management craze, then its long-term effects upon the union movement may be negligible.

At the moment, the unions have their hands full trying to minimise the damage being wrought by the tendering process. Although their primary concern is still with 'saving' public services, some union organisers are beginning to give thought to strategies aimed at building a union presence within contractors' organisations. But penetrating firms such as Pritchard Services, Brengreen Holdings and the Hawley Group will be no easy task. Senior managers within these organisations are convinced of the disruptive effects of public sector unionism; those who were in any doubt about this five years ago have been persuaded by the vituperative campaign waged by the unions since the NHS tendering initiative began. Their employees tend to be poor recruitment prospects for the unions, as the vast majority are part-timers or casual labour.

The overall prospects for union activity within the private sector are unclear. While most contractors have agreed in principle to union recognition, the criteria for recognition are often strict and unions must negotiate on a site by site basis. Given strong competition among unions for members and the general absence of experienced organisers within the contractors' organisations, recruiting these private sector workers will be a long and difficult process. Nevertheless, the unions are optimistic that new membership within contractors' firms can offset some of the major membership losses they have suffered as a result of privatisation. They have been encouraged by developments in Wandsworth, where the T&GWU won formal recognition by Pritchard Services after a long and successful recruitment campaign among street cleaning workers. Whether this signals the beginning of a trend, and whether such recognition can be translated into improvements in wages and conditions of service, remains to be seen.

5 The Mechanics of Competitive Tendering

The previous two chapters have outlined the objectives and strategies of two of the major interest groups in the current debate. In order to understand the nature of local tendering exercises, it is also necessary to examine the procedural routines and issues involved in competitive tendering. This chapter is devoted to a closer examination of the tendering process itself. It describes the mechanics of individual stages of the process, and then moves to an analysis of the major issues surrounding the process as a whole.

Introducing the exercise

Many supporters of the Government's initiative believe that the recent competitive tendering exercises are no more than an extension of the public sector procurement function. They claim that public agencies have always relied on the private sector to fulfill certain duties and that this experience can be transferred directly to the procurement of cleaning, catering, and other maintenance functions. The existence of purchasing and supplies departments within local and health authorities respectively is often cited as evidence of a certain level of expertise in 'contracting out' or 'buying in' public services.[1] This view is partially correct, as both groups of public sector agencies have considerable experience in purchasing equipment and services that they themselves cannot provide on a cost-effective basis. But competitive tendering in the present context involves routines and concepts which are new to most authorities and it is important to identify the characteristics that distinguish it from normal procurement activities.

Public sector procurement exercises are usually fairly straightforward, involving either the purchase of materials or equipment or the commissioning of a specific project. In general the desired output is quantifiable or fairly easily specified. Quality control is the responsibility of the supplier, as the buyer is usually in a position to go elswhere if he is not happy with the quality of the product. Contracting for 'ongoing' services, however, is a much more complex process. Outputs do not lend themselves readily to quantification, making both specification and monitoring extremely difficult. In addition, the bargaining power of buyers vis-à-vis suppliers is very much reduced by the short-term difficulties in changing suppliers. These fairly obvious differences between purchasing a product and purchasing an ongoing service are significant and important to the debate over contracting out. But they alone do not explain the uniqueness of recent tendering activity, as authorities have been purchasing ongoing services (such as window cleaning and pest control) for years without any special difficulties.

One of the factors which distinguishes recent tendering exercises from those that have gone before is the nature of the services involved: all involve significant interface with either an authority's own employees or with its client groups. For example, the continuous presence of large numbers of a contractor's employees on hospital premises poses problems for the operation of the hospital as a unit and may, in the case of certain services, affect the patient environment. 'On premises' issues are less of a concern in local authorities, but there contractors' employees may well interface with local authority clients (the public) on a more regular basis than has been the case in the past. Another factor differentiating competitive tendering in the NHS from traditional procurement exercises is the highly charged political environment in which it is taking place. Authorities are facing considerable scrutiny from central departments, as well as from local interest groups. Every action must be justified and re-justified, which results in a more time-consuming and expensive process than would otherwise be the case.

But the single most important feature which distinguishes current procurement exercises from those that have gone before is the presence of an in-house bid. Tendering exercises have traditionally pitted outsider against outsider, competing for contracts in areas where no in-house capacity or expertise existed. The shift to competition between existing staff and outsiders has fundamentally transformed the tendering process, and has given rise to a number of new administrative developments. The first concerns the tendering process itself, which must involve a much wider range of administrators than would normally be the case in procurement exercises. The development of the in-house tender and the adjudication process itself frequently require the participation of staff from personnel, legal, finance, general administration, work study and the relevant specialist departments in addition to representatives from supplies or purchasing.

The participation of the specialist department in the tendering process is in itself a second and separate development associated with the presence of an in-house bid. The manager of the service which is being put out to tender must play a central role in the tendering process: in many cases he or she will be the only individual with sufficient expertise to develop an accurate specification, ensure a workable in-house tender, and analyse alternative methods of provision offered by outside contractors. But such a pivotal role can raise fundamental conflict of interest problems, as it is the jobs of both the specialist manager and his or her existing staff which are likely to be affected by the award of the contract to a private firm. A third and equally important issue arising from the existence of an in-house bid concerns industrial relations. Recent tendering processes have frequently been characterised by either industrial action or the refusal of the in-house labour force to cooperate in the process. Not only has this complicated the exercise considerably, but it has often affected relationships between management and employees in related support services.

Competition which involves an in-house bid is thus significantly different from that which does not, and it is sad that the most ardent supporters of the Government's policy fail to recognise this. They tend to rely on American examples as proof of the benefits of competitive tendering without realising that the overwhelming majority of tendering situations in US local authorities and hospitals have never involved an in-house bid and therefore can provide only limited guidance. Competitive tendering in its present British context marks a departure from that which has gone before – both in the US and in the UK – and represents among the most complex, time-consuming, costly, and divisive purchasing exercises ever undertaken by health or local authorities.

The tendering process

Tendering procedures vary widely between the NHS and local authorities and from one local authority to another.[2] Even within a single health or local authority, the precise procedure followed in tendering for one service may be different to that followed at another time for another service. But despite this variation across tendering exercises, all authorities must undertake certain procedural steps and it is therefore possible to examine the tendering process as a series of actions culminating in the award of a contract. This section considers seven phases of the tendering process: pre-tender activity, contract preparation, invitation to tender, in-house tender preparation, adjudication, contract implementation and monitoring. Analytically these phases are discrete events, but in practice they will normally overlap in time (see Chapters 6 and 7). Table 5.1 highlights the key activities likely to occur during these phases, each of which is described in greater detail below.

Stage 1: pre-tender

The term 'pre-tender' generally refers to the period immediately following the decision to subject a particular service to competitive tendering. It is in many ways the simplest and least controversial of stages, but it is also one of the most important. It involves identification of responsibilities, policies and objectives and failure to clarify any one of these adequately can give rise to significant problems during the later stages of the process.

One of the very first tasks which takes place in an authority is the identification of two sets of individuals: those who will be responsible for the tendering process and those who will implement it. Organisational responsibility for tendering in local authorities is usually left to a generalist committee, such as Policy and Resources, which is able to take an independent view of the merits of contracting out, whilst the team organised to implement the process usually consists of representatives from finance, administration, personnel and specialist functions. Organisational responsibility in the NHS is slightly more difficult to define due to the multiplicity of management levels but, in general, responsibility for competitive tendering falls to the district management team which

TABLE 5.1   An outline of the tendering process

Stage	Key issues/activities
Pre-tender	Organisational responsibility Tendering policies Staff consultation procedures Type of contract
Contract preparation	Conditions of tender Contract document Specification
Invitation to tender	Type of invitation Site visits
In-house tender preparation	Staff involvement Avoidable costs
Adjudication	Capability assessment Technical assessment Financial appraisal
Contract implementation	Terminating in-house provision Contract commencement
Monitoring	Responsibility and control Type of monitoring system

will be supported by guidance and assistance from its regional counterparts. The NHS tendering team itself, like its local authority counterpart, consists of representatives from relevant areas such as finance, personnel, supplies, general administration and specialist departments.

Although responsibility for the day-to-day operation of the tendering process falls to administrators, it is generally the local or health authority members who set the policies which guide and direct it. There are at least three specific areas which require statements of tendering policy early on in the process. The first involves the timing of the exercise itself. Realistic scheduling of the tendering stages is important for the authority's administrators, for the in-house team and also for the contractors. Many authorities have found that developing a workable and acceptable tender for the in-house team can take more time than allowed, and have been forced to contract out as a result. Occasionally contractors have had problems meeting tender submission dates, only to find that the adjudication period was later extended from one to several months.

A second area in which policies are established before tendering begins is personnel. Because both in-house and external tenders generally involve lower levels of staffing, the highly emotive issues of redeployment and redundancy will inevitably be raised. As a result, authorities' policies in these areas are usually carefully spelled out to those likely to be affected, so that they may take an informed opinion on the merits of the in-house tender and begin planning for their own post-tender future. The third and final area in which policies are normally clearly specified is finance. At the end of the day, the decision to award a tender will be based partially upon financial quotations from the respective tenderers. As described in later sections of this chapter, financial comparisons are more complex than one would imagine and therefore open to criticism on any number of counts. Laying down clear financial criteria will not ensure against this sort of criticism, but it is likely to minimise it.

In addition to the major policies outlined above, a number of procedural issues are also addressed early on in the tendering process. One of these concerns the establishment of appropriate staff consultation procedures, an important element in keeping the channels of communication open between in-house staff and management. As noted in Chapter 2, the DHSS has taken a somewhat ambivalent view of the extent to which staff should be consulted during the tendering process. Its reluctance to emphasise the importance of staff consultation has been interpreted, probably correctly, as a response to the trade unions' strategy of non-cooperation with the tendering process. But local administrators suggest that the importance of staff consultation throughout the tendering process cannot be over-emphasised. They note that many of the major examples of industrial action have resulted from a failure to consider staff views and the presentation of new conditions of employment as a 'fait accompli', and that those contracts that have been awarded without disruption have generally been characterised by careful and continuous communication with staff interests.

Another 'procedural' issue which is generally addressed during the pre-tender phase is the type of contract that the authority wishes to administer. 'Fixed price' contracts, where the contractor is paid a fixed sum on an annual basis, have dominated public sector bidding to date. This is partly because of their advantages in terms of budgeting accuracy, but also because the Government has expressly stated its support for this type of contract. However, numerous other types of contractual arrangements do exist. As noted in Chapter 2, for years the majority of contracts in the NHS have been 'management fee' arrangements. Under this system, the costs of labour, materials and expenses are charged directly to the client, and a management fee – which includes the contractor's profit margin – is levied on this cost total. A third 'limitation guarantee' approach is beginning to receive serious consideration by the public sector. A hybrid of the two approaches noted above, it involves a fixed price for the cost of labour and an estimated charge for the cost of materials. Catering is an area particularly suited to this form of contract and one such hybrid contract was awarded for catering services at St Mary's Hospital, Paddington in 1985.[3]

These are by no means the only types of contract available. Certain activities may be better suited to 'unit pricing' where the contractor is paid per unit of output (e.g. pavement construction). Other work is best organised on an 'hourly rate' basis, particularly where outputs are readily visible (e.g. snowploughing). A final approach common to many areas of engineering work involves charging for 'time and materials'.[4] Each type of contract has both benefits and drawbacks. As shown in Table 5.2, the trade-off is frequently between cost-savings and accurate budgeting on the one hand and the flexibility to adjust to different needs, more advanced technology, and changes in costs (both up and down) on the other.

Stage 2: contract preparation

The second stage of the tendering process involves preparation of the contract documents. It is by far the most technically exacting portion of the exercise and therefore the most time-consuming, taking anywhere from 12 to 24 weeks. There are three parts to what are generally referred to as the contract documents: the conditions of tender, the contract and the specification. The general rules

TABLE 5.2   Types of contracts: advantages and disadvantages

Type of contract	Advantages	Disadvantages
Fixed price	Accurate budgeting	Little flexibility in labour or material usage; may encourage cost-cutting
Management fee	Flexibility in labour and material usage	Incentive to maximise costs; difficult budgeting
Limitation guarantee	Flexibility in material usage	Little flexibility of labour
Unit pricing	Incentive to minimise time; easy budgeting	May lead to cost-cutting
Hourly rate	Needed for unpredictable volumes of work	Incentive to extend time and cost; difficult budgeting
Time and materials	High standard of service	No incentive to save; difficult budgeting

which govern the competitive tendering process are referred to as the *conditions of tender* and are unlikely to vary dramatically from one authority to another. The conditions of tender focus on the behaviour of contractors and generally prohibit things like collusive behaviour among competitors or the canvassing of authority representatives. Often they will indicate what background information about the company should be made available and what sort of bond or guarantee is required.

The *contract* itself defines the conditions which will bind the authority and the successful tenderer, and lists the responsibilities and liabilities of both parties. The first area that contracts deal with is the provision of equipment, premises and supplies. A number of authorities require contractors to either buy or lease existing plant; others give them free use of it. Similarly, some authorites are willing to provide a site for the contractor at little or no rent; others will charge the market rate. A related area involes the purchasing of supplies. In the case of the NHS, the buying power of the organisation as a whole is significantly greater than that of any single contractor; it may therefore be to the authority's advantage to continue purchasing materials from its own suppliers and sell them at cost to the contractor. In the case of local authorities it is often just the opposite, with large contractors wielding comparatively greater buying power.

The second issue that the contract must deal with is future changes to the contract price. These will generally fall into two categories: fluctuations and variations. Fluctuations can be seen as changes to the contract price which will be made at periodic intervals. The simplest case would be that of an annual increase in line with the rate of inflation; more complex arrangements would involve adjustments to the contract price based on changes in the cost of one or more factors of production. Though more difficult for an authority to administer, contracts which tie prices to the cost of raw materials (or other factors) are the only ones which offer the prospect, albeit remote, of a price reduction over the life of the contract. Variations clauses also refer to changes in the amount paid by an authority to contractors. They anticipate and prepare for any changes in the type of service required and for changes in its volume or frequency. Such variations in payment are by no means uncommon, and will normally result from events such as closure of a hospital ward or addition of a new housing development to an authority's refuse collection area.

The third issue which contracts deal with in great detail is what might be termed 'self-protection'. This includes a range of safeguards to ensure that the standard and continuity of the service is not affected over the lifetime of the contract. Three areas will generally be covered: penalty and reward clauses, insurance and performance bonds, and default or termination. Penalty and reward clauses are designed to ensure that standards of service specified in the contract documents are maintained. Failure to do so, as reported either by the authority's monitoring representative or by end-users of the service, will generally result in a deduction in monthly payments to the contractor. Insurance usually takes the form of deeds of guarantee or performance bonds. Deeds of guarantee, often required from subsidiaries of large companies, generally state that the parent company will be responsible for any losses or damages which result from default by the contractor. The term 'performance bond' refers to a given sum of money which is posted by the contractor and held by a third party, often a bank, over the lifetime of the contract. If and when the contractor withdraws from its commitment to fulfill the terms of the contract, this money will go to the authority and help it to set up an in-house service or to find a new contractor. Although the Government has expressed its general disapproval of performance bonds on the grounds that they add to the cost of a contract, several local authorities have required bonds valued at between 5 and 15 per cent of the contract price.

Default and termination clauses exist to protect the authority in case of withdrawal or unsatisfactory performance by the contractor. Default clauses usually give the authority the power to take one of three actions in case of unsatisfactory performance. It may (1) force the contractor to do a certain part of the work again or (2) bring someone else in to do it or (3) undertake the work itself until such time as it believes the contractor is able to manage it. In all three cases the authority retains the right to charge the contractor for all costs. Termination clauses give the authority the right to end the contractual arrangement if the contractor goes bankrupt or fails to provide the adequate level of service. Again, the authority will be able to charge the contractor for all costs associated with termination. Although both default and termination are important issues, even the most strongly-worded clauses will not prevent the disruption that will occur when a contractor pulls out or is terminated – particularly when there is no immediate replacement and an in-house service must be reinitiated.

The *specification* is the third and most technical portion of the contract documents. It describes when and where the work will be done, and may also give suggestions as to how to do it. In theory, there are two general types of specifications: technical and performance. Technical specifications set down details of how a particular service is to be conducted; in the case of refuse collection, for example, this might involve specifying methods of collection, hours to be worked, street routes to be followed, number of vehicles to be employed, etc. Performance specifications are much more general and indicate only the level of output that is required. Using the same refuse collection example, the authority might only state the number of collections it requires per household per week. In practice, however, these two approaches to specification are fairly extreme and authorities generally feel most comfortable somewhere between the two. They will specify details which are sufficient to give them some control over the service, but will refrain from circumscribing the contractor to too great an extent.

Some authorities have asked contractors to respond to both detailed ('standard') and general ('creative') specifications. Such an arrangement allows the contractor to put forward an innovative approach to service provision, but permits the authority to compare this approach to a more traditional one. However, experience to date has shown that the detailed tender is nearly always successful and that contractors are reluctant to waste their time preparing an alternative or 'creative' tender. Another approach which can be followed by authorities involves preparation of tenders at two or three different levels of service. This allows the authority to consider the incremental costs of higher levels of service, and to select the tender it believes provides the best value for money. But this approach places significant additional costs in terms of tender preparation and adjudication upon contractors and authorities respectively and has therefore been of limited appeal in Britain.

The specification document itself is generally long and detailed, and is likely to be understood only by those directly involved in service provision. Nevertheless it is considered to be one of the most important documents of all, as it specifies the precise obligations of the contractor and forms the basis for any complaints registered by the authority. It is usually prepared by the relevant specialist on the tendering team, often the current services manager, with help from legal advisors and other interested parties. Developing the document is rarely straightforward and generally takes a considerable amount of time. This is because management information systems are often poor, particularly in the NHS. Many administrators have very little concrete information about the performance of the present in-house service and are forced to establish both financial and operational data through a comprehensive review of the existing service before drawing up the specification. Those administrators who have this information to hand early on in the tendering process, usually as a result of bonus scheme reviews, are often able to shorten the tendering period dramatically.

Stage 3: invitation to tender

New entrants into the cleaning and catering industries have made the job of identifying suitable contractors particularly difficult. Very few of these firms have significant commercial experience in the UK; even fewer have relevant UK experience. Many are subsidiaries of larger companies, and information about their financial situation often lies buried within the parent company's accounts. As a result of these two factors, very little may actually be known about new firms. Authorities have not been dissuaded from inviting these companies to tender, but they have been cautious about awarding substantial contracts to them.

A variety of methods are used by authorities to invite tenders for services. The most comprehensive method employed is an 'open invitation', which generally involves advertising in newspapers, magazines and trade journals. This usually stimulates a large number of responses, a high percentage of which tend to come from firms clearly not suited to take on the service in question. 'Selective invitation' is therefore the preferred method, particularly for large contracts. In the past, this has involved approaches to the relevant trade association or direct approaches to the contractors themselves. More recently, authorities have come to rely on lists prepared by neighboring authorities or, in the case of the NHS, by the regional management team. Some send out prequalification questionnaires to the contractors to find out more about their abilities and experience. Others take what might be called a 'semi-selective' approach, inviting a number of the larger companies to bid alongside some of the more promising smaller firms while soliciting additional responses through the media. In many cases, particularly in rural areas, a concerted effort is made to include at least one local contractor on the tender list.

Regardless of which approach is taken, the criteria used by authorities to invite and later to shortlist companies tend to be similar. Among the key criteria are financial stability, relevant experience in other areas, management ability, and company characteristics such as location, history, size and structure. After considering these issues, authorities select a number of companies (usually five or six) which they feel are competent to undertake the work. These companies are then sent a copy of the contract documents and asked to reply by the specified date – usually six to eight weeks hence. Some authorities then hold meetings with invitees as a group, so that any questions regarding the specification or conditions can be answered; this helps to ensure that contractors understand fully the needs of the authority and will not submit incomplete or inappropriate bids. Other authorities use the tender preparation period to complete site visits to selected contractors. This usually involves a visit either to the contractor's premises (in the case of laundry services) or to another authority's premises where the contractor is presently employed (in the case of cleaning and catering services).

Stage 4: in-house tender preparation

The period between the issuance of contract documents to contractors and the receipt of completed tenders sees the production of the authority's own in-house tender. Like the specification, this is a technical document and involves extensive participation from the relevant specialist departments. The functional manager tends to play a central role in the preparation of this tender, supported by representatives from the authority's finance and work-study departments. Involvement from the same individuals who were active in devising the specification is common.

The extent to which staff interests should be involved in drawing up the in-house tender has been open to dispute. As noted earlier, the Government has attempted to minimise the trade unions' role and has suggested that the workforce should be 'kept informed' but should not participate actively in the process. Nevertheless, administrators have usually tried to involve staff interests fully throughout the process. Some have met with a stiff rebuke from the workforce during the tender preparation stage or even after the contract has been awarded in-house; others have found staff involvement productive and have successfully developed in-house tenders acceptable to the workforce. Even with the cooperation of the staff, however, in-house tendering has proved a complicated exercise due to the variety of costs which might or might not be incorporated in the final calculation. Advice on how to handle costs has come from a variety of sources including professional associations, individuals with experience of contracting and, of course, government departments. Despite such advice, or perhaps because of it, the methods of pricing in-house tenders have varied from area to area, much to the displeasure of contractors and government departments.

According to the Chartered Institute of Public Finance and Accountacy (CIPFA) publication, *Management Guide to Contracting Out Services in Local Government*, an in-house tender put forward by an authority should include only what are referred to as 'avoidable costs', costs which would not be incurred if the contract was awarded to the private sector.[5] These costs are not always easy to identify, as not all avoidable costs will appear on the functional budget; for example, many operating costs relating to the service will be carried on the authority's central budget. Furthermore, costs may be unavoidable in the short term but avoidable over a longer time scale, as is often the case with offices, depots and other physical facilities. It is worthwhile examining the concept of avoidable costs more closely, as it has been at the centre of a number of disputes about the validity of authorities' financial comparisons. Avoidable costs can usually be broken down into three areas: direct current, indirect, and capital costs.

Direct current costs include many of the variable costs associated with the operation of the service. The cost of salaries and wages, including national insurance and pension contributions, form a large proportion of direct costs; other variable costs which can be directly attributed to this particular service, such as heating, telephone and consumables, are also included. Calculations of these costs is usually fairly straightforward, both in local authorities and the NHS.

Indirect costs refer to the functions which are provided centrally for the service department. Because finance, purchasing, personnel, maintenance and transport operations are provided for a number of departments simultaneously, the costs of these services cannot be attributed directly to any one area. These indirect costs, also referred to as 'common costs' or 'overhead costs', can therefore pose problems for the tendering team. Some may be wholly avoidable given the contracting out of one service; many will be partially avoidable. Those that would clearly be saved by the contracting out of the service (e.g. payroll processing or auditing) are often excessively high due to inefficiencies in central provision. Inclusion of excess indirect costs can have a negative effect upon the competitive position of the in-house service as against that of the contractors.

Capital costs are the final and most complicated area of avoidable costs. Capital cost calculations must take into account the value of assets which would be disposed of as a result of contracting out. This issue is not quite as relevant for health authorities, who receive money for capital investment from the DHSS and do not include depreciation as a charge in their annual accounts, as it is for local authorities, who themselves fund capital investment and depreciate assets as would any commercial concern. Public finance experts emphasise that authorities should take into account the actual value, not the book value, of assets which would be disposed of as a result of contracting out; whether this present value exceeds the 'historic cost' value depends both on the rate of depreciation employed and the 'saleability' of the asset in question. They also suggest that authorities' calculations of capital cost include the cost of assets which would not have to be acquired as a result of contracting out. Calculation of these specific costs requires the use of discounted cash flow (DCF) techniques to take into account the value of money over time, despite the fact that such techniques often involve selection of a somewhat arbitrary discount rate.

The issue of capital costs is a highly technical one and is of primary interest only to financial minds in local government. However, it is important from an analytical standpoint insofar as it highlights the scope which authorities have to influence the outcome of the tendering process. Both the discount rate employed in calculating these costs and the time which is chosen to go to tender are open to manipulation, and can have a dramatic effect upon the competitiveness of the in-house bid. The timing of this tender is particularly critical in the case of assets with little or no resale value. Early in the life of major assets, it may be cheaper to stay in-house: loan charges are considered a sunk cost until assets need to be replaced. Later on, however, significant costs involved in asset replacement may tilt the balance in favour of a private contractor.[6] It is therefore possible to manipulate contract periods to show in-house provision in a particularly favourable light; it will also be possible to bias the financial calculations in the other direction.

Stage 5: adjudication

The deadline for receipt of in-house and external tenders marks the beginning of what is sometimes referred to as the 'adjudication' period. Adjudication involves evaluation of the submitted tenders and selection of the winning bid, and usually sees the participation of numerous functions or departments. The general, but by no means the only, pattern involves the establishment of an adjudication panel made up of a senior administrator, a senior financial officer, a management services officer and other functional representatives. Occasionally, these panels also include trade union representatives or the manager of the relevant specialist department. The panel's job is to consider reports on each tender from relevant functional departments. It is possible to identify three analytically distinct parts of the adjudication process. The first is a capability assessment, the second a technical assessment, and the third a financial appraisal.

The *capability assessment* assesses the bidder's capability to undertake the type of contract which has been put out to tender. Several criteria are commonly used to determine how capable a contractor is of performing to the requisite standard during the lifetime of the contract. The primary considerations are commercial ones and include the contractor's financial position, level of investment in equipment, and other commitments which might affect performance on the job. Personnel considerations are also important. Authorities attempt to ensure that the contractor has adequate staff, often by examining the ratio of supervisory to service personnel. Many investigate the general quality of company management and the specific competence of the manager who will be responsible for the contract. Frequently an authority will examine the contractor's personnel code to determine whether or not the firm is likely to follow established policies on health, safety, and training.

A *technical assessment* forms the second phase of the adjudication process. Responsibility for analysing the technical merits of both in-house and external tenders usually falls to the relevant specialists. Their task is to determine whether or not the specification has indeed been met and, if so, whether the contracting firm can be expected to implement its proposals at the quoted price. One of the most popular measures used to analyse tenders is the employee performance index (PI) as specified by the British Standards Institute. Used throughout the NHS, this technique specifies a 75 PI level as normal with a 100 PI level indicating a suitably motivated staff. It is thought that levels much above this cannot be sustained for extended periods of time. By comparing a contractor's proposed performance levels with current ones, and taking into account the lower wages and rewards accruing to staff, authorities are able to isolate the most unrealistic bids. Many find that contractors overlook one or more aspects of the specification and, as a result, quote at a lower price than would normally be expected.

The third and most contentious stage of the evaluation process has been the *financial appraisal*. It is not, as might be thought, a straightforward comparison of the prices quoted by shortlisted candidates. Contractors' bids need to be adjusted to make them compatible with one another and with the in-house tender. The method of adjusting these figures varies due to differences in the way authorities have chosen to treat redundancy, monitoring and overhead costs. In general, however, authorities begin by ensuring that contractors' prices are comparable (i.e. that they have all covered the specification comprehensively). Other costs associated with contracting out, such as VAT, monitoring costs and any overhead costs (for example, water and heat), are then added.[7] Where contracting out would allow disposal of certain assets, the value of these assets is then been subtracted from the sub-total; where it would not, the notional costs of redundant equipment might be added. The final adjustment which needs to be made involves redundancy and early retirement costs. These payments will vary according to the size and age profile of the in-house workforce, but they are usually quite significant due to the large number of workers who choose early retirement over employment with a contractor. Many authorities follow DHSS guidelines and show the total costs of these payments 'below the line' so that they may be taken into account in judging the longer-term benefits of costed options. One possible format for a financial appraisal is shown in Table 5.3.

Although authorities' approaches to financial appraisals vary considerably, the choice of approach is not critical as long as all of the relevant figures are comparable. This permits the tenders to be ranked accurately in terms of cost, an undertaking which does not – contrary to popular belief – signal the end of the adjudication process. Financial rankings are only one among many considerations used by adjudication panels to arrive at their decisions, and there is evidence to suggest that technical and capability assess-

TABLE 5.3   Financial appraisal format

	£
Contractor's price for contract period	2 520
Adjusted for comparability	2 340
Add overhead costs associated with private contractor	+30
Add EEC levy (1%)	+23
Subtract income from disposal of capital assets *or*	+30
add notional costs of redundant equipment	—
Add monitoring costs	+45
Subtotal	*2 468*
Add redundancy costs*	+345
Add early retirement costs	+300
Total cost to authority	**3 113**

* This would reflect the net cost to the authority after taking account of amounts recovered from the Department of Employment.

ments, as well as interviews with shortlisted contractors, play an equally important role in the decision-making process. Although comprehensive statistics are not available, it appears that only a minority of contracts are awarded to the lowest bidder; indeed the Managing Director of one of the most successful contracting firms recently boasted that his company had never won an NHS contract on price. His comments, together with the evidence provided by authorities' internal adjudication papers, suggests that authorities may be looking for value for money, despite the government's exhortations to accept the lowest tender.

Any number of ways can be employed to identify 'value for money', and much will depend on the particular objectives and needs of an authority. In general, each of the shortlisted bidders is scrutinised carefully and key strengths or weaknesses noted. One health authority highlighted ten areas 'where careful analysis of the tenders submitted by cleaning contractors was required'. These included:

1   the cost of providing the services
2   the total hours allowed

3   input hours per 100 square metres
4   terms and conditions of service
5   implications for existing staff
6   union recognition
7   satisfactory staff training manuals
8   site visits where appropriate
9   proposed staffing levels
10   the receipt of satisfactory references

The in-house tender is frequently amongst the shortlisted options. Where this is the case, the unquantifiable organisational effects involved in moving from an internally to an externally provided service are usually identified. (These effects might include improved management in other service areas or declining morale among the wider local authority workforce.) After taking the relevant 'spin-off' considerations into account, the adjudication panel recommends giving the contract to one particular tenderer. This recommendation is then passed on to the local council committee or district health authority that is empowered to award the contract; in most cases, endorsement of the recommended bid is fairly straightforward. Following this endorsement, authorities notify both successful and unsuccessful contractors of their decision. Notification is frequently done by way of a letter, although some authorities believe that a meeting with unsuccessful contractors helps to prevent queries from contractors and from the relevant government department. Rarely if ever are contractors shown the financial calculations or the adjustments which have been made to their quoted prices.

Stage 6: contract implementation

Arrangements for implementation are fairly simple where the in-house team has been awarded the contract. The quoted price becomes the service's budget over the contract period, new work schedules are implemented, and any reductions in staffing totals are achieved through a combination of redeployment, voluntary redundancy, early retirement and natural wastage. However, implementing the contract where it has been awarded to a private contractor is much more complicated. Transitional arrangements generally involve two major areas: termination of in-house provision and commencement of the private service.

Terminating in-house provision is always an unhappy business, and the brunt of it generally falls on personnel administrators. The task of making so many people redundant simultaneously is made difficult by the natural sympathy which many personnel officers, who know individual employees well, feel for members of the in-house team. But beyond the emotional difficulties, making arrangements for each and every employee is time-consuming and costly. All too frequently, the individual employees are not fully aware of the options and personnel staff must conduct lengthy discussions in which they explain the situation and solicit feedback on personal preferences.

Three avenues are traditionally open to the individual whose job is being terminated: redeployment, employment with a contractor or voluntary redundancy. Redeployment within the given authority is occasionally possible, depending on the individual's skills and the authority's current vacancies. Those who can be redeployed remain eligible for the benefits associated with continuous work with the same employer, but are not eligible for redundancy payments. Employment with a contractor is a second option; in most cases where a contract is awarded to the private sector, the contractor is keen to take on a certain proportion of the experienced in-house staff. Several authorities ask contractors to promise to interview all staff who want to continue in their jobs, and personnel staff participate in setting up these interviews between the award of the contract and its commencement. The third option open to in-house employees involves redundancy or early retirement. As noted in Chapter 4, this is often the most suitable option for older employees, particularly those who have accumulated many years of continuous service.

While arrangements are made to terminate in-house provision, authorities must prepare for commencement of the contract by the private firm. Contractors frequently ask to spend time getting to know the particular routines and physical characteristics of the new working environment. Occasionally, authorities have failed to cooperate with contractors' needs during the period prior to commencement and this has had disastrous consequences for the start of the contract. Typical of the problems experienced by some contractors were those reported by Mediclean's Managing Director some time after his firm began a domestic services contract at St Helier's Hospital in Carshalton, Surrey. Hospital staff reportedly failed to tell the contract manager where the cleaning machines were stored (eventually Mediclean staff found them 'hidden' in a crutches cupboard). The firm could not arrange for a telephone to be installed prior to contract commencement and was therefore unable to advertise for staff. Many of the pre-existing staff accepted jobs and then did not show up for work. Mediclean was then told that it could not employ its own 'beeping' system, as this would interfere with the hospital's existing personnel paging system.

While not all contracts have been characterised by such significant transitional problems, most have run into what contractors like to refer to as 'teething pains', an analogy that is not entirely accurate. Whereas teething pains are unavoidable, many of the problems that have characterised the early days of both health service and local authority contracts could have been avoided. Sometimes they have been the fault of the authority, which has either left too short a period of time between contract award and commencement or has failed to cooperate with the contractor. In other cases, they have been the fault of the contractor, who has not done sufficient 'homework' during this period. In general, however, the onus is on the authority to take precautionary measures to ensure that contractors have adequate time both to hire and train the necessary staff and to become familiar with the necessary routines and standards. Too many authorities have learned first-hand that contracts which begin badly can take a painfully long time to improve.

The transitional period is also the time when arrangements needed to monitor the performance of the private contractor are usually established. The change from in-house to external provision is a major one, both for the organisation and the individuals involved, and nearly all authorities experience a certain amount of turbulence. Financial control, reporting and performance supervision systems are required at an early stage, as the worst problems have generally been reported in the weeks following contract commencement. One very experienced American municipal administrator suggested that "plan for the worst and you will not be disappointed" should be the motto for the transition from in-house to contractual services.[8] Administrators in the health service and local government might take comfort in the fact that a certain amount of chaos during the transitional period appears to be universal.

Stage 7: monitoring

Monitoring the contract is considered an integral part of the competitive tendering process. As one DHSS circular noted, 'however much skill, knowledge and care is put into detailed written specifications, they will always be tentative until they are in operation.'[9] This holds true for all contracts, regardless of whether they have been awarded in-house or to a private contractor. Contractors agree that surveillance is important, and suggest that monitoring systems and the cost of providing them should apply equally to in-house and private contractors. Although this approach appears perfectly logical, it can be argued that monitoring is more important when the contract is awarded privately than when it remains in-house.

There are two major reasons why this should be so. The first is a question of performance levels. There are a number of factors which, taken together, could lead the contractor to achieve lower standards of service than those met by an in-house staff. A lack of knowledge or experience is one possible factor. This can manifest itself in a number of ways: failure to perform a job in the most efficient manner, lack of understanding of the risks involved, inability to handle a crisis, difficulty in communicating with other staff and client groups, etc. Another factor is the commercial profit motive. Commercial contractors must work to rigid time and cost schedules to secure what appear to be very slim margins. As a result, flexibility for the users of the service may be limited; any unforeseen crisis or additional work is likely to draw resources away from other areas of the contract and might therefore be handled hastily. The second reason why monitoring may be particularly important when dealing with private contractors has to do with the potential consequences of poor surveillance. Inadequate monitoring of in-house staff is unlikely to lead to much other than waste and inefficiency; staff are fully conversant with their jobs and will continue to do them, although possibly at an unsatisfactorily slow rate. The implications of poor monitoring of contractors are more serious; pressure to keep costs down and lack of experience, particularly in a hospital environment, could lead to serious health and safety risks.

Both of these concerns, the likelihood of reduced service standards and the implications of poor oversight, are difficult to quantify and British contractors would argue that they do not therefore justify more rigorous monitoring. But experience in America has shown that such concerns are not purely theoretical and that special monitoring systems are indeed needed for contractual arrangements. One experienced local adminstrator in the US noted: 'One of the hardest aspects for citizens, elected officials, and even managers to understand is that contractual services are harder to administer than in-house services. In reminding themselves of that fact, some contract administrators have a habit of saying "contractors don't think".'[10]

Responsibility for monitoring the performance of contractors is generally placed with an experienced and qualified individual or team. Because these activities require familiarity with both the authority's policies and the service itself, the job tends to fall to a specialist manager and frequently to the individual who was running the service prior to the tendering exercise. The precise type of monitoring required by an authority will vary according to the nature and location of the activity being undertaken. Cleaning in a hospital environment clearly requires more sophisticated and rigorous monitoring systems than street cleaning or refuse collection. This is partly because of the magnitude of health risks in hospitals, but also because activities like street cleaning and refuse collection are to some extent self-monitoring: if the job is not being done properly, then a local authority can be sure that numerous complaints from concerned taxpayers will alert it to the situation. In general, however, the importance of sound monitoring systems is universally recognised throughout the local authority and health service network. Even the Government, despite its strong support for the private sector, has recognised the importance of them; one paper circulated by the DHSS noted that 'apart from the specification, the most significant factor in achieving value for money from a contract for domestic services is the development of an effective contract monitoring system'.[11]

Procedural issues

The preceding pages have looked at the major stages of the
tendering process and have noted that certain procedural issues
have been open to dispute among interested parties. In practice, the
NHS tendering process as a whole has been criticised as unfair by
contractors and public sector employees, both of whom exhibit
what might be called paranoid attitudes toward the tendering
process. Contractors believe that they are at a serious disadvantage
when competing against in-house tenders. They argue that in-
house tenders do not take into account all relevant costs, that
specifications are unduly complicated, and that adjustments made
to their quoted prices during the adjudication process are unfair
and unrealistic. All these problems, they suggest, stem from the
Government's lack of interest in the outcome of the process and its
use of them as a 'tool' to force local authority savings. Many health
service administrators are equally unhappy with the process. They
feel that the Government has continually changed the rules of the
tendering game to make it more difficult for the in-house team to
compete, and cite the removal of VAT on private contracts and the
abolition of the Fair Wages Resolution as support for their belief.

It is hardly surprising that those who stand to gain or lose most
as a result of the tendering process are its greatest critics. Satisfying
both contractor and service administrator is difficult, if not impossible, as any concession to one side will have a negative effect on the
competitive position of the other. The dynamics of this situation
are nicely illustrated by recent events in the NHS. Contractors have
found themselves putting in extremely competitive (and in some
cases unprofitable) bids, only to lose the majority of contracts to
the in-house labour forces. Because they have nothing to lose and
everything to gain, contractors have complained continuously to
ministers and departments responsible and have based their complaints on either 'unfair' aspects of procedures or on procedural
irregularities. Ministers have been fairly receptive to these complaints and either have acted to restrict procedural variations or
have intervened on the contractors' behalf in a particular tendering
situation. Both types of political intervention have left the in-house
team in a considerably weakened position.

The complaints that have prompted this political interference
have been varied and numerous. Contractors have complained

repeatedly about the type of contract selected, the nature of the specification, and the presence of restrictive clauses which limit their commercial freedom. Financial issues have also been a focus of their attention, particularly the allocation of relevant costs and the adjustments that have been made to quoted prices during the adjudication process. Ten of the most familiar complaints put forward to the DHSS by the companies and their trade assocations are shown in Table 5.4 and discussed below.

VAT

Value Added Tax was introduced on health authorities' contracts with private firms in 1973. This had a significant effect upon the economics of both fixed price and management fee contracts, putting the contract service industries at a tremendous competitive disadvantage and contributing to the steady decline in their share of the NHS market between 1974 and 1983. When it became clear that the Government would endorse fixed price contracts for its NHS initiative, the companies lobbied hard for the abolition of VAT in the health service sector. In 1983, just prior to the start of NHS tendering initiative, the DHSS announced that it would refund VAT paid by health authorities on ancillary service contracts.

Bidding freedom

Contractors in both local and health authorities have continuously complained about the restrictions placed upon them in bidding situations. These restrictions range from clauses which indicate how a job is to be done or how many people are to be employed to clauses which require a contractor to rent and utilise certain types of equipment (for example, refuse trucks or depots). The Government has taken a strong stand against such behaviour in its advice to health authorities and is likely to prohibit such restrictions in local authority documents if and when mandatory competitive tendering is introduced in that sector. However, the Government's major removal of restrictions involved the abolition of the Fair Wages Resolution. This left contractors free to pay any wage rate at all, greatly improving their competitive position against authorities, all of whom must pay nationally negotiated wage rates. As

TABLE 5.4 The competitive tendering process: key procedural issues

Issue	Contractor complaint	Departmental action
VAT on private contracts	Unfair handicap in public sector bidding	Abolished 1983
Bidding freedom	Restrictions imposed by authority limit creativity in personnel and technical matters	Departmental advice; Fair Wages Resolution abolished*
Type of contract	Fixed price contracts unsuitable for certain areas (e.g. catering)	Hired consultants to investigate
In-house awards	Authorities overlooking lower private bids or making new investment to lower in-house price	Overruled by DHSS on a case by case basis
Capital costs	Cost of capital should be included in health authority in-house tenders	Recommendation of standard Treasury investment appraisal procedures
Monitoring costs	Monitoring costs should apply equally to in-house and external contracts	—
Overhead costs	Management support costs not included in in-house tender	—
Redundancy and retirement costs	Long-term costs should not be written off over lifetime of con-tract	Revised guidance from DHSS
Prequalification procedures	Unnecessarily complex and repetitive	—
Overspecification	Specifications are unnecessarily lengthy and often exaggerate level of service needed	—

* Against contractors' wishes.

noted in Chapter 4, this was a move which contractors had lobbied against because of its damaging effects upon industry margins and public relations, and one which was soon neutralised by the agreement of many health service contractors to continue to match Whitley rates of pay.

Type of contract

As noted earlier in this chapter, the Government has specified fixed price contracts for all three ancillary services, much to the displeasure of certain industries. The catering industry has been the most vocal critic, and has all but withdrawn from tendering for many NHS contracts. The government was forced to bring in management consultants Coopers and Lybrand to examine ways to increase private participation in tendering exercises for catering services. The firm's report, completed in 1985, has prompted the DHSS to issue formal advice to health authorities recommending the award of larger contracts which offer catering contractors significant economies of scale.

In-house awards

Contractors have complained bitterly to the DHSS about two forms of 'suspicious' in-house awards. The first involves the award of a contract to the in-house team on the basis of an internal tender that is substantially higher in cost than those submitted by private contractors. The second involves an award to an in-house team that has been able to propose a slightly more competitive price on the basis of substantial capital investment. The DHSS has investigated both types of complaints on an individual basis. In cases where suspicions of internal bias are confirmed, the Department has generally overruled the internal award and demanded that the contract be awarded to the lowest contractor. These events are documented more fully in Chapter 6.

Capital costs

Contractors tendering for work in the NHS, particularly those in the more capital-intensive areas of laundry and catering, have always been unhappy about the treatment of capital costs in the NHS. Local accounting practices tend to reflect the fact that capital expenditures are met centrally and most decisions, including those associated with contracting out, are based upon the net effects upon an authority's revenue account. Despite government pressure to employ more rigorous investment appraisal procedures, there is a strong tendency not to do so and depreciation of capital assets rarely has a significant impact upon NHS tendering decisions.[12] Many health service administrators admit that this unsystematic treatment of capital costs presents one of the truly significant biases against contractors in bidding for NHS work.

Monitoring costs

Contractors firmly believe that monitoring costs should apply equally to in-house and external tenders. Most authorities add them only to the external contractors' prices, on the assumption that monitoring costs are built into the in-house tenders. Since the NHS initiative began, contractors have lobbied the DHSS to look into the way that monitoring costs are handled by health authorities. To date, however, the Department has expressed no real sympathy with the contractors' views and in its own 'Framework for the Comparison of Costs' has specifically excluded them from the list of items to be included in the in-house tender.[13]

Overhead costs

Readily identifiable overheads, such as payroll processing, telephone, and secretarial support costs, would normally be included in any in-house tender. Contractors argue that these are only a few of the relevant indirect costs and that many other management support costs should be, but are not, included in costing the in-house tender. They cite such things as training centres, research establishments, and senior management costs as items which support the individual service without ever being charged against it. But calculating the relevant costs of these items is not as easy as it might seem and contractors have yet to suggest a logical or appropriate way of allocating these costs over the range of health authority activities.

Redundancy and retirement costs

Although redundancy and retirement costs are generally accepted as a legitimate cost to be added to the contractors' quoted prices, there is some dispute as to how they should be treated. Contractors complain that by writing off redundancy costs in the first year of a contract, authorities can make contracting out look significantly less attractive than it would look if these costs were amortised over a longer period of time. They also have complained that the costs associated with retirement, particularly pension costs, should not include payments to a retiring individual beyond the lifetime of the contract. They argue that these later costs, which can only be estimated with the help of actuarial tables, will be offset by continued savings made by the authority after completion of the contract. Both of these points have been accepted by the DHSS, which plans to issue further advice on this subject to authorities in 1986.

Pre-qualification procedures

As noted earlier, many of the companies tendering for NHS work are either newly established or new to the UK market. Health authorities tend to know very little about them and have therefore felt it necessary to undertake fairly comprehensive pre-qualification procedures. Contractors and their trade associations have continuously complained that these procedures are unnecessarily complex and that they should not need to go through such procedures with each and every district authority. They have suggested, and indeed have lobbied hard for, the establishment of a 'list of approved contractors' by the DHSS. But the Department views this primarily as an attempt by the larger contractors to minimise or eliminate competition from smaller and newer competitors and has therefore not been particularly receptive to the idea.

Overspecification

Many contractors have complained that the specification documents developed by authorities are unnecessarily lengthy and complicated. They argue that the time involved in responding to such specifications is excessive, and that some authorities use this technique to discourage private contractors from competing for the service. They also claim that authorities exaggerate the level of service needed (for example, the number of pieces of laundry to be processed per week or the number of times a hospital corridor must be cleaned) so that they can put in competitive bids and still operate within the budget if they are awarded the contract. However DHSS advisors report that overspecification, where it does exist, is rarely intentional and that it has tended to work against the in-house team: experienced contractors often recognise that an authority has overspecified and will price their job based on what they see as 'a sensible interpretation of these specifications', while those preparing the in-house tender often stick quite literally to the wording of the specification.

The ten issues outlined above are by no means the only concerns which have been voiced by contractors tendering for health service work. The DHSS also reports a constant stream of complaints about suspected procedural irregularities in specific cases. These typically involve the disclosure of contractors' quotes to the in-house team in advance of the tender deadline or the receipt of an in-house tender after the deadline for bids. However standing back from the substance of the complaints themselves, it is apparent that the highest frequency of complaints has occurred during periods when the public sector has won an overwhelming majority of contracts. In contrast, complaints have been fewer and farther between when 'the going is good' for contractors, as it was for cleaning contractors early on in the NHS tendering initiative. This lends support to the DHSSS administrators' belief that contractors will continue to find problems with various aspects of the tendering process throughout the remaining months of the Government's initiative.

An overview

The number and variety of complaints from contractors could easily lead one to believe that the tendering process has been stacked against them from beginning to end. The reality, however, is that contractors are in a very weak position to compete in certain areas and in a very strong position to compete in others. This is borne out by reports from regional authorities across the country which describe 'feast or famine' situations: some services attract the interest of a wide range of contractors and others attract little or no response. Cleaning work in urban areas has generally been oversubscribed, while the majority of catering contracts have attracted minimal interest and many have had to be awarded in-house by default. Overall, however, the contractors appear to have had a reasonable rate of response to their complaints about procedural irregularities and most (if not all) of the interventions from ministerial and departmental levels have helped to enhance their competitive position.

Although government involvement has clearly made it easier for private firms to win contracts, it would be wrong to suggest that the competitive position of public sector authorities has been totally undermined. They retain substantial freedom to influence the tendering process by determining the standard which must be met, the timing of the process itself, and the financial techniques which will be used to adjust tender prices and calculate future savings. These procedural powers can be, and on many occasions have been, used to influence the outcome of the tendering exercise. Although central government has attempted to minimise this influence by banning certain procedures and overruling 'suspicious' decisions, such intervention cannot possibly remove all traces of local discretion. Administrative processes, by their very nature, can never be wholly free from manipulation in terms of the way they are implemented. Furthermore, from a purely practical standpoint, the Government could not hope to identify systematically individual authorities' influence over the tendering process with the unsophisticated approach to monitoring employed by the DHSS (see Chapter 6).

The debate over the fairness of the competitive tendering process is likely to continue throughout the life of the current initiative. Contractors will continue to try to win the Government's ear and administrators will continue to be able to manipulate the tendering process in a variety of subtle ways. But it is important to recognise that the debate over procedural fairness is, in large part, artificial and irrelevant. It is merely a convenient battleground upon which the real battle over resources (i.e. over contracting out) is being fought. Contractors, authorities and trade unions are undoubtedly more interested in outcomes than they are in procedures. The only party with a genuine interest in the process itself is the Government. It is not primarily concerned with winners or losers, nor with the fairness of the current tendering mechanisms. Its primary concern is that the process operates smoothly and in as competitive a fashion as possible, so that cost-savings will be maximised and its own economic objectives will be met.

6 Competitive Tendering in the NHS

The introduction of mandatory competitive tendering in 1983 came as a blow to health service administrators, but not as a surprise. Since 1979, the NHS had played host to privatisation initiatives, attempts to improve management and efficiency, and an attack upon local autonomy. Prolonged industrial action by ancillary workers in 1982 had coincided with a major reorganisation which abolished area health authorities. Further change in the way the service was run looked imminent with the appointment of the Griffiths Inquiry, whose brief was to suggest improvements in NHS management practices. These and other events which preceded the introduction of the tendering initiative help to explain both the initial opposition with which health authorities greeted the policy and, paradoxically, their longer-term reluctance to fight it.

The historical setting

The past twenty years of the National Health Service's history have been littered with attempts by governments to find a structure for providing efficient and effective health care across Britain. Created in 1948, the NHS enjoyed a 'honeymoon' period throughout most of the 1950s. By the early 1960s, however, the original tripartite division of responsibilities between local authorities, executive councils, and the hospital service had come under criticism. Many felt that a unified structure more closely resembling that of local authorities was needed. Calls for reorganisation continued throughout the remainder of the decade, but it was not until the 1974 reorganisation that significant changes were implemented. Area health authorities were set up to coincide with local authority boundaries and districts constituted a new tier under the area authorities. Teaching hospitals were integrated into the unified structure, and both Family Practitioner Committees and Community Health Councils were established. Functional hierarchies, teams of managers representing the major services at district, area and regional level, were created in an attempt to promote 'consensus management' decisions.[1]

The emphasis of the 1974 reorganisation was primarily on increasing delegation within the NHS and no formal line relationship existed between functional managers at the various levels. This emphasis was reaffirmed by the Labour Party, which came into power later that year committed to increasing local autonomy within the service. A Devolution Working Party was set up by the Secretary of State and various other reports were commissioned to examine the role of the DHSS. But nothing came of these deliberations during the lifetime of either the 1974 or the 1976 Labour Government. The period saw a deterioration in industrial relations as economic growth came to a halt and cash limits were introduced, events which threw the existing strategic planning system into chaos.

The first real proposals for change came with the publication of the Green Paper *Patients First* in 1979. It recommended a curious combination of increased devolution of power and greater accountability to Parliament and the Secretary of State. While recognising the disruption that central guidance could cause, the document endorsed some fairly substantial organisational changes, many of which were implemented in the second major reorganisation of the health service in 1982. This Conservative initiative attempted to simplify and tighten the NHS structure: area health authorities were abolished (although regional management teams remained) and functional hierarchies were removed. The district health authorities became the basic planning bodies, and local or 'unit' management was strengthened. The planning system was changed: more immediate operational and forward programming over a two-year period replaced the previous more comprehensive three-year strategic planning cycle. Although smaller in scope than the 1974 changes, the reorganisation created an equivalent amount of disruption within the NHS. As one well-respected NHS publication noted, 'the term confusion rather than local flexibility seems to be the most appropriate one with which to describe the events surrounding the formation of a substantial part of the new unit level structure over the following 18 months to 2 years.'[2]

Two other sets of Conservative policy initiatives have occurred within the NHS, one concerned with increasing reliance on the private sector and another directed at improving managerial performance. 'Privatisation' policies have included increasing the percentage of pay beds, encouraging management of NHS hospitals by private firms, closing uneconomic hospitals, selling off residential NHS accommodation, introducing private auditors and contracting out ancillary services. Such moves have not only served to boost the fortunes of the private medical sector, but they have also opened a new market for firms providing a variety of non-medical services. Many administrators fear that these numerous privatisation initiatives represent only the tip of the iceberg and that more comprehensive attacks on the system, and indeed the concept, of national health care are likely to occur.

A second set of recent initiatives in the NHS has been directed at improving managerial performance. Some of these management exercises, such as the Financial Management Initiative and the Rayner Scrutinies, have been implemented on a government-wide basis; others have been developed specifically for the health service. As shown in Table 6.1, nearly all have been directed at improving the efficiency of the health service by introducing new techniques of management.

The scope and impact of both privatisation and management initiatives have varied. Some have been nothing more than 'experiments' undertaken on a limited scale; others have been implemented across the whole of the health service and have caused comparatively greater organisational friction and upheaval. But quite apart from the individual changes these initiatives have wrought, they have assumed a collective significance of considerable consequence. The sheer number and frequency of these initiatives has sent a strong and unambiguous signal to health service administrators that the government considers the NHS to be a legitimate, and indeed an important, component of its campaign to restore strength to the British economy.

Conflicts between central and local authorities are nothing new to the NHS and have often been seen as a natural occurrence in an organisation built upon fairly paternalistic assumptions about the nature of medical authority. But the increases in central interfer-

TABLE 6.1   Some recent NHS management initiatives

Initiative	Description
Rayner scrutinies	Investigations into the efficiency of catering, transport, centralised storage, certain aspects of payment collection services, and other areas
Regional reviews	Annual meetings between ministers, regional health authority chairmen, and regional officers, which aim to monitor efficient use of NHS resources
Performance indicators	New measures of how well medical, financial and administrative resources are managed. Useful in comparing local areas and in monitoring performance
Optional appraisal	A new and more rigorous approach to investment appraisal in the NHS, which takes into account the opportunity cost of capital investment
General managers	The appointment of general managers at all levels of the health service aims to improve the standard of NHS management by introducing personnel and techniques from the private sector
Competitive tendering	Mandatory tendering for domestic, laundry and catering services aims to improve efficiency and management in the ancillary sector

ence which have occurred in recent years are unprecedented. Many attribute this new 'interventionist' approach on the part of the Government to the arrival of Norman Fowler at the DHSS in 1982, and highlight the fact that previous ministers had actively encouraged devolution of decision-making power. Whatever its causes, this new approach has had a significant impact upon both the tenor and the development of the current debate. Competitive tendering has *not* been viewed as an isolated event by health service administrators; it has been seen as one of many privatisation and management initiatives which together constitute a broadly-based attack upon local autonomy and discretion. But while the comprehensiveness of the attack aroused hostility among administrators, it also convinced them of the absolute determination of the Government and thus the futility of opposition activity. This helps to explain why many of the most vocal and articulate critics of government policy have taken very little action to frustrate or disrupt its implementation.

The ancillary services: a profile

Over the past two decades, the NHS has accounted for a growing share of public expenditure. Its costs have doubled in real terms between 1965 and 1984, rising from 4.1 per cent to 6.2 per cent of GNP. In 1985, it accounted for approximately £14 000 million worth of expenditure annually and constituted about one-fifth of all public expenditure. Expenditure within the NHS is clearly divided into two types. 'Capital expenditure' refers to the costs of new buildings and equipment and accounted for about 6 per cent of all NHS expenditure in 1984–5.[3] The remaining costs of running the NHS fall under the general heading of 'revenue expenditure'. This includes both the cost of patient care and services, generally referred to as 'clinical' activities, and the general and administrative services needed to support the activities of a hospital, often referred to as 'non-clinical' activities. Clinical services have traditionally accounted for the largest share of revenue expenditure and their percentage increased from about 58 per cent of all revenue expenditure in 1974–5 to 63 per cent in 1981–2 – a reflection of skyrocketing medical costs.

Ancillary services fall within the non-clinical segment of revenue expenditure. The term 'ancillary', which literally means 'subservient' or 'subordinate', is a confusing one, as it does not refer to all hospital services ancillary to patient care; the administrative costs of running a hospital, maintaining patient records, and training staff are generally excluded from consideration under this heading. Furthermore, the number of services defined as 'ancillary' will vary from authority to authority. In general, however, the largest portion of hospital ancillary expenditure is accounted for by six areas: building maintenance, catering, cleaning, engineering, gardening and laundry services. In 1983–4 these areas were responsible for 1.3 billion pounds of revenue expenditure in England alone, as shown in Table 6.2.[4]

TABLE 6.2 Ancillary service expenditure: England (1983–4)

Ancillary service	Total expenditure (£000s)
Cleaning and domestic	428 900
Catering	353 500
Engineering	257 000
Building maintenance	163 700
Laundry	66 000
Gardening/farming	23 500
Total	**1 292 600**

Source: Computed from *Sixth Report from the Social Services Committee* (1984–5), House of Commons, 39.

The costs of ancillary services vary significantly from one district or regional authority to another. Proponents of contracting out attribute this to widespread inefficiencies in service provision, but others argue that these variations reflect geographic and demographic factors, as well as the impact of local decisions as to the quantity and quality of service needed. Evaluating these opposing arguments is difficult as accounting variations, particularly in relation to the apportionment of overheads, prevent reliable comparison between authorities.

There are approximately 240 000 workers employed in ancillary health service work in Britain; this represents roughly one out of five NHS personnel. A large number of these, probably around 45 per cent, are part-time workers. Staffing totals in the ancillary service sector have risen more slowly than in other areas and are now falling. Figure 6.1 shows that between 1974 and 1983 ancillary service numbers increased by only 1.9 per cent; during the same period medical and nursing staff numbers rose 30.7 and 27.5 per cent respectively. Since 1982, ancillary totals have been declining. Between April 1983 and April 1984, for example, the number of

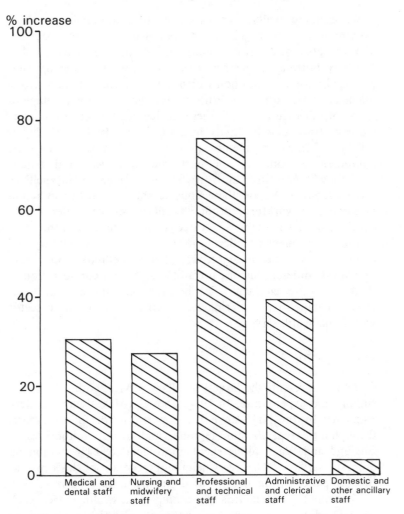

Figure 6.1 Health service manpower trends: 1974–83
Source: Computed from *Compendium of Health Statistics, 5th Edition* (London:
Office of Health Economics, 1984), 76.

whole-time equivalents in the UK fell by 1.2 per cent. This was
primarily a result of a 6 per cent drop in the number of ancillary
workers in England, which offset increases in other parts of the
country.

Wages in the ancillary service sector have traditionally been low, even by health service standards. As noted in Chapter 4, current Whitley rates for catering, laundry and domestic assistants fall at the very bottom of the health service scale and low pay has provided a foundation upon which the unions have built a strong ancillary service presence. With among the highest percentage of union members in the NHS, these services have acted as a cornerstone of trade union activity in many hospitals. Union officials attribute their strong membership showing in this sector to the continued 'exploitation' of part-time, unskilled, and female workers who constitute an overwhelming percentage of ancillary service labour. Despite these considerable similarities in remuneration and workforce profile, ancillary services differ significantly from one another. The three services which form the focus of the Government's tendering initiative – cleaning, laundry and catering – have different objectives, different methods of operation, and keenly different historical traditions. A brief consideration of their respective characteristics helps to explain why attitudes toward competitive tendering have varied from sector to sector within the health service.

Domestic services

Cleaning represents the largest ancillary service, both in terms of staffing and expenditure. In 1984, about 110 000 domestics were employed by the NHS on either a part-time or full-time basis throughout Great Britain; regional and district authorities in England and Wales alone spent approximately £436 million on domestic services.[5] The overwhelming percentage of this expenditure (90 per cent) can be attributed directly to the costs of labour.

There are three standards of cleaning in the health service, each geared to different areas within a hospital: 'high risk' areas include all operating theatres, 'clinical' areas include both in-patient and out-patient departments, and 'non clinical' areas include administration offices and staff residences. The basic job of a domestic cleaner concerns the provision of cleaning services to all five of these locations. Frequently, domestics are expected to provide additional support duties for nursing staff, such as serving meals, attending patient baths, washing dishes, making tea and arranging flowers. Occasionally they will be asked to undertake housekeeping duties, such as distributing linen or issuing uniforms and protective clothing. Because of the variety of these duties, hospital cleaning workers are often viewed as part of a team providing an environment which is conducive to convalescence. They usually maintain a close working relationship with other ward personnel, particularly the ward sister. In addition to playing a part in the immediate world of the patient, cleaners are part of numerous other hospital spheres including fire safety, occupational health, patient transport, emergency and disaster procedures.

Traditionally, the job of the hospital cleaner was inseparable from the other activities within a hospital. Up until the 1960s, there was no domestic services hierarchy and responsibility for cleaning services rested with senior nursing administrators. Individual cleaners were allocated to wards and departments; ward sisters and departmental heads were responsible for their training and supervision. During the early 1960s, this situation began to change as many administrators recognised the need to reduce the nurse's workload. Some chose to appoint an internal domestic manager to undertake supervisory duties previously carried out by ward sisters. Others decided to try outside contractors who promised to supply the personnel and expertise needed to carry out these same supervisory duties.

This marked the beginning of contract cleaning in the health service. As noted in Chapter 2, it grew rapidly as a result of the large number of hospital administrators who were experiencing problems recruiting qualified supervisory personnel. Pay scales for domestic supervisors were low and varied according to the size of the unit they controlled; as a result, those who managed smaller units did particularly badly and usually jumped at an opportunity to move to a larger hospital. As one early convert to contract cleaning noted in 1964: 'Domestic superintendents are as hard to find as good cooks and harder to keep.'[6] Most of the early private arrangements in the NHS were management contracts which, because the cost of labour did not change (as employees continued to be paid directly by the NHS) and the cost of management rose (due to the higher salaries paid to contractors' supervisory personnel), were nearly always more expensive than in-house services. Commercial interest in these early NHS cleaning contracts was limited, and the few firms attempting to break into the market rarely came into direct competition with one another. Arrangements with private cleaners were frequently made on the basis of a vague specification, after a simple comparison of in-house costs with a quotation provided by one contractor.[7] Throughout the 1960s and 1970s, the Crothall company dominated the NHS market for private cleaning. On the basis of its New Zealand experience, it gained an early foothold in the NHS and, by 1973, held 90 per cent of this very small market. But reorganisation and the imposition of VAT on contracts put a halt to growth in this market. By 1979, when the Conservative Government came to power, only three private contractors were active in the domestic services area of the NHS and only 40 or so contracts were in private hands. These contracts represented only 2 per cent of the NHS market for domestic services and were primarily based in London and the South-east. Over the next few years, the position of these three contractors seemed to deteriorate as several long-standing cleaning contracts were cancelled in favour of a return to in-house provision. This adverse change in contractors' fortunes was an important motivating factor behind the determined campaign by contract cleaners to convince the government of the merits of private provision.

Laundry services

Laundry work constitutes the smallest NHS ancillary service, both in staffing and expenditure terms. In 1983–4, some £66 million was spent on laundry services. Dry cleaning accounted for about 4.5 per cent of this total; the remaining expenditure reflected costs incurred in the washing of bedding and clothing. Laundry services are clearly less labour-intensive than cleaning, with only about 40 per cent of the total cost of a laundry service being directly attributable to wages and benefits of employees. Over 9000 workers were employed in the NHS laundry sector in 1984, a great number of them on a part-time basis.[8] Many have come to the NHS after a significant amount of private sector experience. As with domestic cleaning, the great majority of the workforce is female.

NHS laundries process about 750 million articles each year, or about 15 million per week. There are two distinct types of NHS laundries. Centrally-located, modern hospital laundries generally undertake 300–400 000 pieces of laundry per work week, and often serve between five and seven hospitals. Other more antiquated laundries, many in need of re-equipping, serve one or two hospitals only. Both types will occasionally cater to hospitals in neighbouring district authorities and both must meet significantly different requirements than commercial laundries. Because they handle large amounts of foul and infected laundry, they must employ 'barrier-washing' techniques to separate these items from uncontaminated pieces. They must also provide for relatively fast 'turnaround' of items, typically returning laundry within 48 hours of its collection. The processing cost of each item can vary anywhere from 8 to 20 pence per piece depending upon the age of equipment, geographical coverage of the laundry, and level of employee remuneration.

Laundry managers are paid according to the number of pieces they process over a given time period. Wage rates for laundry workers in 1985 stood at £1.75 per hour or £70 per week. Nearly 70 per cent of all laundry staff were on incentive bonus schemes, and these schemes generally added about 25 per cent to the basic wage of laundry workers. Despite the low wage rates, it is estimated that less than 10 per cent of NHS laundry workers belong to a union. As a result, this sector has not exhibited any significant degree of trade union activity.

The history of NHS laundry services is interesting, as it highlights the well-established tradition of using private contractors to supplement in-house provision. Prior to the creation of the NHS in 1948, nearly 60 per cent of hospital laundry work was done by private firms. Few of these firms were of significant size; most were locally-based and did not incur significant transport costs. With the formation of the NHS, however, 1200 independent laundries were brought under one organisational roof. Many of these were old and could not cope with increasing volumes of laundry. A substantial programme of NHS laundry closures began in the 1950s and gathered pace during the 1960s and 1970s. The 'big hospital' programme of the early 1970s, which saw large, modern laundries built onto new hospitals in an attempt to achieve self-sufficiency, accelerated the pace of closures. Only about 430 NHS laundries remained operational as of 1985, one-third of the number which existed thirty-five years ago.

Older hospital laundries were phased out only gradually, however, and those which remained open during the 1950s and 1960s continued to have trouble coping with peak demand periods. Many were forced to look to private contractors to supplement their in-house capacity. Flatwork (consisting of pillow cases and sheets) was frequently sent out, while clothing and infected items continued to be washed in-house. Thus began the partnership between NHS hospital laundries and private contractors that has existed ever since. But despite the peaceful and relatively stable nature of this partnership, private laundry contractors, like their domestic service counterparts, suffered a decline in their NHS market share in the early 1980s. In 1980, private contractors were responsible for just over 14 per cent of expenditure on NHS laundry work; by 1984, they held less than 10 per cent of this same market. For this reason, contract launderers were as keen as contract cleaners for the Government to encourage greater use of private firms in ancillary service provision.

Catering services

NHS catering workers feed some 600 000 'customers' in 2000 locations on an average working day. Approximately 15 per cent of these customers have special diets, which require separate preparation of food. In 1983, catering services provided an acceptable standard and variety of meals to both normal and 'special' patients within a budget of approximately £1.10 per person per day.[9] Aggregate catering costs for authorities in England and Wales in 1983–4 totalled £375 million. Roughly 60 per cent of this expenditure can be attributed to labour costs. In 1983 there were approximately 37 000 catering 'operatives', who were supported by 1400 managers and about 650 clerical workers. As with the other major ancillary services, the catering workforce is predominantly female and includes many part-time workers. Union representation is patchy, and turnover is high.

Catering is generally considered the most efficient of ancillary services. Between 1974 and 1982, NHS catering teams fed 10 per cent more people with 7 per cent fewer staff and still managed to reduce real costs by 12 per cent. Catering services declined as a percentage of total NHS expenditure, while the contribution return on staff catering shot up.[10] The improvement in catering performance is generally attributed to the managerial skill of NHS catering managers. Most enter the health service with college degrees or professional catering qualifications, and many are recruited from well-respected private sector catering firms. These managers used the wider voice assigned to functional areas by the 1974 reorganisation to lobby successfully for new catering equipment, and this equipment has played a vital role in the dramatic reduction of operating costs.

The efficiency of in-house services, combined with the tremendous purchasing power of the NHS, makes catering the most difficult service for a private contractor to penetrate. However, this has not always been the case. During less efficient periods, particularly during the late 1950s and 1960s, catering contractors found it relatively easy to break into the NHS. Guaranteeing expertise not always found in the health service, they were able to build up a reasonably strong track record of management contracts in hospital catering by the mid-1960s. But the growth of contract catering in the NHS was brought to a halt in the late 1960s and early 1970s. Several catering firms were found to be putting in good managers at the start of the contract, and then replacing them with less experienced managers who could not maintain service standards. This behaviour, characteristic of many contract service industries, convinced hospital administrators that improvements to the in-house service should precede consideration of contracting out. By the late 1970s improvements in equipment and productivity had led to significant in-house savings, and only a few isolated health authorities were using contract caterers. The situation facing catering firms deteriorated further between 1980 and 1982, when nearly all of the remaining catering contracts were terminated and returned to in-house provision.

Summary

The relationship that existed between private contractors and the health service throughout the 1960s and early 1970s was fairly straightforward: the private sector was called upon when the public sector needed it. Four reasons featured most prominently in decisions to employ alternative methods of service provision for ancillary services:

1 to relieve burdens on existing staff or facilities
2 to provide manpower in areas of labour shortages

3   to provide better qualified supervisory personnel
4   to improve services undergoing significant problems

The most common answer to these needs was a management fee contract, which avoided the industrial relations and accountability issues associated with full contracting out. Evidence indicates that competition for such contracts was not particularly fierce, and that incumbent contractors were in a fairly strong position to hold on to the work when the contract period drew to a close. Private firms were often more expensive than in-house provision; as late as 1970, one of the major areas of concern was the higher wages paid by private firms to their employees. The contrast between contracting out as it existed then and as it exists now could hardly be more vivid.

The situation began to change in the middle of the 1970s, and the last decade has seen a consistent weakening in the position of contractors within the NHS. Functional hierarchies, set up by the 1974 reorganisation, gave the key ancillary services stronger voices at district level and made it harder for contractors to establish a foothold in new areas. Those authorities that had employed contractors grew dissatisfied with these arrangements and many reverted to in-house provision. As shown in Table 6.3, the pendulum was clearly swinging away from contractors as the Government began its NHS tendering initiative. The percentages of work undertaken by private contractors in the three major ancillary services had declined steadily between 1980 and 1983, as had the aggregate value of these contracts. The value of domestic service contracts in the NHS fell from £9.6 million in 1980 to £8.4 million in 1983; over the same period the value of laundry contracts dropped from £7.2 million to £6.4 million and the value of catering contracts from £1.0 to £0.8 million. These years saw the major contractors lose some of their oldest and most profitable public sector contracts and, although the total value of these contracts was small, their loss served to compound the problems of static or declining private sector markets for their services. This helps explain why contractors in all three areas assigned such tremendous significance to the opening of the NHS market.

Table 6.3   Private provision of NHS ancillary services: 1980–4

Year	Domestic services (% NHS expenditure)	Laundry (% NHS expenditure)	Catering (% NHS expenditure)
1979–80	2.4	14.1	0.2
1980–81	2.5	12.0	0.3
1981–82	2.1	11.7	0.2
1982–83	2.0	11.5	0.2
1983–84	2.0	9.2	0.2

Source: *Hansard*, 16 November, 1982, col. 131W; 7 March 1983, col. 327W; 28 November 1984, col. 535W and *Sixth Report from the Social Services Committee*, House of Commons, 1985.

The implementation of mandatory tendering

The responses of health authorities to the DHSS circular on competitive tendering have exhibited an all too familiar variety of management styles. These can be summarised as follows: get on with it and learn as we go along; employ management consultants to do all or most of the work involved; buy a computer 'package' which promises to relieve us of most of the work involved; play for time and hope to profit from the success/ mistakes of the foregoing when finally forced to act.[11]

These few sentences, written by a regional health administrator in September 1985, appropriately describe the introduction of competitive tendering into the NHS. Tendering for ancillary services has involved a tremendous amount of work and many authorities have never undertaken an exercise like this before. Little central guidance has been forthcoming; as a result, a number of authorities have delayed the tendering process as long as possible. These factors have contributed to making competitive tendering a more salient and more controversial issue than any of its proponents had expected. The remainder of this chapter examines the implementation of the policy in the health service. It considers both the nature and impact of opposition to it, and documents the effects that these and other factors have had upon the policy to date. Several case studies are used to highlight the key features of both government and opposition campaigns.

Introducing the policy

Mandatory competitive tendering became government policy for English and Welsh health authorities on 17 September 1983. All district health authorities were asked to draw up plans to submit cleaning, laundry and catering services to competitive tender by the end of 1986. These plans were to be sent to regional authorities by February 1984 and would form the basis of regional timetables which were to be submitted to the DHSS by April 1984. As might have been expected given the Government's clumsy handling of health authority views during the consultative stages (documented in Chapter 2), the initiative got off to a slow start. Several health authorities refused to submit timetables by the specified date; others submitted documents which contained incomplete programmes or asked for an extension to the specified deadline. Although the specific reasons for health authority opposition varied from area to area, most were critical of the timing, cost and likely impact of the exercise. Many felt that because a major disruption to the existing service could have long-term ramifications in terms of employee morale and the standard of service, the risks associated with contracting out far outweighed its potential benefits. Several suggested that the emphasis should be more on the quality of a service than upon its cost.[12]

Initial opposition by the health authorities was not primarily drawn along party political lines; one regional administrator noted that, 'all the authorities are unhappy about it; it's not a right–left thing'. Only about half of the 192 English authorities submitted timetables by the February deadline, and a number of districts flatly refused to comply with the circular. But despite fierce opposition from certain quarters, a large number of health authorities did submit timetables within a few months of the government's deadline. By mid-May 1984, 164 of the 192 English authorities (85 per cent) had submitted timetables; two-thirds of the Welsh authorities had also cooperated. Nevertheless, the reluctance on the part of some regional and district health authorities to put forward genuine proposals for contracting out services worried DHSS administrators and pressure was put on the regions to speed up activity in recalcitrant districts.

Within the first six months of the implementation period, while many authorities were venting their anger in the health service press, a number of others went ahead with mandatory tendering exercises. Some were new hospitals, required by Circular HC(83)18 to go out to tender before recruiting an in-house service team. Others were established hospitals, whose previously existing private contracts came up for re-tender very soon after the Government's policy was made official. For a third group of authorities, competitive tendering was a prerequisite for capital investment: the DHSS circular required all authorities who wished to make more than £0.5 million worth of capital improvements to existing laundries to go out to tender first. A fourth group of pioneering authorities might be labelled 'true believers', anxious to be among the first to go out to tender. Some were in need of significant savings to meet financial targets; others felt that tendering might offer a solution to their time-consuming and disruptive industrial relations problems.

This peculiar mix of motives put the contractors in a fairly strong position. Some hospitals had no in-house service to speak of; others were quietly keen to make radical changes to the one which existed. Both of these factors contributed to a string of early victories for the contractors. Cleaning contractors did particularly well during this period, winning all 12 contracts to be let in 1983 and 7 of the 9 to be awarded in the first quarter of 1984. But progress was not as rapid as some proponenets of contracting out would have liked. Most of the early tendering activity was limited to the South-east and focused on domestic service contracts only, giving rise to suspicions that authorities were 'dragging their feet'. In March 1984, the Tory Reform Group published *High Noon in the National Health Service*, a pamphlet which argued that hospitals and health authorities were going out of their way to delay the tendering process. It claimed that the contracts which had been won since the start of the initiative were 'freak' incidents, and that authorities were reluctant to put large and potentially lucrative contracts out to tender. These claims were fundamentally correct: most authorities had scheduled smaller units and hospitals for tendering before larger ones, in an attempt to 'test the water' and gain experience before undertaking major tendering exercises. The DHSS, which by then had received a majority of timetables, was well aware of this fact but ignored the pamphlet's plea for a switch to a mandatory contracting out policy.

Opposition grows

As the NHS initiative gradually gained momentum, contractors grew increasingly dissatisfied with the outcome of tendering exercises. Some of this dissatisfaction was directed at health authorities who had awarded contracts in-house under 'suspicious' circumstances, but much of it was aimed at DHSS administrators who contractors felt were responsible – both as architects and enforcers of the policy – for the problems they had experienced in trying to win contracts. This second stage also saw the development of major opposition activity by the trade unions. Early on, the unions focused on developing and circulating information about the tendering process and strategies for fighting it. By the spring of 1984, however, they were prepared for action.

London formed the focus of the unions' early opposition campaign. Industrial action began at Barking Hospital in London in March 1984. This was a curious place for the first confrontation, since Barking had employed a private cleaning contractor for many years and had not experienced any special problems. But the Government's tendering exercise had transformed the competitive environment significantly and Crothall, the existing contractor, was forced to put in a highly competitive bid when the contract came up for re-tender. The company won the contract, but was placed in the awkward position of having to make dramatic cuts in the wages and benefits of existing employees. These workers walked out in protest at the company's action, and their experience soon became an important symbol of the effects of contracting out upon ancillary workers. Not long after Barking's domestics walked out, their counterparts at Hammersmith Hospital followed. Hammersmith had never had contractors, and the unions' main objection was to competitive tendering itself. They expressed their opposition by adamantly refusing to cooperate in the process and by mounting a divisive strike which spread quickly to other ancillary services. The reputation of Hammersmith Hospital made it highly visible to the general public, and the unions' national organisations seized upon it as the second *cause célèbre*. Events at Hammersmith are examined later in this chapter.

The unions did not rely exclusively upon evidence of deteriorating conditions for its members to support their case against contractors. Throughout 1984, the unions collected and disseminated any evidence they could find about contractors' failure to maintain standards. Much of the material they came up with was relatively minor, reflecting early 'teething pains' rather than legitimate failures. Nevertheless, the information was widely publicised and formed a critical part of the unions' early campaign to undermine the credibility of contractors in the eyes of health authority administrators. This campaign coincided with a steady increase in the number of in-house successes in the first half of 1984. Although the union campaign was unrelated to the change in contractors' fortunes (the growing number of in-house wins simply reflected the fact that older hospitals, many with a long tradition of in-house provision, had begun to go out to tender), it aroused considerable concern among contractors. Companies saw that their success ratios were dropping steadily and began to complain bitterly to DHSS officials and ministers about both structural and procedural irregularities.

Laundry companies felt handicapped by the peculiar treatment of capital costs in the NHS. They brought to the attention of DHSS administrators cases where they believed health authorities were deliberately spending money on new equipment in order to be in a competitive position at the outset of the tendering exercise. They also queried cases where the in-house tender price undercut the lowest external bid by a suspiciously small margin. Catering contractors, having failed to win any of the first half dozen contracts to go out to tender, directed their anger at the fixed price contract. They claimed that catering did not lend itself to fixed price arrangements, due to variations in dietary needs and foodstuff costs, and asserted that few such arrangements existed in the private sector. Some hinted that they would be selective in tendering for contracts; the largest contractor, Gardner Merchant, actually withdrew from its two existing contracts in November 1984 and refused further tender invitations. Complaints from contract cleaners focused on procedural, rather than structural, irregularities. Their criticism was primarily directed at authorities which had awarded contracts to the in-house team at prices higher than those submitted by the private sector, though they also complained about the length and complexity of the contract documents issued by tendering authorities.

The DHSS was not particularly responsive to complaints from contractors. Although it conceded that a number of in-house wins were suspicious, its information and monitoring systems were not sufficiently comprehensive to pinpoint irregularities at their source. Senior managers in contracting firms complained that when irregularities were pointed out to key civil servants 'they cooperated without enthusiasm' and that 'DHSS administrators feel a kindred spirit with the NHS employee'. Contractors soon began directing complaints about in-house wins to the relevant ministers. Both Kenneth Clarke, Minister for Health, and John Patten, Parliamentary Undersecretary of Health, appeared to be far more receptive to these complaints than departmental administrators and sent a steady stream of enquiries to the chairmen of regional and district authorities, asking them to review particularly 'suspicious' decisions to award contracts in-house.

Occasionally, ministers went so far as to overrule an existing award and order that the contract be placed with an outside contractor. These interventions revealed the full extent of government interest in the tendering initiative, and showed its willingness to interfere in the local adjudication process. Several of these 'political' decisions involved awards to in-house laundries whose tenders had involved some element of re-equipping to achieve maximum savings. Despite the fact that in each of these cases the in-house tender seemed more cost-effective in the long run then any private sector bid, ministers argued that capital expenditure could be put to better uses and overruled these awards. A slightly different situation arose on the domestic services side, where ministers challenged certain in-house awards on the grounds that the lowest tender had to be accepted unless there were exceptional reasons for not doing so. This selective enforcement of lowest tender criteria angered many authorities who felt that such blatantly political interference removed the last vestiges of local discretion from service delivery decisions.

Ministerial intervention contributed to a general improvement in the performance of contractors against in-house teams in the latter part of 1984. Most of the tendering activity remained in the South-east, where cleaning contractors were based and where laundry contractors had excess capacity. As a result, competition in both of these areas was keen and in-house teams stood little chance of beating contractors on price. By March 1985, eighteen months after the initiative began, contractors had won 52 per cent of all contracts that had gone out to tender. As expected, their performance was strongest in domestic services, the most labour-intensive area, and weakest in catering, where they had won only 3 of the 29 contracts that went out to tender.[13]

Recent developments

The remainder of 1985 saw the pendulum swing once again in the direction of in-house labour forces. This success reflected a greater understanding by the in-house teams of the nature of private sector competition: watching others go through the process made many less reluctant to cooperate with management in devising an acceptable in-house tender. Another reason behind the improved performance of direct labour was the shift in tendering activity from the South-east towards the North of England. Better success ratios in the North can partly be attributed to differences in political outlook, but they are also a reflection of a more serious unemployment situation, a comparatively stronger trade union movement, and poorer geographic coverage by the major southern-based contractors.

This later turn in the tendering tide affected the behaviour of contracting firms in two ways. First, it caused them to become more selective about which contracts to compete for and which deadlines to meet. Most were inundated with invitations to tender; thus the opportunity costs of tendering for contracts likely to be awarded in-house escalated. Secondly, it brought a rash of new complaints to the desks of both DHSS administrators and ministers. As noted in Chapter 5, contractors accused authorities of laying down unnecessary conditions of service, of overspecifying and of adopting inappropriate, unduly rigorous monitoring systems. In addition, queries about 'suspicious' in-house awards continued. One trade association indicated its intention to register queries with the DHSS about the validity of every in-house award not based on price. Another offered to fund an independent check on any authority which awarded a major contract in-house.

The rising number of in-house awards and increasing dissatisfaction among contractors were no doubt important factors behind the increase in central intervention which occurred during 1985. Ministers continued to step in to overrule questionable decisions, but also began to issue blanket directives about procedural techniques and the content of contract documents. One of the major issues that occupied ministerial attention was the presence of fair wages clauses in many contract documents. In the year following the abolition of the Fair Wages Resolution, trade unions put considerable pressure on authorities to specify 'fair wages' in their contract documents and more than two dozen authorities adopted such clauses. Unions firmly believed, and ministers soon came to agree, that this move would help to cut the competitive floor out from under the private contractor. In May 1985, Kenneth Clarke denounced fair wages clauses as tendentious and meaningless. He asked regional chairmen to remove these requirements, on the grounds that they constituted unreasonable interference in the relationship between contractors and their employees. According to the DHSS, authorities were to go no further than ensuring that contractors are competent and that they offer adequate rates to recruit appropriate staff.

Another area in which ministers sought to limit local discretion involves action on unsatisfactory performance. In early 1985, Bromley DHA cancelled a contract with Hospital Hygiene Services for domestic services at Orpington Hospital. In doing so, it became the first authority to terminate a major cleaning contract awarded under the NHS initiative. This action was brought to ministerial attention and an instruction not to take action on existing cleaning contracts was immediately sent to health authorities by ministers. Any authority considering cancelling a contract was directed to consult the DHSS first.

Despite the general improvement in tendering outcomes for in-house staff, this phase of the tendering initiative saw unions continue to wage war upon contractors through the media. Addenbrooke's Hospital in Cambridge was the focus of industrial action in the South throughout much of 1985. Major industrial action also occurred in a variety of areas in the North. In most cases the unions demanded complete reappraisals of the tendering process and refused to cooperate even after the authority awarded the contract in-house. Such pressure from the unions led at least two health authorities, Sunderland and York, to temporarily suspend their tendering programmes.

A summary of progress

This whole exercise, which has now been underway for around four years, has involved a considerable amount of management time and effort; has caused disruption and discontent, not exclusively among NHS staff directly employed in these services; and to date has not brought home the bacon. The real impact of competitive tendering, for better or for worse, has yet to be seen.[14]

This was the conclusion of the House of Commons Select Committee on Social Services after examining the results of the Government's policy in mid-1985. At that time, only 222 of an expected 2000 tendering exercises had been carried out, and almost half of all health authorities had yet to put their first service out to tender. This slow progress explained the rather limited savings which had been reported. The DHSS estimated that £18.6 million per year had been saved by the middle of 1985, representing just under 2 per cent of the £950 million spent annually on the three ancillary services. In-house wins accounted for £6.1 million or 33 per cent of the savings total; contractors' victories were responsible for the remaining £12.5 million. Savings were most significant in the cleaning field: the £14.8 million in savings represented 3.5 per cent of that service's annual budget, while laundry and catering savings accounted for only 2.3 and 0.4 per cent of their respective services' budgets.

There are some obvious reasons for the unexpectedly slow progress of the initiative. Most authorities were reluctant to put large contracts out to tender too quickly. Their reluctance stemmed from three basic factors: disapproval of the policy, anger over the lack of consultation during its development, and the lack of guidance offered by central sources. Leaving aside the political issues surrounding the policy itself and its handling by the government, perhaps the most significant factor which prevented authorities from moving quickly was the lack of 'commercial' guidance issued by the DHSS. Although the department published model contracts and offered the services of its professional cleaning, laundry and catering staff to individual authorities, this was insufficient support for the great number of authorities which had little or no experience of this form of competitive tendering.[15] Few authorities wanted to pioneer the process; most waited to see the problems encountered by other authorities. Those that did venture ahead of the pack proceeded extremely cautiously, taking problems and objections raised by participating parties very seriously indeed. One health administrator likened the process to 'reinventing the wheel, 192 times over'.

Another important factor that contributed to the lack of substantial progress was the absence of a viable monitoring mechanism. Although the original circular had requested that comprehensive regional timetables be sent to the DHSS by April of 1984, no formal structure was established to monitor the progress of events promised by these schedules. Responsibility fell primarily in the lap of a shortstaffed unit at DHSS headquarters in London. Its administrators were forced to adopt a 'fire-fighting' approach to the task at hand and were kept busy investigating isolated cases of 'suspicious' authority behaviour brought to their attention directly by contractors or indirectly by ministers. Although additional feedback was received through the Department's Regional Liaison Division, monitoring remained haphazard. Rather late in the day, the Department recognised that the absence of any sort of systematic monitoring was a mistake and asked for progress reports to be supplied by regions on a quarterly basis beginning 1 January, 1985. But DHSS sources reported that throughout 1985 complaints from contractors remained one of the major channels of information about tendering irregularities. As noted by the Tory Reform Group,

> No one at the DHSS seems to have anticipated any problems in the impartiality of the tendering process to judge from the skeleton staff at the DHSS responsible for supervising a switch in management control of almost £1 billion worth of contracts. Contractors are amazed at the low key approach taken by the DHSS in London.[16]

Although numerous authorities had fallen behind on their timetables, tendering activity picked up in the latter part of 1985. Figures produced at the end of the year showed that over 500 separate exercises had been completed since the tendering programme had begun; 60 per cent of these involved domestic service contracts. As shown in Table 6.4 savings totalled £41.8 million per annum, with in-house wins accounting for 57 per cent of the total. The most significant progress was reported in the cleaning and laundry fields, where savings accounted for 7.6 per cent and 7.1 per cent of these services' respective annual budgets. Catering remained a difficult area for contractors. By the end of 1985, they had won only 7 of the 126 contracts awarded in this area. Savings as a result of the tendering process amounted to only 2.3 per cent of the NHS annual catering budget, a reflection of the relative efficiency of pre-existing services. Prospects for future savings are mixed. Although aggregate savings will undoubtedly continue to rise as the remaining NHS services are put out to tender, savings as a percentage of the cost of the previous arrangements are expected to decline in all three service sectors.

TABLE 6.4   NHS competitive tendering results: to December 1985

	In-house		External		Total	
Service	No. of contracts	Savings (£m)	No. of contracts	Savings (£m)	No. of contracts	Savings (£m)
Domestic	221	15.9	97	16.5	318	32.4
Catering	119	4.6	7	0.5	126	5.1
Laundry	56	3.2	19	1.1	75	4.3
Total	**396**	**23.7**	**123**	**18.2**	**519**	**41.8**

Source: DHSS estimates.

Case studies

Having established the trends in tendering activity at national level, it is necessary to examine the impact of the tendering initiative at local level. The three case studies which follow explore in greater depth the dynamics of the NHS tendering process. It should be emphasised that none of the situations described can claim to be representative of events in other areas; indeed no such 'typical' situations exist. The overriding characteristic of the NHS tendering process has been its variability, with personalities, tactics, politics and historical tradition all playing significant roles in determining local outcomes. The case studies provide an insight into the influence that the attitudes and behaviour of key participants have had upon recent tendering exercises. The first study focuses on Hammersmith Hospital, a prestigious London teaching hospital which was among the first to experience prolonged industrial action as a result of the tendering exercise. The second study looks at the experience of North West Hertfordshire Health Authority, one of the first districts to go out to tender for laundry services. The third and final study describes events at the Bethlem Royal and Maudsley Hospitals, which together have amassed over 50 years of experience with private sector contracts.

Hammersmith Hospital

Hammersmith Hospital is part of the Hammersmith and Queen Charlotte's Special Health Authority. Located adjacent to Wormwood Scrubs prison in West London, it is recognised worldwide as a centre of medical excellence because of its postgraduate medical school and its pioneering role in open heart surgery. Like other hospitals, Hammersmith found itself facing a severe shortage of ·cash in 1984 and needed an estimated £665 000 worth of savings to balance its budget for the coming year. The district management team was determined that these savings should not have a direct effect upon the quality of patient care and, as a result, turned its attention to improving the efficiency of ancillary services. Among its other distinctions, Hammersmith had the most expensive hospital cleaning force in the country as measured in costs per square foot. With an annual service cost of close to £1.2 million, both management and staff recognised that savings needed to be made.

Behind the high cost of the service lay severe over-staffing problems, a product of the peculiar industrial relations situation which had existed at Hammersmith for many years. Ever since the 1973 ancillary workers' strike, the unions' voice in hospital affairs had been strong. In the mid-1970s union officials won a number of battles for the ancillary service community and caused constant disruption through frequent calls for day or week-long industrial action. Although the situation at Hammersmith quieted down somewhat between 1978 and 1980, Hammersmith remained, as one union spokesman put it, 'a cesspit of industrial relations'. However, the situation at Hammersmith changed significantly following the arrival of a substantially new administrative team in 1982–3. Younger, more commercially-minded individuals moved into senior management positions and showed an interest in abolishing the restrictive practices which existed throughout the ancillary service network. The combination of a management team determined to deal firmly with the unions and a serious financial shortfall set the stage for Hammersmith's leap into competitive tendering.

The decision to proceed with tendering was actually taken in July 1983, two months before the Government's final tendering circular was published. Local trade unionists knew that competitive tendering was likely to result in dramatic reductions in staffing hours and the number of positions and, in an attempt to delay the tendering process, asked management to prepare a bonus scheme. But the unions overlooked the fact that the specification developed by management in preparing the bonus scheme was precisely the specification which needed to be drawn up prior to going out to tender. Far from delaying the tendering process, preparation of the bonus scheme and its immediate rejection by the unions only accelerated it. It gave hospital management an excuse to push ahead with the tendering process, and invitations to tender on the basis of the bonus scheme specification were issued almost immediately. The unions were angry and, as one senior Hammersmith administrator noted, 'quite rightly, because we had foisted something upon them'.

In line with their previous warnings, both NUPE, with 140 members, and COHSE, with 40, instructed their members not to cooperate with the exercise and sent letters explaining their position to health authority members. While members refused to accede to their demands for a suspension of the tendering process, they were keen that an in-house bid should be considered alongside those from contractors and asked the domestic service manager to prepare an in-house tender on behalf of the employees. This tender was opened in early June alongside those of the contractors. As authority deliberations began, the overwhelming majority of the in-house staff took industrial action. Joined by women from Barking Hospital, where another controversial tendering exercise was underway, the Hammersmith strike organisers succeeded in gathering between 1500 and 2000 people outside the hospital on the first day of action. Within a week of this initial demonstration the strike had spread to other ancillary services. Catering workers refused to serve food on paper plates (one of the labour-saving schemes adopted to lighten housekeeping duties during the strike) on the grounds that they were a health hazard; porters refused to push trolleys loaded with paper plates. A large number of workers in both portering and catering departments joined the domestics on the picket line during the last week of June.

The hospital administrators were determined to maintain services at Hammersmith. They brought in agency cleaners to supplement the small number of domestics who continued working and recruited volunteers from within the hospital itself. Senior catering staff were forced to take over the preparation of meals, while an assortment of volunteers was assigned to serving and delivering them. Some essential supplies could not easily be delivered, but the services themselves continued to operate. By this time the unions had met with health authority members, who they believed were more sympathetic to their cause than the management team. In response to union demands for longer term negotiations on costs and staffing levels, the health authority requested a meeting between staff representatives and management, at which appropriate costing schedules would be agreed. Staff and management representatives met five days later but did not reach any real agreement, and all attention became focused on the next action of health authority members.

The SHA convened in mid-July to consider the adjudication report alongside financial and conditions of service comparisons. The panel's report concentrated on comparing the in-house tender to those from two contractors that had priced below the in-house figure of £663 100. The financial comparison used by the panel, shown in Table 6.5, indicated that the difference between external and internal tenders could be put down to the additional cost of Whitley conditions of service. Many authority members were sceptical of rushing out to contract and felt that the additional cost of Whitley conditions, estimated at £66 000, was worth spending. As a result, they recommended that the in-house tender should be accepted on the condition that the existing staff offer a firm commitment to work it. The management team was given instructions to negotiate freely with the workforce so long as the cost of the final package remained within the in-house tender cost of £663 100.

Although these negotiations were expected to be completed by the next SHA meeting in August, in the event they dragged on into September. Both sides made concessions during this period. The district management team revealed 'Option 3', a revised in-house tender which increased the ratio of full-time to part-time workers

TABLE 6.5 **Hammersmith Hospital: financial comparison statement**

	In-House (£000)	Firm C (£000)	Firm F (£000)
Tender base price	562	464	430
Tender base price for period of contract	1 688	1 393	1 289
Additional monitoring costs	61	61	61
Notional cost of equipment not required	—	30	30
VAT adjustment—1% EEC levy	—	14	13
Adjusted tender price	1 749	1 498	1 393
Add			
Redundancy costs	80	103	103
Early retirement costs	160	206	206
Tender comparison price	1 989	1 807	1 702
Tender comparison price averaged over 3 years	663	602	567

Notes:
1. The In-House tender does not include provision for the 1984 wage award.
2. Provision for inflation over the contract period has not been made.
3. Overhead costs are assumed to be the same given either outcome.
4. It has been assumed that early retirement costs will be in the same ratio as redundancy costs between the in-house and external tenders.
5. On advice from the DHSS, early retirement costs are assumed to be £2100 per employee in the first year and £1100 in subsequent years.
Source: Hammersmith and Queen Charlotte's Special Health Authority, *Domestic Services—Hammersmith Hospital*, Report to the Special Health Authority, 18 July 1984.

dramatically and added another £10 000 to the adjusted per annum cost of the in-house tender. The unions agreed to work a scaled-down version of the first in-house tender for a trial period of three months, but only on the condition that the appropriate level of bonus payment would be made. Later, when it became clear to the unions that there was not much hope of further concessions from the management team, they offered to accept 'Option 3' if it was brought into effect in two years' time. However neither of the union proposals particularly appealed to the district management team who, after 3 months of protracted negotiations, placed little faith in the will or ability of the unions to deliver on their promises. At a special meeting called early on the day the authority was to meet, the adjudication panel recommended that Mediclean be given the contract. The SHA members endorsed the recommendation and awarded Mediclean the contract at a price of £464 200 per annum over a three-year period. The cost to the authority, including redundancy and monitoring costs, was estimated at £602 400 per annum. This represented an annual saving of £571 000 or 49 per cent of the original in-house service's cost.

As shown in Table 6.6, the changes in manpower scheduling which resulted from the switch to Mediclean were dramatic. Mediclean domestics were to be on duty less than half the time that the in-house staff had been, which meant that medical and nursing staff no longer received any 'extras' and that 24-hour cover was virtually abandoned. Some Hammersmith administrators claim that this has led to a 'patchy' standard of cleaning, in that public areas are kept spotless while less visible areas are filthy, but others have stated that the previous in-house team provided an even poorer service. Reconciling these views is not easy, as biases both in favour of and against contractors remain strong. The competitive tendering exercise only widened the rift that already existed within the hospital's administrative ranks between members of the 'paternalistic' school and their more commercially-minded counterparts. Little consensus was achieved in the months following the completion of the exercise.

The unions claim to have learned lessons from the Hammersmith fiasco. With the benefit of hindsight, union organisers agree that their techniques and strategy were somewhat misdirected and that turning Hammersmith into a national *cause célèbre* and refusing to cooperate with the in-house tender worked to their members' disadvantage. However, none is convinced that a different set of tactics would necessarily have saved the jobs of their members. One union organiser noted recently: 'It wasn't the kind of strike that you form a Strike Committee and expect to win. They knew they were going to lose . . . the kamikaze attitude was heartening.' At the moment, the unions' main concern is rebuilding their organisation at Hammersmith. Their penetration of Mediclean to date has been low and, in the absence of organisers within the Mediclean workforce, will probably remain so in the short-term future. Not

TABLE 6.6   Hammersmith Hospital: comparison of domestic service contracts

	Previous in-house service	Mediclean contract
Annual cost	£1 174 000	£603 000
Employees: full-time	122	28
part-time	78	130
supervisors	7	–
Total	207	158
Total hours	6 170	2 802

Source: Various SHA documents.

easily discouraged, however, NUPE representatives have made regular Thursday appearances outside the gates of the hospital in an effort to stir domestic workers' interest. How long it will be before their efforts begin to pay off, if indeed they ever do, remains to be seen.

North West Hertfordshire Health Authority

North West Hertfordshire Health Authority earned notoriety as the first health authority to go out to tender for laundry services after publication of the government's tendering circular. Unlike their Hammersmith counterparts, North West Hertfordshire administrators did not want to go out to competitive tender for their laundry services; they were forced to as a result of the DHSS requirement that authorities undertake tendering exercises before spending £0.5 million or more on capital improvements. The district had agreed upon a rationalisation scheme for its laundry services in June 1983, three months before the final circular was published. The rationalisation programme involved expenditure in the region of £500 000, but it was expected that the plan would save £100 000 per year once it was fully implemented. Electricity costs would be reduced by 20 per cent, and the elimination of 17 jobs would save an additional £85 000 per annum.

Two significant elements of capital investment – a new distribution point (linen room) and a new tunnel washer – were required. The planned purchase of the tunnel washer, at a cost of £250 000, created problems for the authority. Because such washers are made to measure, a decision to purchase one is irrevocable. Hospital administrators feared that regional or departmental intervention during the nine-month period between commission and installation of the unit could force them to go out to tender and possibly leave them with no in-house workforce to use this expensive piece of machinery. As a result, the authority decided to complete the tendering exercise in advance of making a final purchase commitment. It took advantage of a three-month cancellation period offered by the washer's manufacturer and proceeded to order the new equipment with the intention of completing the tendering process within the three-month deadline.

About a month after the DHSS had issued its final tendering circular, the health authority issued invitations to tender to eight private contractors whose names were supplied by regional administrators. Although the authority itself had sizeable in-house laundries, hospital management specifically asked contractors to quote for laundry work done on their own external premises. The legal and technical work involved in drawing up a specification to allow contractors to use the authority's existing equipment and premises would have been substantial and would have prevented the authority from meeting the deadline imposed by the tunnel washer's manufacturer.

Following issuance of the invitation to tender, an in-house tender was drawn up by authority administrators. Trade unions flatly turned down an invitation to participate in the tendering process, claiming that they were not in the business of negotiating themselves out of jobs. But it was more by default than by conscious decision that the local members found themselves excluded from the in-house tendering process. Union activity had never been particularly strong in the laundry service, and the predominantly female workforce had traditionally abdicated responsibility for welfare issues to full-time trade union officers. In this case, few workers showed any real interest in competitive tendering and union officers stepped in on behalf of the in-house employees and took the decision not to participate in an in-house tender. The in-house tender was eventually put together by the domestic service manager and the deputy treasurer and consisted of a shortened version of the rationalisation programme. All changes, including the installation of the tunnel washer and the resulting redundancies, were to be made within a three-year period. Eight tenders were received by the authority in mid-December 1983. Quoted prices varied dramatically from £8.60 to £15 per 100 articles processed, with the in-house tender clearly the lowest. However, in contrast to events at Hammersmith, the adjudication panel decided that agreement by staff to work the rationalisation plan was necessary *before* the in-house tender could be endorsed. The panel asked that negotiations with union officials take place in the run-up to the Christmas period in an attempt to reach agreement before the DHA meeting scheduled for early in January. As these negotiations began, it was clear that neither the union officials nor their members were in a particularly strong position to fight the in-house tender: their choice was between losing 17 jobs or losing 30. As one administrator noted: 'They were negotiating with their arms behind their backs.' Union officials were forced to back down from the policy of non-cooperation with an in-house tender and by the New Year an agreement to accept the tender on certain conditions, shown in Table 6.7, had been reached. This agreement allowed the authority's adjudication panel, meeting later that week, to recommend that the health authority award the contract to the in-house team.

The authority took a number of steps to insure that its decision would not be challenged. In advance of the contract award, the deputy treasurer of the health authority discussed the in-house tender with the DHSS laundry advisers in the hope that this consultation would protect the authority from departmental and ministerial queries at a later date. In addition, the authority sent a letter to contractors explaining the outcome and held a 'debriefing meeting' with them about a month after the contract had been awarded. But these precautions were insufficient to protect the authority totally. One contractor voiced suspicions about the validity of the financial calculations to John Patten at the DHSS. The Department asked for all documentation, but found everything in order and gave the authority the 'all-clear'.

However the debate about the validity of the in-house tender continued. Soon after the in-house 'contract' started, the authority was forced to send a small batch of laundry out to private contractors due to delays in installing the tunnel washer.[17] Infor-

TABLE 6.7   North West Hertfordshire DHA: agreements made with trade unions

1   Health Authority will seek to maintain policy of no redundancies.

2   Staff reductions will be the laundry services' maximum contribution to future manpower targets.

3   Staff will be considered for early retirement.

4   Staff will be offered suitable comparable positions in other departments.

5   The bonus scheme at Hill End Hospital laundry will be unaffected.

6   Certain regular overtime will be protected for a limited period.

7   Excess travelling time and costs will be considered for staff redeployed.

8   Health Authority will seek to maintain the agreed staffing levels for the duration of the laundry contract.

Source: North West Hertfordshire DHA, *Letter from Deputy District Administrator to Laundry Staff*, 28 December 1983.

mation about this incident reached contractors and they were quick to capitalise on it in the media. Simon Rawlins, director of the leading laundry trade association, suggested in *The Sunday Times* in late July 1984 that North West Hertfordshire's in-house laundry 'couldn't cope'. A week later the newspaper published a reply by the district administrator, which contained an explanation of the exact circumstances of the disruption. A copy of this letter was sent by the Chairman of North West Hertfordshire Health Authority to Kenneth Clarke, in what appears to have been an attempt to stave off further ministerial enquiries. Clarke reported his satisfaction with the contract, and the matter was finally laid to rest.

The aftermath to the North West Hertfordshire laundry tendering exercise is interesting and shows the difficulties which many managers of in-house 'contracts' face. Although preliminary figures produced at the end of the first year showed that the service had kept well within its annual budget, the linen services manager reported severe constraints arising from his position within a public sector organisation. 'They want me to be a commercial contractor, but they won't let me do anything outside of the norm,' he noted recently. The first problem appeared when several hospitals served by the laundry made claims for lost articles, an item not covered by the in-house budget. Although private sector firms can take out insurance against such claims, regulations forbid NHS laundries from doing so. A second issue arose when laundry machinery experienced a breakdown. Although the laundry budget must include payments for energy (£114 000) and maintenance (£75 000), the service's manager has no control over the speed with which the hospital's works department responds to mechanical problems. This inability to control machinery down-time has reportedly had a serious effect upon the laundry service budget. A third constraint reported by the current service manager concerns a similar lack of control over the accounting function. As of mid-1985, he had not been given financial data on his performance for the first quarter of 1985, nor had the final figures for the first year of the contract's operation been received. 'If I can be privatised,' he noted in mid-1985, 'so can the finance department and so can the works department.'

Bethlem Royal and Maudsley Hospitals

The Bethlem Royal and Maudsley Special Health Authority boasts the only specialist postgraduate teaching hospital for psychiatry in the country. Made up of two hospitals – the Maudsley, in Denmark Hill, London and the Bethlem Royal, nine miles away in Beckenham, Kent – it is also the only health authority to have experience in contracting out more than one major ancillary service over an extended period of time. For over twenty-five years, the authority has contracted out all or part of five services – catering, cleaning, laundry, gardening and transport. Until recently, it experienced little change in terms of the operating environment in any of these areas. But the growth of the contract industries and the introduction of competitive tendering have fostered significant changes in the way that the services are performed at the hospitals. These changes have been most notable in the fields of catering and cleaning.

Catering   The Bethlem Royal and Maudsley Hospitals' experience of contract catering dates back to the late 1950s. Like other small hospitals, they found recruitment and retention of qualified supervisory staff particularly difficult during a period of full employment due to NHS catering salary scales, which were based on the number of beds within a unit. These personnel problems, and the close ties which had always existed between the hospitals' Board of Governors and the City of London, led to a decision to approach John Gardner, a private contractor which provided catering services through a number of restaurants in the City. The original arrangement with John Gardner began at the Bethlem Royal in 1957 and was extended to the Maudsley one year later. As a management fee contract, all operating costs plus a management fee were paid to the contractor at the end of each month and catering workers were given a choice of remaining on the hospital payroll or taking up employment with the contractor. Conditions varied little between the two; Gardner observed NHS pay scales and hours, and all changes in rates of pay were agreed upon by hospital management. The change from in-house to external provision thus aroused little opposition from the unions or indeed from the workers.

Gardner held on to this contract for the next twenty-five years, during which time its business in institutional catering expanded rapidly and it became part of the Trusthouse Forte Group. Much of its success in holding on to the contract for such a long period of time can be attributed to the absence of any real competition. Although the contract was occasionally redefined, Bethlem and Maudsley did not once go out to 're-tender' during this period. The contractor had little incentive for efficiency; one administrator noted, 'we simply paid the management fee and picked up the bill year after year'. This relaxed attitude changed somewhat in the early 1980s as a result of the appearance of new and viable competitors in the contract catering field. In the summer of 1984, despite Gardner Merchant's arguments that it could not afford to invest in the contract with no guarantee of future work, the authority went ahead with a competitive tendering exercise for its catering services.

By this time the Government's mandatory tendering directive had come into force and the authority was forced to adopt a fixed price approach to the contract. Although this placed a new burden of estimating the appropriate amounts of food required upon contractors, the absence of an in-house competitor ensured that there was considerable interest from the private sector. After narrowing the field down to five firms, the authority shortlisted Gardner Merchant and Spinneys, a new arrival on the UK contract catering scene. But Gardner Merchant was unhappy about undertaking the contract on a fixed price basis and, one hour before the award decision was to be announced by the SHA chairman, the main Trusthouse Forte Board decided to withdraw from the procedure entirely. The contract fell by default to Spinneys.

The departure of Gardner Merchant and the arrival of Spinneys saw the first real changes in catering services at the Bethlem Royal and Maudsley in 25 years. A cook-chill system was introduced which allowed much of the food to be prepared ahead of time and enabled the firm to operate with three fewer cooks than had previously been the case. A system of individual choice was introduced for patients, but it placed too great a burden upon nurses and gave way to a system of more limited choice based upon a menu. Rates of pay for existing staff were increased, although a shorter workweek (37¼ hours) was introduced. Conditions of service, previously in line with Whitley Council provisions, changed significantly: sick pay was reduced to between one and two weeks after six months of work, holiday entitlement fell to two weeks plus ten public holidays, and shift allowances were abolished. Trade union membership was encouraged and the contractor set up appropriate consultative machinery enabling it to communicate effectively and directly with staff interests.

Early reports by hospital administrators indicated that the change to a new contractor was a positive one. The quality of the service to patients improved; staff meals became cheaper and involved larger portions. Spinneys reportedly instituted effective site management and displayed an unusual willingness to satisfy staff interests. Despite the fact that in some cases take-home pay fell as a result of new manpower schedules, there was little resistance from staff to the changes. Even union officials admitted that the catering service had improved considerably as a result of the switch in contractors, though they continued to voice suspicions that the new contractor may have been 'front-loading' the contract to gain positive publicity.

Cleaning Cleaning services at the Bethlem Royal and Maudsley exhibited many of the same problems which plagued catering supervision during the 1950s: recruitment of competent managerial staff was time-consuming and difficult due to the rigidity imposed by Whitley salaries and conditions of service. In an attempt to increase the authority's 'freedom of manoeuvre', a fairly informal contractual arrangement was made with Crothall in 1962 to clean the Maudsley Hospital. (Bethlem Royal continued to be cleaned by a direct labour force until the mid-1960s, at which time it too became the subject of a contract awarded to Crothall.) The arrangements with Crothall changed little throughout the late 1960s and early 1970s. By the mid-1970s, however, there was a general feeling that the specification needed to be tightened and that more competitive prices might be put forward by Crothall's competitors. The contract was put out to tender for the first time, and since then has been put out to tender every three years. Three firms – Crothall, Strand and Initial – have held the contract, although the workforce itself has not undergone dramatic change. As one administrator noted recently: 'Domestic contracts have changed without ruffling a feather.'

While each tendering exercise has witnessed an improved specification and additional cost-savings, the hospitals' domestic contract specifications remain fairly general documents in comparison to those being developed by other authorities. One administrator noted: 'When we did our domestic contract, we had no guidelines. Since then, many people have looked at ours. Now we're in a position to look at their contracts.' This loose specification document is responsible for an unusually casual approach towards monitoring the domestic contract. The onus to report unsatisfactory performance is on ward staff, all of whom were given a copy of the specification at the start of the current contract. Penalty clauses are virtually non-existent, and variations clauses are not invoked unless absolutely necessary. As one administrator commented: 'If we can't cost it, we can't penalise them.'

Other areas   Cleaning and catering are not the only services performed by contract at the Bethlem Royal and Maudsley Hospitals. Neither hospital has its own laundry facilities and both have been forced to rely on external laundries. As psychiatric hospitals, however, they produce a limited amount of laundry and the total cost of the laundry contract is not more than £50 000 annually. Transport between the two hospitals and gardening at the Maudsley also remain in private hands; these contracts are valued at between £15 000 and £20 000 each. Recently, the authority went out to tender for internal auditing services and awarded the contract to one of the largest UK-based accountancy firms.

In general, the health authority's administrators are happy with the level of service they have received from contractors. They report that the primary benefit is the flexibility to deal with new circumstances and suggest that staff now have training opportunities they would not otherwise have. But they also acknowledge that there have been problems with these services over the years, foremost of which has been the lack of competition from contract service firms and the informal nature of contract specifications.[18] The consequent poor levels of efficiency have only now come to the forefront of authority debate.

The Government's competitive tendering initiative has had a significant impact upon the nature of contractual arrangements at Bethlem and Maudsley. For the first time the authority has been required to produce a more detailed specification and to test the market at regular intervals. These changes have clearly affected the relationship which formerly existed between contractor and authority. 'Now,' said one administrator, 'if they do additional work in one area, we expect they'll skimp in another.' But despite the 'commercialisation' of the relationship between the authority and the contractor, Bethlem Royal and Maudsley administrators continue to exhibit a low key approach to contract monitoring. 'Profit anyway is a great self-monitor for contractors,' one noted in mid-1985. It will be interesting to see whether this hands-off attitude to contractors will remain throughout future retendering exercises.

An assessment

Current NHS tendering exercises mark a significant departure from the sort of exercises undertaken five, ten or even twenty years ago. The scope of the national initiative and the political will that lies behind it have made the environment in which tendering takes place more volatile than ever before. Whereas in previous years there existed very solid rationales for switching to private contractors (usually a scarcity of labour, problem with the existing service, or absence of supervisory talent), today's service provision decisions are based on much more fragile and delicate foundations. Very often a decision to award a contract either in-house or externally can be traced to the attitudes of one or two individuals or to the strategic decisions of one particular interest group. The preceding case studies illustrate clearly the tremendous impact which the attitudes and indeed the personalities of individual participants have had upon the tendering process. As might be expected given the nature of decision-making in the health service, the strongest influence has often been exercised by senior hospital managers. This was certainly the case at Hammersmith Hospital, where the domestic service tendering exercise was 'driven' by a commercially-minded management team determined to make long overdue economies in the ancillary service sector. Senior administrators set the tone of the exercise and, despite reluctance from some administrative quarters, succeeded in convincing the unions that they meant business. Even now, there is some feeling at Hammersmith that key hospital managers wanted their unit to be among the first to go out to tender under the Government's new regulations. One administrator commented that the management team may have been 'trying to score brownie points' by endorsing government policy so enthusiastically. Another suspected that the DHSS may have encouraged or 'sponsored' this early tendering exercise as an example to other authorities.

Administrators also played a central role in the tendering exercise carried out at North West Hertfordshire, though their attitudes were somewhat different from those displayed at Hammersmith. The district management team exhibited a paternalistic and almost protective attitude toward the existing staff and service, and showed a subtle desire to keep the service in-house. This desire was evident in the decision to ask contractors to bid for laundry services conducted exclusively on their own premises, a move which imposed additional transport costs on contractors and seemed to be built on the assumption (or perhaps the hope) that the in-house team would be awarded the contract. Had a private contractor been able to undercut the in-house tender, the authority would have been left with three laundries and millions of pounds worth of highly specialised equipment. In the event, this dangerous but clearly legitimate gamble paid off. One administrator noted: 'We took the view that if we had tried to be Machiavellian in any way, we'd be found out. We decided that we had to beat the contractors at their own game.'

The attitudes of health authority members have frequently been as important in determining the outcome of service awards as those of district administrators. In both Hammersmith and North West Hertfordshire, authority members voted to award the contract to the in-house team despite the unions' adamant refusal to cooperate with the tender preparation exercise; this move was particularly notable at Hammersmith, where the in-house bid was significantly higher than those proposed by several of the private contractors. These events highlight the fact that the sympathies of health authority members have frequently lain with the existing workforce, often to such an extent that the authority has agreed to pay a premium to retain the direct labour organisation. Although the Government has continually put pressure on regional and district authorities to prevent such behaviour at local level, ministerial attention is selective and the practice continues to be widespread.

Union attitudes and behaviour are a third factor which has had a dramatic impact upon tendering outcomes. At Hammersmith Hospital, a highly unionised workforce – used to getting its way with administrators – reacted violently to the straightjacket imposed by the competitive tendering exercise. Failure to cooperate with the tendering process led to the preparation of a radical, and in union eyes unsatisfactory, in-house tender by management. The refusal to accept a more generous version of this tender during the negotiations following the first and second SHA meetings frustrated the attempts of health authority members to keep the contract in-house and alienated some of the more sympathetic administrators. One senior administrator at Hammersmith noted: 'At an early stage, we were prepared to make the in-house tender work. As time wore on, many people got less comfortable with the in-house tender. I could see that there were big forces at work against us.' Rather different tactics were adopted by the unions in North West Hertfordshire. Union officials felt they had to accept the substance of the changes arising from the in-house tender and focused instead upon securing the best possible arrangements for members given this situation. Compromises were made on both sides during an intense ten days of negotiations and agreement was reached in time for the district members to act positively on the adjudication panel's recommendation of an in-house award.

Both these experiences are a far cry from that of the Bethlem Royal and Maudsley SHA. For twenty-five years, the health authority has dealt with cleaning, laundry and catering contractors in a straightforward and uncontroversial manner. Throughout this entire period, the personal attitudes of hospital managers, trade unionists and health authority members have had very little impact upon the outcome of tendering decisions. However, the Government's tendering exercise has clearly had an effect upon the authority's approach to service provision. Tender specifications are tighter, trade unions are more active, prices are clearly more competitive and the relationship with contractors has become more commercial and less easy-going. But despite these changes, the apolitical and seemingly detached approach to service provision has remained. Senior administrators exhibit no preference for one method of delivery or another, in striking contrast to the clear-cut opinions exhibited by their counterparts in many other authorities. The hospitals' House Governor noted recently: 'We should have the variety which suits our patients best as long as there is fair comparison and as long as the pressing need for financial economy is not overlooked.'[19]

This brings us to one of the central ironies of the present NHS tendering initiative. Although the Government has based the entire exercise upon its ability to produce savings and has emphasised repeatedly the need to award contracts to the lowest tenderer, the economics of contracting out have actually played a limited part in contract award decisions. In Hammersmith, the authority repeatedly tried to award the contract to the in-house team at a price well above those offered by the private sector. In North West Hertfordshire, the in-house bid was marginally cheaper than the lowest private bid but it is likely that contractors would have come up with even cheaper bids had they been offered the use of existing laundry facilities. At Bethlem Royal and Maudsley, the original motivation for using private contractors was not to achieve savings but to break free of the constraints imposed by the Whitley Council system of salaries which had consistently failed to attract competent managers. In these and many other areas, a desire to achieve maximum economies has *not* been the driving force behind either the tendering process or the switch to private service provision.

7 Contracting Out in Local Authorities

The local government context

The primary task of local authorities throughout the Western world is the provision of services to the local community. The number and range of services provided at this level vary across countries and generally reflect both the welfare objectives of the state and the division of responsibilities between central and local political units. However, certain services are almost universally provided at local level: education, housing, police protection, fire-fighting and refuse collection among others. Revenue to fund these services comes primarily from a combination of local taxes (usually property or sales tax) and central government grants. Although the vast majority of these services are offered on a free or subsidised basis to local citizens and are carried out by in-house labour, a small number of services are often provided by voluntary or private means. Under private arrangements, companies either sell their services directly to the public under contract to a local authority (for example, franchised refuse collection in part of the US) or sell the service to the local authority and then provide it directly to consumers (for example, contract refuse collection in the UK). Until recently both the number of municipalities committed to private arrangements and the volumes of work they represent have remained static.

However, in both North America and Western Europe increasingly stringent financial constraints upon local authorities have focused attention upon the protected position of local authority workers and have stimulated interest in alternative methods of service provision. The most significant moves toward 'contracting out' have occurred in the US, where a number of Democratic and Republican-controlled municipalities have switched to private

209

modes of provision for certain public services.[1] In nearly all cases, the decision to use private contractors has been an economic rather than a political one. Despite the low political salience of the issue, the American municipal unions have argued strongly against privatising local services.[2] Unlike the trade unions in Britain, however, they have rarely attempted to use tendering exercises as a forum in which to fight their case. This is primarily because most tendering activity in American municipalities has not involved union members. The overwhelming majority of tendering authorities have taken a unilateral decision to 'privatise' a service and have solicited quotations solely from the private sector. Until recently, American-style tendering has been virtually synonymous with contracting out.

Although the term 'competitive tendering' has taken on a different meaning in British local government (commonly referring to competition between in-house and external labour), American municipal experience became particularly relevant in the late 1970s and early 1980s. British local authorities began to experience many of the same problems which had plagued their American counterparts in the early 1970s. Dramatic increases in public sector expenditure prompted increasingly stringent financial constraints and caused both white-collar and manual worker trade unions to become stronger and more militant. The impact of these trends in Britain was both severe and widespread, hence any evaluation of the growth of municipal tendering and contracting out must begin by reviewing their development.

The historical setting

The period since World War II has seen tremendous growth in the role of the state in capitalist democracies. Although this growth is partially a result of demographic factors, such as increases in population and the extension of the average life span, much of it can be explained by changes in the economic and social environment. Post-industrial life has been characterised by an increase in leisure time and greater emphasis on education and health. This has led to rising expectations among citizens and to demands for more cultural and sporting facilities, better schools and transport systems, and more rigorous government control over health, safety and environmental hazards. Meeting these demands has required a bigger, and therefore more expensive, state apparatus.

As the role of the state has increased, many of these obligations – particularly those which cannot be effectively carried out on a national basis – have been taken on by local authorities. The growth of local expenditure has been particularly pronounced in Britain, as a result of the country's unitary constitutional structure. No intermediary tiers separate local from national government, thus there is no clear differentiation of responsibilities (as there is under a federalist system) nor is there any significant 'sharing' of responsibilities (as exists in many unitary states which exhibit regional tiers). The net effect of this arrangement is that local authorities in Britain have assumed a wider range of responsibilities than they have in most other industrialised nations.

A variety of statistics clearly illustrate recent changes. Local service provision in Britain has expanded rapidly in the past forty years, with the most dramatic growth occuring in the period between 1950 and 1970. While all public expenditure as a percentage of GDP rose 23 per cent (from 35 per cent to 43 per cent), local expenditure increased by 67 per cent (from 9 per cent to 15 per cent of GDP). Whereas in 1950 approximately one-fourth of all public expenditure was 'local' in nature, by 1970 local expenditure accounted for well over one-third of all public spending. Much of the expansion of local authority services has been financed by grants from central government. Between 1955 and 1975, the percentage of local authority current income for non-trading services arising from central government grants rose from 50 per cent to 57 per cent; contributions from non-domestic rates fell slightly from 25 to 24 per cent, while those from domestic rates dropped from 25 per cent to 18 per cent.[3]

The expansion of local government activities in Britain .has demanded significant growth in the local authority workforce. Between 1960 and 1975, the number of workers employed in local authorities grew from 1.8 million to 3 million, from 8 per cent to 13 per cent of the working population. This sharp increase contrasts with the relatively static level of central government employment during this period; the size of the local workforce as a percentage of all government workers, excluding those in public corporations, grew from 53 per cent to 61 per cent.[4] However, much of the growth at local level was due to a significant increase in the number of part-time workers in local government. Between 1962 and 1972, for example, the number of part-time workers increased 92 per cent while the number of full-time workers in local government increased only 26 per cent. In 1952, part-time workers accounted for only 18 per cent of all local authority staff; by 1982, they accounted for 34 per cent.[5]

The increasing size of the British local government workforce has proved fertile ground for trade union recruitment. As noted in Chapter 4, public sector trade unions grew dramatically between 1965 and 1980: NUPE membership increased 288 per cent and NALGO membership jumped 228 per cent.[6] The percentage of unionised employees in local government grew from 62 per cent in 1948 to 86 per cent in 1974, making it one of the most unionised workforces in the country.[7] Local government workers became increasingly militant during the late 1960s and early 1970s. Along with employees of public sector corporations, they were among the earliest public sector activists and by the mid-1970s their willingness to take strike action had spread to health service workers and the civil service.

The growth of local service provision and the increase in public sector union militancy have had significant direct and indirect effects upon the financial situation of local government. The direct effect has been a dramatic escalation in the costs of running local government over the past ten years. Simultaneously, central government has moved to exert more rigorous control over grants to local authorities, reducing the proportion of local expenditure funded by central sources and forcing politically sensitive local tax increases. Local authorities have responded by trying to reduce their costs. However staff costs, the most obvious area for savings in a labour-intensive 'business' like local government, have been a 'no-go' area due to powerful municipal unions and nationally negotiated wage settlements.[8] As a result, authorities have been forced to rely on cuts in capital expenditure and increases in fees and charges. In addition, much of the burden of increased local property taxes has fallen upon the commercial and industrial sectors, especially in central urban authorities.

The indirect effect of increases in service provision and union militancy has been changes in central government behaviour in response to these trends. What began as a general reduction in public spending with the imposition of cash limits on central departments in 1976 has escalated to become a carefully targeted attack upon the financial freedom of local authorities. The Local Government Planning and Land Act (1980) instituted a new Block Grant formula, which tied the level of central grants to assessments of local expenditure made by central government. The Government also created a system whereby 'overspending' authorities would have their grant withheld at a penal rate and removed an authority's right to impose additional taxes during the financial year. Neither set of measures proved adequate for the Government's purposes, however, and in 1984 it introduced controversial 'rate-capping' legislation, which allowed it to set a maximum figure for annual property tax increases in selected localities.

Increasing central control over local government affairs has not been limited to the financial sphere. The past few years have also seen the Government interfering in the operation of local services, first by making competitive tendering mandatory for building services and then by forcing local authorities to sell existing public housing stock to sitting tenants. More recently, it has taken the dramatic step of abolishing the metropolitan counties, thus forcing a reorganisation of the structure of service provision in urban areas. Proposals for mandatory competitive tendering for a wide range of local services have also been announced, a move viewed by many local administrators as a logical extension of the government's programme to limit the size and expenditure of local government.

Local government services

The network of local authority services in Britain is well-developed and extensive. About half of local authority service expenditure, or some £10 billion annually, goes to education. Social and emergency services are also major cost centres, accounting for 11 per cent and 15 per cent of annual service expenditure respectively.[9] Other major services include local transport, refuse collection and disposal, school meals, cultural facilities, recreation and planning. Estimated net expenditure for major local authority services in 1985–6 is shown in Table 7.1.

Neither contracting out nor competitive tendering is new to local authority service provision. Local councils have always gone out to

TABLE 7.1 Local authority service expenditure: England and Wales*
(estimated 1985–6 at November 1984 prices)

Service	Cost (£m)	%
Education	10 595	49.0
Police	2 672	12.4
Personal social services	2 386	11.0
Highways, local transport	1 207	5.6
Refuse collection, disposal	587	2.7
Fire	587	2.7
School meals	427	2.0
Galleries, libraries, museums	403	1.9
Parks and open spaces	373	1.7
Environmental health	351	1.6
Town and country planning	330	1.5
Administration of justice	309	1.4
Recreation facilities	268	1.2
Cost of rate collection	155	0.7
Housing **	121	0.6
Cemeteries and crematoria	39	0.2
Unallocated general administration	53	0.2
Other services	780	3.6
Total	**21 643**	**100.0**

* Net expenditure including trading services.
** Other than Housing Revenue Account.

Source: *Finance and General Statistics 1985–1986*, CIPFA Statistical Information Service.

contract for services not available in-house; laundry, pest control, management consultancy and computer support services are a few examples. Private firms have also been brought in to supplement existing in-house staff at peak periods, during strike action or in other 'crisis' situations. Both forms of contracting out have usually involved some form of competitive tendering between potential suppliers. Some indication of the scope and frequency of tendering activity in this sector is given by the fact that an estimated £3 billion of local authority expenditure will be awarded via some form of competitive tendering in 1985–6. Most of these tendering exercises will not involve in-house workforces and most will be completed quietly, at a safe distance from the furore over contracting out.

The recent debate over contracting out has focused exclusively on services which have little or no tradition of external provision. Foremost among these have been a variety of cleaning, catering and maintenance activities. School meal and school cleaning services, the responsibility of county councils and metropolitan boroughs, have been one area of media and trade union attention. Although these areas are particularly controversial due to the involvement of a large number of women working on a part-time basis for very low wages, only a small number of contracts have been awarded in this field and profit margins for contractors are reported to be slim. Nevertheless commercial interest in both services is likely to remain, primarily because these contracts tend to be awarded on a piecemeal basis (five or six contractors may be asked to split up one county catchment area) and thus provide a good opportunity for new firms to establish a track record in the public sector.

But by far the greatest inroads for private contractors have occurred in refuse collection and street cleaning, sometimes referred to as 'public cleansing services'. Each of these services has a history of poor supervision, glaring inefficiencies and high levels of trade union activity. Both refuse and street cleaning services are highly labour-intensive, which means that wage and productivity agreements can have a dramatic effect on total service cost. It is also comparatively easy to monitor service outputs in these areas, particularly in the field of refuse collection. These characteristics, crucial to understanding the private sector's relative success in these sectors, are examined more closely on the following pages. Although particular attention has been devoted to refuse collection (the better documented of the two services), most authorities link all cleansing services functionally and the comments made below apply equally to street cleaning activities.

Refuse collection services: a profile

In 1986, local authorities in England and Wales will have employed more than 40 000 individuals and spent close to £600 million to carry out refuse collection and disposal tasks. Although this represents only about 3 per cent of all local spending, to many citizens it is the most visible and one of the most important services provided by local authorities. Councils have a statutory duty to collect both domestic and trade refuse under the Public Health Act 1936 (they are allowed to make a 'reasonable charge' for removing the latter). Since 1974, refuse duties have been split between local government tiers with the district councils responsible for waste collection and the county councils responsible for its disposal. For the past fifty years, most of the work on the collection side has been carried out by a directly employed labour force. From time to time, however, a number of councils have found that shortages of labour made it necessary to hire private contractors. Most of the contractors they hired, particularly those operating in rural areas, bore little resemblance to the refuse contractors currently competing for work in the major metropolitan areas. The overwhelming majority were small local operators, many of whom relied on unsophisticated collection vehicles.

A good picture of refuse collection in the 1950s and 1960s can be drawn from the report of a Committee of Enquiry set up by Sir Alec Douglas Home in 1963. Its brief was to examine collection practices across the country and its findings were published in 1967 in a document entitled *Refuse Storage and Collection*. The committee sent questionnaires to 1364 local authorities, 64 of whom had some form of arrangement with private refuse contractors. As shown in Table 7.2, 35 of these councils (primarily those in rural areas) relied exclusively on private firms for provision of a comprehensive refuse collection service.

The study found that while some arrangements with contractors were of long standing, others were caused by short-term 'labour difficulties' resulting from a high level of employment and keen competition for labour. A supplementary questionnaire sent to 289 of the 1364 councils indicated that seven councils had switched from contract back to direct labour, four of them as a result of dissatisfaction with contract collection. The Committee report came out clearly against the contracting out of refuse collection to the private sector, and suggested that very small authorities should consider setting up a joint collection service with a neighbouring area or contracting it out to another authority. Among their many conclusions, the committee members noted,

In our opinion local authorities should not leave the collection of house refuse, and any incidental collection of trade refuse, to

TABLE 7.2 Refuse collection arrangements: 1964–7

Type of authority	Direct labour only	Contract only	Both	Total
Urban districts	503	8	4	**515**
Rural districts	399	24	20	**443**
Non-county boroughs	290	2	3	**295**
County boroughs	83	—	—	**83**
Metropolitan boroughs	25	1	2	**28**
Total	**1 300**	**35**	**29**	**1 364**

Source: *Refuse Storage and Collection* (London: HMSO, 1967).

contractors. Collection by contract may relieve a local authority of what is often a worrying responsibility, but it makes it harder for them to ensure a good service. It prevents them from taking direct action on complaints. With control in their own hands they can much more readily see to it that the right kind of vehicles are used and properly maintained, that tidiness is not sacrificed for speed, that there is no totting, and that the men have good working conditions.[10]

Problems with contractors and a more fluid labour market led to a decline in the use of contractors throughout the late 1960s and 1970s and, by the time the Conservatives arrived in power in 1979, only two councils – Maldon and Mid-Bedfordshire – were using private contractors for a significant volume of refuse collection. But while direct labour became more and more the norm in local authorities, refuse collection departments were becoming one of the main targets of accusations of inefficiency in local service provision. Both the tremendous variation in service costs from one local authority to another and the impact which restrictive work practices were having upon attempts to reduce costs and improve productivity came under criticism. Two particular aspects of refuse work were at the centre of this attention. The first was the 'task and finish' system, which allows refuse workers to finish their workday when collection tasks have been completed. The second was the bonus system, under which loaders and drivers qualify for bonuses in return for achieving an agreed-upon performance level based on the number of bins or premises, the volume of refuse, or the amount of time involved in collection.

Both task and finish and bonus sytems make refuse collection jobs more attractive, and this helps explain their development during the period of manpower shortages which followed World War II. Originally devised to facilitate recruitment of necessary levels of manpower, they gained in popularity during the 1950s and 1960s as a relatively 'easy' way to improve productivity and morale among refuse workforces. By the mid-1960s, almost half of all local authorities operated bonus schemes and 30 per cent employed a task and finish system.

In the twenty years since that time, significant developments in refuse collection have occurred. Methods of collection have changed and the capacity of refuse vehicles has increased. The number of commercial premises has declined, refuse has become much lighter, and routes have been adapted to take account of new housing and commercial developments. These changes have generally made the life of the refuse collector much easier. Thanks to the task and finish system, many can finish work at 1:00 or 2:00 in the afternoon – roughly three hours earlier than they would have done previously. However, over the years these changes were not taken into account fully in updating existing bonus schemes. Because bonus schemes quickly became an 'untouchable' aspect of refuse collectors' pay and conditions of employment, implementing the necessary changes often meant risking a head-on confrontation with the increasingly strong and militant local government manual workers' unions. Until recently, the great majority of authorities chose to tolerate a level of inefficiency rather than risk a prolonged disruption of services.

Bonus schemes continue to constitute a major part of the cost of refuse collection services. As shown in Table 7.3, in 1984 they accounted for 25 per cent of all expenditure on labour, which itself accounted for almost half of all refuse collection costs. Most of these bonus schemes were based on productivity levels and work schedules devised years ago and had thus lost any real relationship to improved productivity. In 1984, a report on refuse collection practices by the Audit Commission concluded that there was no relationship between bonus schemes and performance and that refuse forces without such schemes were often more productive than those which had retained them.

This report, *Securing Further Improvements in Refuse Collection*, provided the most comprehensive look at refuse collection since

TABLE 7.3   Refuse collection costs in England and Wales: 1983–4

Type of cost		£m
Labour		240
Basic pay and overtime	(135)	
Bonuses	(60)	
National Insurance and pensions	(45)	
Vehicle Standing		65
Vehicle Running		65
Other		130
Total		500

Source: *Securing Further Improvements in Refuse Collection*, Audit Commission, 1984.

1967. It stated that the costs of refuse collection varied widely across England and Wales due to differences in geography, methods of collection, and the quality of management. Analysing a number of authorities which had privatised refuse collection in the prior few years, the Commission found that:

● the cost of contracted services were all among the lowest 25 per cent of council refuse service expenditure;
● of the eight 'privatised' authorities examined, two had shown worse service as a result of contracting out and one had reported improvement. Five others noted that the contracted service required closer monitoring than that previously associated with the direct labour service;
● most of the contracting out of refuse collection has occurred in areas where industrial relations have proved troublesome; and
● there is no *a priori* reason for the public sector to be any less competitive than the private sector. Improvements in the efficiency of in-house refuse services could save £20 million annually without any change to the existing standard of service.[11]

The Commission's findings came as no surprise to local administrators, several of whom had undertaken reviews of refuse operations as part of the larger cost-cutting exercises which occurred in the late 1970s. These reviews had increased interest in efficiency improvements among service administrators and had led to the development of a number of management tools specifically designed to improve refuse service efficiency. Foremost among these systems was 'ROSS' (Refuse Operation System Simulation), a computer model developed by LAMSAC (Local Authorities Management Services and Computer Committee). Marketed as a 'complete refuse service management system', ROSS was designed to audit existing services, adjust them for changes, and simulate an entirely new refuse system.[12] Although the initial reception to ROSS among refuse service managers was mixed, it has proved a powerful tool in highlighting cost variations between services and has thus given support to the government's case for efficiency improvements and savings.

Contracting out activity

The new-found emphasis on cost-cutting and efficiency led ultimately to the growth of contracting out in local government. Local councils tried a variety of techniques to improve the efficiency of their refuse services. Some secured significant savings through programmes of voluntary redundancy, others through a reduction in the number of refuse vehicles. Several, however, found themselves unable to act on the results of their efficiency review due to union refusals to adapt to changes in the working environment. They turned to competitive tendering as a way to break the deadlock – a move which has had a significant impact upon the wider local government community. The section below offers a general overview of the growth of tendering and contracting out between 1980 and 1985. It also looks at the experiences of the pioneering councils, which have assumed a particular significance in light of the Government's declared intention to make tendering compulsory for local authorities.

Early developments (1980–2)

Although a number of other authorities have recent experience of private contractors, Southend District Council is generally regarded as the pioneer of the contracting out movement in Britain. In 1980, it went out to tender for a variety of public cleansing services as a result of its inability to control its workforce (see Chapter 2). Opposition by the trade unions was strong and media coverage considerable, arousing significant interest among a large number of local authorities who were having problems with their own refuse services. The contract was eventually awarded to Exclusive Services, the lowest private sector bidder, at an impressive level of projected savings. A number of Conservative councils were so captivated by the idea of contracting out that they did not wait to monitor the results of Southend's exercise. Within a year of the contract's commencement in April 1981, Wandsworth had awarded Pritchard Services a substantial street cleaning contract and Kensington and Chelsea had brought in Grand Metropolitan's waste service subsidiary to carry out refuse collection in Chelsea. Wandsworth Council was particularly keen and within a month of privatising street cleaning invited tenders for refuse collection. Whereas the first contract was awarded without serious opposition, the manual workers' unions in Wandsworth decided to launch an all-out campaign against the second tendering exercise. Their industrial action, described later in this chapter, won support from large sections of the council's administrative staff and brought events in Wandsworth to national attention.

Developments in Southend and Wandsworth stimulated interest in privatisation across a wide range of local authorities in late 1982 and early 1983. A survey of 314 authorities conducted by the *Local Government Chronicle* in April 1983 found that although 150 (48 per cent) had recently considered privatisation, 79 of these (53 per cent) had decided to retain the in-house force without ever going out to tender. The great majority (70 per cent) of councils taking privatisation seriously at this early stage were Conservative-controlled, and most of these were located in the South and Southeast. Only 9 Labour-controlled councils (6 per cent) had considered privatisation, and none of them had actually gone ahead with it. As shown in Table 7.4, only 11 councils contracted out a major service between 1981 and early 1983. All 11 contracts involved refuse collection and 5 included street cleaning in the same tendering exercise. During this same period at least a dozen councils hired private contractors for smaller pest control, office cleaning or catering contracts.[13]

Reported savings on these early contracts varied widely. Aggregate savings of £6.2 million were claimed on the 13 major contracts

TABLE 7.4 Local authority interest in contracting out: 1981–3

Political control	Number considering privatisation	%	Number which privatised major service*
Conservative	95	69	9
Labour	9	7	—
Independent	9	7	1
No overall control	25	18	1
	138	100**	11

* Contract in excess of £50 000
** Does not add up due to rounding.

Source: Calculated from *Local Government Chronicle* Survey, 17 June 1983.

let, which represented 32 per cent of the previous cost of these services. Not all large contracts resulted in correspondingly large savings; one council, Babergh, contracted for £1 million worth of housing repairs at an estimated savings of £10 000. In contrast, some of the smaller contracts achieved very big savings; Gillingham, for example, contracted out cleaning of public conveniences and saved £30 000 as a result of a £13 000 contract. Savings were not limited to 'privatising' authorities. Many councils which did not go through with contracting out found that threats of doing so helped them to negotiate substantial savings with their in-house workforces, particularly in the refuse collection field. Others, including Glanford, Bridgeworth, Dover and Stoke-on-Trent, went out to tender for refuse collection and awarded these contracts in-house.

With the exception of Wandsworth's refuse collection contract, most of the awards made during this period saw little effective opposition. Trade union campaigns were fought locally and often included refusals to cooperate with the tendering process and media initiatives aimed at discrediting contractors. Because little legitimate information about contractors' performance was available at this stage (the Southend contract had been in operation for no more than a year), union arguments were built around the potential for declining standards of service and the lack of accountability inherent in private contracting.

Fading interest (1983–4)

Throughout 1983, contracting out was the focus of numerous articles in the local government press and of several professional conferences. Many administrators who were considering contracting out visited Southend, Wandsworth, and other pioneering councils to observe their new arrangements in operation. For reasons not entirely clear, however, the flurry of activity in academic and professional circles did not lead to significant growth in contracting out. To the contrary, the latter half of 1983 and early 1984 saw a significant decline in the volume and value of major service work put out by district councils. During this period only two councils, South Kesteven and the Vale of White Horse, put both refuse collection and street cleaning out to private firms. Two councils privatised refuse only, another three contracted out street cleaning, and half a dozen privatised convenience cleaning. Together these contracts were worth £4.5 million on an annual basis, a drop of almost £7 million from the value of public cleansing contracts awarded in the previous year. As shown in Table 7.5, an increase in school cleaning work compensated somewhat for the drop in public cleansing activity during this period. Two county councils, Cambridgeshire and Kent, and two metropolitan boroughs, Solihull and Dudley, contracted out large volumes of school cleaning work.

Though it is dangerous to draw conclusions about national

TABLE 7.5   Contracting out of major services: April 1983–April 1984

Type of contract	Control Conservative	Independent	Total
Refuse and/or street cleaning	7	1	8
Public conveniences	3	2	5
School cleaning	4	—	4
School meals	1	—	1
	15	3	18

Source: *Public Service Review, Public Service Action* and *Local Government Chronicle.*

trends from such a small number of contracting authorities, it appears that interest in contracting out had faded somewhat by the spring of 1984. The annual survey of privatisation conducted by *Local Government Chronicle* in early 1984 found that only 27 per cent of the 340 respondents had considered privatisation between April 1983 and April 1984, compared with 48 per cent among a similar number of respondents the previous year.[14] Despite the general decline in interest, privatisation continued to result in savings. Savings on large contracts claimed by the authorities participating in the survey amounted to £5.5 million or 39 per cent of the services' previous cost. Many councils continued to use the threat of privatisation to elicit support from the unions for in-house savings packages.

By the latter half of 1984, however, the union campaign against privatisation was significantly stronger. Although industrial action remained localised, the campaign to undermine the public credibility of contractors was taken more seriously by local administrators. Evidence of contractors' failures to live up to commercial promises was growing rapidly and the unions made the most of it. Invocation of penalty clauses was fairly common, as many contractors experienced 'teething pains' at the start of new contracts. Other 'failures' included increases in original contract prices and reductions in employees' wages and conditions, both publicised as proof of the dangerously slim profit margins associated with local government cleansing work. Typical examples of contractors' failures, as defined by the unions, included:

- *penalty payments*   In Ealing, Exclusive Services fell short of the specification set out for street cleaning activities early on in the contract's life. Exclusive claimed that this was due to external factors beyond its control and pointed to the numbers of cars parked on the street overnight, noting that this prevented the use of efficient street cleaning vehicles. Despite its explanation, the firm was fined £18 000 in the first month of the contract's operation. Later, the standard of performance was relaxed somewhat to allow the company to receive the appropriate payments.[15]
- *reductions in pay*   In Wandsworth, Pritchard received large penalties on its gardening contract not long after it began in the spring of 1983. A new 'productivity payment' scheme for

its workers was introduced, under which weekly take-home pay was determined by the amount of work actually completed.[16]

● *deterioration in service standards* In Dudley, a survey undertaken by a local National Union of Teachers (NUT) branch found that 64 per cent of the 146 schools with private cleaners reported a deterioration in the standard of cleaning. Three firms – Initial, OCS and Taskmasters – were accused of failing to provide appropriate materials, training and supervision.

Some of these 'failures' were clearly more serious than others and not all of the unions' claims were justified, as problems in several areas stemmed from poorly written specifications or unforeseen local circumstances.[18] But, legitimate or not, the sheer number of failures publicised by the unions caused many authorities to think twice about the wisdom of contracting out and probably contributed to the slower pace with which it was conducted throughout 1984. By this time, most councils with clear political motivations for contracting out had attempted it; those that remained to consider it were more sceptical of its purported benefits. One chief executive queried at the time, 'Are we expecting too much of privatisation? Are we tending to treat it as the cure-all of the financial problems of local government?'[19]

A reversal of the trend (1985)

Declining interest in contracting out continued into 1985, despite the Government's confirmation of its intention to make competitive tendering mandatory for a wide range of local authority activities. Between April 1984 and April 1985, only four authorities contracted for refuse collection and two of these (Peterborough and Sevenoaks) limited the work to part of their district area. The only other sizeable contract awards were made by Hereford and Worcester County Council and Ealing Borough Council, both of which privatised their school meals service. While the value and volume of contracts continued to decline, the type of firm to which they were awarded changed. Only a fraction of the major contracts awarded during the 1984–5 financial year were won by the large companies which had previously done well in this market. Contracts for catering, refuse collection and vehicle maintenance tended to be awarded to smaller, local firms. Authorities with previous experience of contracting out accounted for a large percentage of the value of these more recently-awarded contracts: Southend, Ealing, Wandsworth, and Hammersmith and Fulham councils were responsible for £6.5 million worth of business in 1984–5, nearly half of the value of all large service contracts (other than building construction or maintenance) awarded to the private sector over this period.

Another survey of trends in local government tendering activity was conducted in April 1985. Its findings confirmed the continued decline in contracting out activity. Large parts of the country – including whole counties – privatised nothing at all between April 1984 and March 1985; only one council in Scotland privatised anything (Orkney contracted out refuse collection at an annual cost of £2000). Over three-quarters (78 per cent) of all responding councils said they had not considered privatising anything in the past year and in some areas 'the drive for privatisation has gone into reverse', with councils awarding work previously done by private contractors to the in-house force. The survey concluded that there was overwhelming evidence that interest among councils in contracting out their services had continued to decline steadily.[20]

As interest in the subject of contracting out faded, union opposition became less visible. The great majority of contracts awarded during 1985 were small and therefore did not pose a significant threat to union membership totals. In addition, many local councils who were reluctant to privatise went out of their way to foster the sort of relationship with the unions needed to achieve increased efficiency and cost savings. Nevertheless, the unions maintained their opposition to contracting out in local government. Their national publicity campaign continued, though its focus shifted from refuse collection issues to the detrimental impact privatisation might have upon standards of school meals and school cleaning. Union organisers began trying to recruit private contractors' street cleaning and refuse collection employees, with the longer-term objective of returning these services to direct labour. The unions also voiced strong protests against the Government's plans to mandate competitive tendering for a range of local services, and it is likely that their opposition campaign will escalate if compulsory tendering legislation is indeed brought into force.

In summary, it appears that the recent debate over contracting out in local authorities has been something of a storm in a teacup. Although a majority of local councils considered privatisation of one or more services in the early 1980s, few took it seriously enough to undertake formal competitive tendering exercises and even fewer contracted out. By the end of 1985, only two dozen local councils had privatised street cleaning or refuse collection and only about half a dozen county councils or metropolitan boroughs had contracted out school cleaning or the provision of school meals. This represents little more than the normal changes in modes of service provision one would expect over time. Indeed, during this same period many councils terminated private provision and returned to an in-house service. For example, Leicester City, Bassetlaw and Enfield reportedly switched from using private to directly employed architects; Burnley, West Midlands and Lancashire Councils returned to in-house provision of office cleaning, and Cambridgeshire County Council terminated its contract for school cleaning.

This balance between public and private provision of local authority services is unlikely to change in the immediate future. Most councillors are pleased with their existing service arrangements, considerably more so than they were five years ago. Contractors are disillusioned with the lack of growth in this market and have withdrawn from heavy sales development activity at local level. As the Pritchard Services Group noted in its 1984 Annual Report,

> Progress in this market has been profoundly disappointing. The number of opportunities to tender for further business was very limited ... Intentionally or otherwise, of those opportunities that did exist during 1984, approximately half contained conditions of tender which discriminated against the private contractor to such an extent that we declined even to bid.

Contractors have instead turned their lobbying attention to central government, whose interest in the subject was confirmed by the consultative document on mandatory local authority tendering issued by the DOE in February 1985. Although follow-up legislation had been expected during the 1985–1986 session, timetabling problems delayed its introduction and it is now expected to arrive in 1986–87. Both contract service firms and local administrators are actively preparing for what has been forecast as the 'second wave' of the contracting out storm.

Case studies

In anticipation of the next round of competitive tendering, it is useful to look more closely at the experiences of individual local authorities. Despite the fact that the vast majority of tendering exercises have occurred in Conservative-controlled authorities in the South and South-east, the nature and outcome of these exercises have varied dramatically. The three cases which occupy the remaining pages of this chapter have been chosen to illustrate the localised nature of both procedures and outcomes. The first case study is built around events in Gloucester, where the in-house team retained the public cleansing contract against significant external competition. The second case looks at the unusual experience of Wandsworth, which has the most ambitious and extensive competitive tendering programme in the country. The final case examines the experience of Bath City Council which, like Hammersmith Hospital, embraced privatisation because of its staff's refusal to cooperate with changes in their working environment.

Gloucester City Council

Like most of its neighbouring areas, Gloucester City Council has a long history of control by the Conservative Party. At the time of the Council's controversial tendering exercise in 1983, the Conservatives had a clear majority on the Council, controlling the chairmanship and all of its committees. While the majority of these Conservatives were from the old-fashioned paternalistic wing of the Conservative party, a few individuals were considered hard-line 'Thatcherites'. These hard-line Tories, encouraged by the recent experience of other contracting authorities, persuaded the Council to undertake a series of efficiency reviews in the early 1980s. By 1983, office cleaning, cattle market cleaning, airport operations, catering and nursery services had come under scrutiny. Two of these services, catering and market cleaning, had been privatised; the others remained with the direct labour organisation. Both of the privately controlled services quickly proved to be failures.

Catering returned to the DLO after the withdrawal of the private contractor. The contract for cleaning Gloucester's cattle market, originally awarded to Initial Services, also proved unworkable and was awarded at a higher price to another firm after Initial withdrew under accusations of poor hygiene in 1982.

These very obvious failures of privatisation did little to deter the ruling Conservatives from pushing ahead with similar exercises in other fields. Although the refuse collection service had been tested and shown to be one of the most efficient in the country, council members and administrators were aware that existing task and finish practices and bonus arrangements could be improved. At a meeting of the Highway and Works Committee in March 1983, members agreed to ask officers to prepare a report on the efficiency of a variety of services, among them refuse collection and street cleaning.[21] Information was to be provided in a way that would allow direct comparisons with other authorities and with private sector firms.

Although the members denied that they were committed to a formal tendering exercise, local trade unions quickly swung into action.[22] By the end of March, representatives of the three major unions – NUPE, T&GWU and NALGO – had met with local members of the Labour Party to formulate a joint strategy to combat any attempt at privatisation. Together they founded the Gloucester City Public Services Defence Committee, whose immediate objectives were to rally support from within the local union membership and to mobilise public opinion in the outside community. Within a short period of time it became clear that the Committee's first objective would be more difficult to achieve than its second. At a mass meeting attended by over 200 Gloucester city employees in early April, numerous union members spoke out *against* opposing the council's privatisation plans. Some felt they would be better off working for a contractor; others cited the futility of opposing a policy supported by central government and suggested that the unions should instead concentrate on securing beneficial redundancy terms. Despite this widespread reluctance to oppose council actions, those attending were eventually persuaded to support a substantial publicity campaign and a 'day of action' to articulate opposition to privatisation.

The 'day of action' coincided with the April Highway and Works Committee meeting and entailed a day-long strike, a demonstration through the streets of Gloucester, and a lobby of councillors as they arrived for the meeting. Although the Committee eventually decided to proceed with plans to compare the costs of both refuse and street cleaning services with private industry, it stopped short of making a commitment to a formal tendering exercise. This may have been due to the proximity of the local elections and the fact that many of the less radical Conservative members were keen to avoid civic controversy. In any case, privatisation became the central issue in the run-up to the local elections in early May. Although these elections saw the Conservatives' majority reduced to one, their desire to proceed with a formal 'efficiency review' was undiminished. With the completion of the report on the efficiency of public cleansing services, the Council decided that this document would form the basis for a specification to be used in a formal tendering exercise. A Privatisation Sub-committee was formed within the Highway and Works Committee and the tendering process was scheduled to begin in mid-summer.

Confirmation of the tendering exercise galvanised union organisers into action, and a mass meeting was called in late June to approve future opposition tactics. The 'mass' turned out to be a misnomer, since only 48 of the 360 workers attended. By this time, it had become obvious that the unions' primary struggle would be with their own membership. The four affected unions (NUPE, T&GWU, NALGO and UCATT) had only six shop stewards between them at the outset of the privatisation debate, an inadequate organisational base upon which to launch a major anti-privatisation campaign. NUPE, the only union to show an interest in leading the campaign, had no membership to speak of in either refuse collection or street cleaning sectors and a rather apathetic membership in other areas. As a result, much of the union campaign had to be organised by NUPE's full-time officials. To create the appearance of a joint union effort orchestrated by the local membership and to divert attention from the activities of its full-time officials, NUPE recruited one refuse worker to become a steward and helped appoint him to the leadership of the appropriate employees' committees.

Union efforts received a major setback when employees met in early July to discuss a proposal for a week-long 'go-slow', during which half of the workforce and its equipment would be removed from service to show what would happen under private contractors. Not only was attendance at the meeting poor, but a majority saw no point in taking further industrial action. Despite promises of generous strike pay for those not working, members voted overwhelmingly against the strike proposal. Much of the reluctance to support an opposition campaign stemmed from the activities of the city's officers, who were doing everything they could to ensure staff cooperation with the tendering process. They had decided that the exact specification to be used in the tendering exercise should be devised with the full knowledge of the workforce and had set up a joint working party at one of the council depots in order to examine the proposed specification. The final specification document reflected concessions by both sides, with the unions' influence evident in the incorporation of a number of clauses which restricted the contractors' ability to undercut in-house costs. These included requirements that the successful tenderer lease both vehicle and premises from the Council, that all vehicle maintenance be conducted at the Council's workshops, that all fuel and lubricants be purchased from the Council at current retail prices and that the contractor pay not less than the basic rate for local authority workers.

Despite the fact that contractors viewed the clauses as a restriction upon their commercial freedom, this specification withstood painstaking scrutiny by the council's Privatisation Sub-committee. The unions' argument that 'if you're doing it commercially, do it right' had a powerful effect upon councillors, most of whom wanted to be seen to be scrupulously fair. Many were concerned about the future of the services if a private contractor should go bankrupt, and saw the retention of vehicles and premises as key factors in allowing a swift transition back to direct labour. The risk of contractor failure was taken more seriously than it had been in other councils, because of withdrawals by contractors operating the catering and cattle market cleaning contracts. In any case, the tender documents were finalised in mid-July and sent to six organisations, including the in-house team. All were given six weeks to develop their proposals, with the deadline for receipt of tenders scheduled for early September 1983.

Although the cleansing services staff decided to cooperate with management in drawing up an in-house tender, the unions continued their campaign to mobilise both internal and external opinion against contracting out. But by this point support for a concerted campaign of opposition had dwindled considerably and a meeting of the Public Services Defence Committee, scheduled for early August, had to be cancelled due to low levels of interest. The lack of support for the unions' opposition campaign proved particularly demoralising for newly recruited stewards, and two resigned during the course of the summer. By mid-August, the entire weight of the opposition campaign had fallen on the shoulders of the unions' full-time officers. One full-time local official confided in a letter to his counterpart in another union at that time, 'I am extremely concerned about the attitude of our membership towards privatisation and I sometimes wonder whether we are banging our heads against the wall ... I can see no point whatsoever in spending a great deal of money financing the campaign where we do not have the backing of the membership.' These officers soon realised the futility of opposition efforts and called no further meetings of the Defence Committee before tenders were received in early September.

By the deadline for receipt of tenders, five firms had submitted bids alongside that of the direct labour organisation. Of the commercial bidders only one proposed a price lower than that of the in-house service, but the manpower schedules suggested on its tender document were considered 'dubious'. With the help of the trade unions, Labour councillors successfully drew the attention of the wider council to the issue of loss-leaders, and the decision to avoid anything that 'smelled suspicious' was a unanimous one. As a result, the Privatisation Sub-committee's recommendation of an in-house award was approved by the Highway and Works Committee in mid-October and ratified by a meeting of the full council one week later.

Gloucester's in-house 'contract' offered the city a saving of £150 000, 15 per cent of the previous service budget, and saw significant changes to the service which had existed prior to the tendering exercise. The number of refuse and cleaning staff was reduced from 69 to 55; some employees accepted early retirement and others were redeployed. Refuse rounds were expanded, and the number of mechanics and vehicles reduced. The workload upon individuals increased significantly, causing a dramatic change in the age profile of the workforce. As the Gloucester City Engineer noted recently: 'In the past we tolerated people on the staff who weren't very strong. Now we're getting past that.' The new scheme is notable in one other respect. One of the effects of the unions' campaign for a 'fair commercial comparison' was the inclusion of penalty clauses in the in-house tender. Failure of the in-house force to live up to the specified standard of service now results in deductions from individual bonus payments.[23] Undesirable as this situation may be to the workforce, most employees felt it was a small concession to make in return for inclusion of substantial restrictions on private contractors in the tendering documents.

Wandsworth Borough Council

Wandsworth Borough is clearly the most privatised borough in London and probably the most privatised local district in the country. Since 1982, it has been engaged in a far-reaching programme of competitive tendering which has led to the contracting out of 15 separate services worth a total of £13 million to contractors annually. The origins of contracting out in Wandsworth date back to the local elections of 1978, when Labour lost control to a Conservative majority pledged to reduce local rates by removing bureaucratic inefficiency. Though the Council's Conservatives were originally considered 'moderate' by the unions, the tenor of the new group was soon transformed by the growing stature of a number of young Tory councillors. It soon became clear that the politics of Wandsworth – previously considered a fairly safe Labour area – were to change radically.

Privatisation first entered the Council's vocabulary in 1980, but only as a threat to promote the adoption of a revised bonus scheme in the refuse collection service. A similar programme of savings was under negotiation with street cleaners one year later when the council announced its intention to compare a revised in-house service budget to outside tenders. Though some lobbying and industrial action occurred, they were limited in scope and the workforce eventually agreed to cooperate on a package of in-house savings which entailed a loss of 30 jobs (from 130 to 100) and a more flexible work schedule. In December 1981, the Council compared this proposal to bids received from thirteen companies. The adjudication process eventually boiled down to a choice between Pritchard Services, the cheapest outside tenderer, and the in-house workforce. Despite the significant package of internal savings which had been negotiated, the contract was awarded to

Pritchard in January 1982 at an estimated saving of £2.4 million over a five-year period.

As the street cleaning contract commenced in March 1982, the Council committed itself to inviting tenders for its refuse service. By this time the unions had realised the futility of competing in what had clearly become a highly charged political environment and refused to participate in the tendering process. Instead they decided to launch a major campaign demanding an end to the tendering process and no privatisation.[24] Thanks to a history of strong cooperation among white-collar and manual worker unions in Wandsworth, it was relatively easy to mobilise support for the campaign. NALGO, whose members in Wandsworth were threatened by similar staffing cuts, pledged its all-out support and a Liaison Committee was set up to coordinate the activities of white-collar and manual worker unions. In early April 1982, a meeting of some 2000 council workers endorsed a plan for industrial action to coincide with the dispatch of tender documents to contractors. Two weeks later, the strike began in full force. An estimated 90 per cent of NALGO's members stopped work and refused to answer telephones, process rate demands or perform other administrative services fairly critical to the council's day-to-day existence. They were joined by large numbers of manual workers, most of whom remained out for several days.

The strike affected virtually every aspect of the Council's activities and received wide coverage in both local and national press. Wandsworth was forced to bring in agency staff for a variety of administrative tasks and to hire private contractors to undertake refuse collection. These contractors found the task more onerous than they expected, as Council refuse workers received sufficient support from neighbouring councils and from the GLC (Greater London Council) to make local disposal of the refuse very difficult. Contractors were ultimately forced to rely on refuse sites as far away as Kent, and several withdrew from these temporary contractual arrangements. The confrontation became particularly vicious in the run-up to the local elections in early May. Pritchard, the company already employed on the street cleaning contract, reported assaults on staff and a series of guerrilla attacks upon its depot. Tyres were reportedly slashed, sugar was put in fuel tanks, fuel lines were cut, and vehicle ignition keys were taken.

The 1982 local elections, heavily influenced by the national swing towards the Government in the wake of the Falklands War, returned the Conservatives to power in Wandsworth. Labour's failure to take back control of the Council proved demoralising to many union members and within a week of the election NALGO called off its intensive campaign. Other unions in turn reassessed their campaign strategies and felt forced to drop their demands for an end to the tendering process. Under some pressure to salvage a deal from the Council, they eventually agreed to a return to work on the conditions that they would be able to see the tenders when they were opened and would be given a chance to put in their own bid. When the unions did receive details of the tenders in mid-June, it was clear that they would not be able to compete with contractors on a cost basis. As a result, they developed a scheme which offered what they termed 'value for money' and submitted it alongside a detailed critique of the tenders put in by the contractors. At a meeting of the Council's Policy and Resources Committee in mid-July, this late union submission was considered alongside the tender put in by the lowest private bidder, Grand Metropolitan. To no-one's surprise, the Committee recommended that the contract be given to Grand Metropolitan and the full Council formally awarded the contract the following day.

The potential cost reductions from the new refuse contract were considerable and encouraged the Council to conduct similar reviews of other services. Next on the Council's list was what is generally known as 'mobile gardening' – the maintenance of roadside verges, small parks, housing estate gardens, and other limited expanses of greenery. Like refuse collection, this service had seen significant cuts in the 1980–1 period, when the entire gardening workforce had been reduced by half. The remaining gardeners submitted a viable and competitive bid when the council went out to tender late in 1982, but were undercut by a bid from Pritchard Services. Despite the fact that the adjusted difference between the in-house bid and the lowest private bid was only 9 per cent, the Council awarded the five-year contract to Pritchard at a cost of £1.75 million.

By the end of 1982, Wandsworth had privatised three services traditionally carried out by direct labour. Although each exercise had strengthened Conservative councillors' belief in the tendering process, it soon became evident that contracting out was not the unqualified success which many had claimed it would be. The street cleaning contract, the earliest award made to the private sector, became a source of serious trouble almost as soon as it began in 1982. Despite a six-week 'penalty free' period, Pritchard amassed 1894 default notices in the first six months of the contract, costing the firm close to £8000 in fines and causing the council significant anguish. As the Chief Executive of Wandsworth noted recently: 'We had a lot of trouble with them. It was a loss-leader and they had to put money into it. It took them a while to realise they had to train managers. We closed our eyes a bit and gave them time to prepare.' The Council eventually bent over backwards to help Pritchard improve its performance. Six months into the contract it set up 'penalty free zones' which the company was to use to 'train its managers'. It also overlooked what to some appeared to be highly erratic hiring and firing policies. Although the firm originally declared its intention to provide a good service with 63 employees, contract troubles forced Pritchard to raise the number of staff and within one year of the contract's commencement it employed 85 workers. It is estimated that this alone added £500 000 to the cost of running the contract.[25]

Grand Metropolitan was experiencing a different set of problems on its refuse collection contract. Immediately after the company was awarded the contract, NUPE and the GMWU challenged its wage structure by bringing a claim under the Fair Wages Resolution (1946) to the Department of Employment. The Central Arbitration Committee found in favour of the unions and ordered Grand Metropolitan to raise its payments to individuals by between £6 and £8 per week and to reduce the standard work week to 39 hours. But the company was never forced to implement the CAC decision in full, as Wandsworth Council immediately began negotiations with its existing contractors to erase the Council's fair wages clause from their conditions of contract. Grand Metropolitan's failure to honour the CAC decision alienated the workforce, which had already launched a stream of complaints about shortages of equipment. In November 1983 the company fired six refuse workers for undisclosed reasons; this compounded existing problems and resulted in yet another strike by refuse workers. To Grand Metropolitan's credit, it dealt with the problem more swiftly than the council ever could have; the company soon reinstated the six men on a temporary basis and their colleagues returned to work.

Contrary to all expectations, mobile gardening – the smallest of the three privatised services – proved more troublesome than either street cleaning or refuse collection. The gardening contract began quietly in March 1983. However as soon as the six week penalty-free period had expired, a deterioration in the standard of service became evident. Over the first three months of the contract, Pritchard notched up numerous penalty points and was fined £35 000. The second three months were worse, with fines totalling an additional £73 000. In July, Pritchard attempted to do something about the unprecedented level of penalties and raised the number of workers from 38 to 51, a level of staffing 40 per cent higher than that associated with the previous in-house service. It also instituted a new productivity scheme, a piecework payment system designed to ensure that specified work was completed. The new scheme's removal of fixed minimum payments for gardening work sparked outrage among Pritchard's employees and precipitated industrial action. The mobile gardeners refused to complete their appointed rounds and the standard of service sunk to a still lower level. Inadequate performance by the contractor led to payments of £27 600 being withheld during August alone.

Although the dispute was eventually settled, Pritchard Services was put on probation. In late August, the Council notified the firm that if it did not clear the backlog of gardening work and show signs of satisfactory performance by the end of October, the contract would be terminated. By the time that this deadline arrived, it had become clear that Pritchard would lose the contract. A letter was sent to Pritchard Services informing the company that the contract was to be terminated as of 1 November and that the premises were to be cleared two weeks later. A second tendering process was set in motion, based on a new contract that would begin in mid-February, 1984. This 'repeat' tendering process proved interesting, as two of the firms which had tendered previously came up with signficantly lower bids the second time around. One of the two, R. B. Tyler of Ware, was eventually awarded the contract. Its winning price, £428 000 for five years, was a full £175 000 lower than its earlier bid.

While this tendering process was underway, the Council undertook discussions with Pritchard Services in an effort to recover the costs of terminating the contract. The Council's primary concern was the cost of hiring temporary gardeners to undertake the planting and maintenance work that needed to be done before the new contract began in February. In theory, this cost should easily have been covered by the £70 000 performance bond (20 per cent of the contract price) that Pritchard had posted with Bank of America. But when Wandsworth wrote to the bank calling in this bond, Pritchard applied for and received an injunction to prevent payment to the Council on the grounds of breach of contract. At the hearing on the case, in December 1985, the court found in favour of the Council. But Pritchard immediately appealed against the ruling and was granted another temporary injunction. This second hearing is not expected to take place until early in 1987. To date, Wandsworth has received no contribution at all toward the costs involved in terminating the contract.

But the problems which Wandsworth encountered in its first three privatisation initiatives did little to dampen the Council's enthusiasm. The process of identifying suitable areas and putting them out to competitive tender continued at a vigorous pace throughout 1983 and 1984. By the end of 1984, five additional services had been put out to contract: cleaning at community centres and public halls, park cleansing, vehicle maintenance, housing caretaking, and public convenience cleaning. A number of these contracts caused significant controversy, though none as heated as that which characterised the refuse collection exercise. Several tendering exercises carried out during this period resulted in victories for the in-house staff. Gully cleansing and street lighting remained in-house due to competitive bids from the existing workforce. Laundry services remained in-house as a result of the lack of interest shown by the private sector.

The momentum of both privatisation and tendering drives continued through 1985 and five additional services were privatised. As one senior Wandsworth official noted: 'We cut our teeth on street cleaning and have never looked back.' The council estimates that aggregate savings since the start of its campaign total £5 million, almost 80 per cent of this from privatised contracts. Reductions in service costs have varied from 9 per cent to 45 per cent with an average saving of 28 per cent. Table 7.6 summarises the projected financial effects of the tendering programme over a period of five years.

The privatisation programme has also had a significant effect

TABLE 7.6   **Wandsworth Council: five-year savings from privatisation and competitive tendering**

	Cost of service before tendering (£000)	Saving (allowing for severance) (£000)	%
Savings through privatisation			
Housing caretakers	17 400	3 200	18
Refuse	16 900	7 500	44
Street cleansing	6 000	1 400	23
Estate management	5 400	800	15
Mechanical workshops	3 500	1 500	43
Social services catering	3 200	400	13
Mobile maintenance unit	2 700	700	26
Public convenience	2 000	500	25
Social services cleaning	1 900	800	42
Battersea Arts Centre	1 200	700	58
Cleaning/attending at public halls	1 100	500	45
Office cleaning	1 000	400	40
Libraries – cleaning and attending	900	400	44
Litter picking (notional)	600	200	33
Agency punching	300	100	33
Subtotal	64 100	19 100	30
Savings through competitive testing against private sector			
Mechanical workshop	7 900	2 300	29
Estate management schemes (building works maintenance)	6 900	1 300	19
Social services transport	5 600	1 400	25
Latchmere Leisure Centre	2 600	200	8
Print unit	1 200	140	12
Street lighting	1 100	500	45
Skips and abandoned vehicles	500	30	6
Gully cleansing	400	70	18
Subtotal	26 200	5 940	23
Total	**90 300**	**25 040**	**28**

Notes:
- These savings are calculated to show the largest saving for each service measured against the higher of current expenditure, current budget or proposed expenditure.
- These figures reflect cost levels at different points in time.
- Savings figures include sales and receipts from equipment, vehicles, etc.

Source: Calculated from figures provided by Wandsworth Council Finance Department.

upon staffing levels in the borough. Combined with the earlier policies of freezing jobs and natural wastage, it helped the borough to reduce staff from 3300 to 1600 between 1980 and 1985. The reduction in staffing has had a dramatic effect upon trade union membership. GMBATU estimates that it lost 1000 members in the borough during this period; NUPE estimates that it lost about 200. Although these and other unions are trying hard to recruit individuals now working for private contractors, it is unlikely that the numbers of new recruits will do more than offset the losses likely to occur during future 'efficiency review' exercises in Wandsworth.

Bath City Council

Bath City Council covers an area of 7000 acres, including some 180 miles of roadway, and its refuse service is responsible for collection from some 37 000 properties. Like nearby Gloucester, its Council was for many years controlled by a moderate Conservative group. Industrial relations were generally good, with the Council taking care to keep the trade unions happy. This stance provided stability and continuity in service provision, but it also led to glaring inefficiencies in certain local services. Refuse collection clearly provided the most dramatic example. The bonus system had rarely been adjusted and was dramatically out of line with those of neighbouring authorities. In addition, an outdated task and finish system had been in operation for some time. Tasks had grown easier with the development of lighter-weight refuse and more sophisticated collection vehicles, but work schedules had not been amended. Levels of overtime were known to be excessive and served to exacerbate the situation.

By late 1980, the standard of Bath's refuse service had deteriorated and complaints from citizens had become more frequent. In November, Council members asked for a formal review of the refuse collection service. The report, prepared by the city engineer's department and presented to the Council in June 1981, identified several alternative methods of refuse collection. Although refuse collection by contract received only a passing mention in the report, Council members were intrigued by the idea and asked for a fuller investigation of the subject. They also asked the city engineer to examine any savings which might be made within the in-house service.

An 'Action Committee', consisting of the supervisors of the cleansing services, shop stewards, workers' representatives and the city engineer, was set up to examine the scope for internal savings. The plan it devised allowed for savings of £80 000 on a budget of £550 000 (15 per cent); it called for the removal of one vehicle, the redistribution of the remaining work, and the removal of 16 of the 73 existing staff. Originally reluctant to accept such significant changes, the workforce agreed to the plan after trade union area officials were consulted. This proposal was presented to the Council's Public Protection and Works Committee in December 1981, alongside an analysis of the costs and benefits of privatisation. Though the quotations put forward by private firms offered savings of £40 000 more than the in-house plan, the city engineer stressed that the difference between the external and internal costs was primarily a function of local authority pay and conditions. On his recommendation, the Committee gave the go-ahead to make savings in the existing in-house service in place of privatisation and stated that the position would be reviewed in a year's time.

Negotiations with the unions over redundancies took place over the four months between the Committee's decision and the commencement of the new arrangement. All went smoothly until October 1982, two or three days before the plan was to go into operation. At that point, a trade union steward told the city engineer that his colleagues would not work the new scheme and argued that workloads were unrealistic. But council officers insisted that the new scheme at least be tried for a period of time, and went ahead with its implementation. The unions responded with a form of covert industrial action, whereby each day a crew would not finish its new rounds. Not recognising that this action was intentional, service administrators told refuse collectors to continue with the next day's rounds and allowed work left undone to be completed later at overtime rates. The unions realised that they were not getting anywhere with the Council and instituted a ban on overtime. This caused the situation to deteriorate rapidly, and the Council was flooded by more than 200 calls a day from irate citizens. The trouble continued for four weeks, with the unions adamant that they could not manage the newly-assigned workload.

By this point, Council members were extremely anxious about the backlog of refuse and called a meeting with the city engineer to address the situation. They decided to offer the workforce a one-off payment of £8000 to clear the backlog, so long as employees would work the negotiated scheme while management tried to identify problems. The workforce agreed and began to clear the backlog. Although the unions had previously stated that removing the build-up of refuse would take three weeks, it took only three days. Furthermore, all rounds were completed easily by 2:00 p.m. It was at this point that both councillors and officers realised that the unions had been observing a 'go slow' policy since the implementation of the new work schedule. This realisation pushed the Council to request that a formal tendering exercise be undertaken straight away.

Bath City Council invited tenders for its refuse collection service in December 1982. Because this service was linked from a budgetary standpoint to the street cleaning and public convenience services, contractors were invited to tender for any of the individual services or for all three simultaneously. The Council specifically requested that the direct labour organisation put in a bid, but the unions declined and the city engineer was forced to put one together on their behalf. His proposal was eventually considered alongside those of thirteen other firms, including two local ones. The private bids were spread widely, and many were cheaper than the revised cost of the in-house service. The two lowest bids, at £350 000 and £370 000 respectively, each shaved more than £100 000 off the cost of the scheme which the unions had so adamantly refused to work. By this point, few Council members wanted to take the risk that the unions might walk out again and most were convinced that contracting out was the only option. After interviewing the shortlisted contractors and visiting several other local authorities where contracts were operating, Bath opted for the lowest bid and awarded the contract for all three services to Pritchard Services at an expected saving of at least £1 million over a five-year period.

Pritchard began the contract in May 1983 with 32 men, 41 less than had been previously employed by the Council, and with vehicles and equipment that were purchased from the Council. A variety of 'teething troubles' occurred soon after the contract's commencement. It took time for Pritchard staff to learn the appropriate routes and to find out where individual refuse bins were stored. Staff turnover was high, which served to slow down the educational process. However substantial increases in staffing (estimates vary from 30 per cent to 70 per cent) occurred in the early days of the contract. Within six weeks, a great majority of the problems had been sorted out and the number of complaints had returned to an 'acceptable level'. Since that time there have been occasional hiccoughs, but no more than existed prior to privatisation and the Council is generally satisfied with the contractor's performance. Unlike Wandsworth, however, Bath Council has not viewed its success in the public cleansing sector as a stepping-stone to further privatisation. The Council feels that it has fulfilled the sole objective of the exercise – an improvement in the efficiency of its cleansing services.

An assessment

These three case studies highlight several important features of local government tendering to date. Perhaps the most obvious feature is the concentration of contracting out activity in the South. Although efficiency reviews occurred throughout the country between 1980 and 1985, only in a small number of primarily Conservative-controlled authorities did they lead directly or indirectly to privatisation. As the Audit Commission report on refuse collection noted, many of these authorities exhibited strong trade union activity. But the push to privatise has generally arisen less from a desire to weaken strong trade unions than from a desire to remove the inefficiences which this trade union presence has fostered. Although the motives of Wandsworth Council have been called into question by its local administrators and trade unionists, the objectives of Bath and Gloucester were clear. Neither had a history of the sorts of industrial relations problems that would encourage an attack upon the trade unions; both looked upon tendering exclusively as a means to improve the efficiency of the refuse service. Their experiences are considerably closer to the experiences of most tendering authorities than are those of Wandsworth.

The case studies illustrate that the first step in moves to tendering is often an efficiency review. Nearly all such reviews have led to the conclusion that existing routines needed to be changed and that staffing levels were excessive. Although most authorities have used this evidence to recommend substantial programmes of savings, the longer-term effect of these efficiency reviews has varied tremendously from council to council. Frequently, the recommended savings have been 'offered' to the workers. In some cases, acceptance of these savings has signalled the end of the issue; this may well have been the case in Bath had its refuse workers not reneged on their agreement to work the scheme. In other areas, the unions' acceptance of a package of savings has not deterred the council from going ahead with a formal tendering exercise at a later date; Wandsworth's street cleaners and mobile gardners both accepted efficiency savings only months before tendering exercises began. And in still other authorities, the recommended savings have not been accepted by the unions – a situation which has nearly always precipitated a formal tendering procedure.

These experiences suggest that the actual results of an efficiency review play only a minor part in determining the ultimate effect of the exercise. Much more important are the political will of the council and the response of the unions to changes in the service's operation. The manifestation of the council's political will can take two forms. The first is a party political approach, which relies on Conservative Party policy and Government exhortations for support. It has been most clearly evident in the events occurring in Wandsworth. Local officials there have suggested that it was unlikely that any of the major services would have remained in-house; one senior Wandsworth administrator, now among the strongest supporters of the privatisation programme, admitted that 'It did smell too much of politics at the time.' Much of the debate over party-political motives has focused on Christopher Chope, former leader of the council and now Conservative MP for Southampton, Itchen. Not only did he lead the drive for privatisation in Wandsworth, but he carried his campaign to the House of Commons and has played a major role in promoting mandatory tendering legislation for local government.

But political will as a driving force behind tendering events has also taken a more neutral form. Many councils have used threats of privatisation to re-establish firm control over trade unions and thus give themselves more flexibility in service decision-making. Contractors are well aware of this, and express their anger at the fact that they are being used by local authorities to 'put the screws on' direct labour organisations. They cite evidence of this behaviour in the large number of authorities who have approached them only to withdraw their interest once the threat of redundancy has had the desired effect upon existing staff. Much to the frustration of contractors, this tactic has generally been successful and has led to solid agreements on efficiency savings in numerous authorities in both the South and North of England. In a minority of cases, however, 'sabre-rattling' techniques have backfired and authorities have gotten more than they bargained for as a result. In these areas, threats of privatisation have prompted stiff opposition from the unions, forcing councillors to undertake a formal tendering exercise and to privatise the service.

A second critical variable, the local union response to threats of contracting out, has also played a significant role in determining the outcome of tendering activity. Although the national policy of most unions is one of strict opposition to the tendering process, support for this has been patchy and union officials know they cannot enforce it. As a result, union strategies have varied from area to area. In highly unionised and militant areas, cooperation with management has not been considered; in Wandsworth, for example, unions believed that 'an attempt to compete with contractors on their own terms was a blind alley and a practical impossibility'.[26] However, in less politicised areas cooperation has been frequent. In Gloucester, for instance, the unions' objective (by default) was to 'win that tender playing the Tory game', which was achieved by lobbying for inclusion of a variety of 'commercial' clauses.

The experiences of Gloucester and Wandsworth nicely illustrate two of the most difficult facts for the unions to accept. The first is that where they have cooperated in the tendering process – due to apathy, goodwill, or a belief that than can actually win – they have frequently been successful in retaining the contract. Often the in-house bid has been selected over cheaper bids from private contractors, as was the case in Gloucester, suggesting that many authorities are still willing to pay a premium to retain direct control over their own services. The converse has been equally hard for the unions to swallow. Where local branches have refused to cooperate with either efficiency reviews or with competitive tendering, they have rarely retained the service. In Bath, the unions' refusal to implement the efficiency review recommendations and to cooperate with tendering led directly to privatisation. As Bath's city engineer noted: 'The great tragedy of this thing is that if the men had followed the agreed route they would still be working for me.'

These two factors, the political will of the council and the attitude of trade unions, are not independent of one another and in any given authority some sort of relationship will exist between the two. But that need not affect the basic conclusion drawn from these case studies – that each factor has played an important part in determining the outcome of service provision decisions. The interaction between the two explains why authorities with similar political outlooks and service requirements – such as Gloucester and Bath – have ended up with totally different modes of service provision, and why authorities with very different political temperaments and service needs – such as Wandsworth and Bath – have ended up with the same mode of provision (and, coincidentally, the same contractor).

Although the outcomes of tendering decisions have been somewhat unpredictable, most local authority tendering exercises have led to improvements in the cost-effectiveness of the refuse service. In some cases, councils are now getting a better standard of service for the same expenditure on refuse; in others, they are receiving the same standard of service for less money. These improvements are visible both where services have been awarded in-house and where they have been contracted out. Although the appeal of private provision as an alternative to existing modes of provision has been limited, where it has been undertaken it has generally proved effective. These two facts are not unrelated. The main reason why contracting out has been successful in local government is that it has been employed in only those councils whose previous service delivery systems were not responding to the needs of the wider community. Selective use of both tendering and contracting out techniques has offered local authorities new solutions to some very old local service problems.

8 An Overview of the Debate

The events documented in previous chapters have touched on a number of important issues: the use of central power for ideological ends, the decline of local autonomy, the growth of private provision of public services and the role of bureaucratic and trade union interests in service provision. This concluding chapter stands back from the details of competitive tendering exercises and explores these wider issues. It puts recent events into historical perspective by evaluating their impact and significance and by highlighting some of the lessons which can be drawn from the experiences of the health service and local authorities.

Alternative perspectives

Two major political arguments have fuelled the recent debate. 'New right' views have provided the foundation upon which the Conservative Party has built its tendering and contracting out policies. A 'traditional left' approach has been equally significant as a backdrop to the unions' campaign of opposition. Both approaches have been set out chiefly by polemicists, rather than theoreticians, with little analytical rigour.

The 'New right' view

The Adam Smith Institute and other Conservative think-tanks perceive public bureaucracies as necessarily inefficient suppliers of services and thus assign great significance to the growth of competitive tendering and contracting out. Applying microeconomic theory to bureaucratic behaviour, new right supporters argue that government agencies have no pecuniary incentive to efficiency as there are few if any means of measuring their 'non-market' outputs, i.e. products for which the consumer does not have to pay. As agencies are monopoly suppliers, the bargaining power of their clients/customers is limited and competitive pressures are non-existent. The bureaucracy retains a monopoly of information both about the benefits generated by its activities and about the costs of providing public services. As a result, demands for resources cannot be rigorously evaluated by external bodies.

Given the lack of external constraints upon agency activity, the new right argues that bureaucrats are free to pursue personal goals: higher salaries, perks, status, power, patronage and what is generally referred to as an 'easy life'. All but the last of these goals give bureaucrats clear incentives to increase the size of the administrative budget both on the 'micro'-scale (within their particular division or unit) and on the 'macro'-scale (across an entire department). Budget-maximising activities cannot easily be scrutinised due to the absence of external information on costs. Furthermore, they receive tacit or visible support from the politicians most directly involved in regulating agencies, who are eager to increase spending when it appears to favour their constituents and are equally reluctant to cut back on existing spending if their supporters are involved. As a result, public agencies inevitably oversupply public service output – providing services at levels beyond those which citizens need or have demanded.[1]

Privatisation, or the shift of emphasis to the private sector, is seen as a remedy to bureaucratic oversupply, the primary cause of inefficiency in service provision. Contracting out serves to break up the 'block' budget, thus reducing budgetary discretion dramatically. It requires public agencies to specify and justify the need for services more precisely than they have done in the past, revealing information about the nature of current operations and the costs of providing a certain level of service. This lifts the veil from what had previously been a very hidden system of resource allocation and allows the public greater scrutiny of and control over the distribution of public funds. Though not as desirable as contracting out, competitive tendering brings a measure of cost consciousness into the public sector environment, forcing public agencies to emulate the cost-saving measures traditionally adopted by private firms. New measures undertaken may include abolishing restrictive work practices, decreasing staff, tightening supervision, or increasing individual workloads.

New right theorists assert that both contracting out and competitive tendering pose considerable threats to the bureaucracy. They signal an end to its monopoly of public services' operational data, which will inevitably result in a loss of autonomy and decision-making freedom. The introduction of competition means that bureaucratic decisions about the type or level of service necessary will be scrutinised carefully by external sources and analysed against competing claims for resources. This is likely to lead to a reduction in the size of the overall service budget and a real or perceived decline in the specific service's bureaucratic status and organisational importance. Downward adjustments in the level of service provided will occur, particularly in areas where the oversupply of outputs has been severe, and may have a negative effect upon the relationship which previously existed between bureaucrats and their relevant client groups. Together these changes will impose dramatic constraints upon bureaucratic behaviour.

If bureaucratic interests are as one-dimensional as the new right suggests *and* the growth of private provision and competitive tendering has as negative an effect upon these interests as is claimed, it would be logical to expect that bureaucratic opposition to the Government's initiative would be very strong indeed. However, this has not proved to be the case in either NHS or local government tendering. As noted in previous chapters, opposition to tendering from policy-level administrators has generally been limited and has not had a significant impact on the tenor of the national debate. Dunleavy has interpreted this quiescence as indicating that bureaucratic interests are not as strong or as one-dimensional as new right theorists have made them out to be and suggests that privatisation is consistent with the 'bureau-shaping' objectives of senior administrators.[2]

The evidence presented in this book supports this conclusion, by showing that bureaucratic interests are more complex and varied than the new right suggests. The case studies in both local government and the NHS demonstrate that bureaucratic motives can vary widely. At Hammersmith Hospital, the competitive tendering exercise caused a rift between two groups of senior hospital administrators with very different objectives: one was eager to privatise the service, the other to retain it in-house. Whereas

Wandsworth administrators were proud to be masterminding the most ambitious 'savings' exercise in local government, in contrast Bath's administrators succeeded (temporarily) in convincing the authority to keep refuse collection in-house at a cost significantly higher than that proposed by private contractors. The presumption that bureaucratic behaviour is driven primarily by budget-maximising considerations does not seem to hold up in the face of recent tendering experience. Hence the new right's primary justification for a major shift in methods of service delivery – the need to remedy inefficiencies resulting necessarily from bureaucratic oversupply – is less clear-cut than the theoretical literature suggests.

But in addition the new right asserts that private provision of services is inherently more efficient than direct provision. Private firms are single purpose organisations with a clear and effective measure of performance – profitability. The commercial profit objective shifts the emphasis from the supply of services to the demand for such services in the marketplace and ensures a more rigorous approach to the issue of costs. As smaller and more independent units, private firms are in a comparatively strong position to negotiate freely with trade unions and are therefore less likely to be hampered by restrictive agreements and rapidly rising wage demands. Private firms' greater flexibility and responsiveness to changes in the market or in technology will result in slimmer and more efficient services.[3]

The new right's argument for the inherent efficiency of private provision does not hold up in the face of the evidence presented in previous chapters. The history of private provision of ancillary services in the NHS suggests that private firms (such as those under contract to the Bethlem Royal and Maudsley Hospitals) were no more efficient than the direct labour organisations which existed at other hospitals. It was not until the NHS tendering directive came into force that the extent of pre-existing inefficiencies under contractual arrangements became apparent. At Barking Hospital, for example, the Crothall company held the domestic services contract from 1972 until 1983. The hospital's decision to go out to tender in 1983 forced Crothall to revise radically both its labour schedule and its conditions of service in order to present a competitive bid. This it did, successfully knocking 40 per cent off the previous contract price and retaining the contract. Similarly dramatic price reductions have been put forward by incumbent contractors in other areas, though not all have been as successful as Crothall was at Barking. Some have lost their existing contract to newer contractors; others have seen previously privatised services revert to in-house provision.

Despite evidence of private sector inefficiencies, the new right's supporters argue that the increasing popularity of contracting out demonstrates the public's recognition of the inherent superiority of private provision. They suggest that the shift in the balance between public and private provision is a permanent one, and that recent developments mark the beginning of a new era in the relationship between citizens and the state. To support this contention they point to new privatisation initiatives in local government (for example, Merton Borough Council has recently considered privatising its entire finance department) and to a more commercial orientation in the health service. But the new right has not yet explained why certain services have returned from external to direct labour, nor have they explained how these new and enlightened public preferences will make themselves felt under a government of a different complexion. Until they do, their conclusions about the permanence of the contracting out phenomenon must remain tentative at best.

The 'traditional left' view

The views of the traditional left on this issue begin from a very different set of premises. Bureaucrats do not budget-maximise nor do they oversupply public service outputs.[4] To the contrary, public provision has important advantages over private provision. Public servants are imbued with a 'public service ethos', one which manifests itself in high levels of loyalty to the organisation and devotion to its clients – the public. Individual integrity and enthusiasm are translated into effective on-the-job performance. The unions assert that the high-quality service provided by direct labour is in sharp contrast to that provided by contracting firms: the pursuit of profit, the primary motivation of commercial organisations, is a recipe for poor performance as costs will always be minimised in order to maximise profit margins.[5]

The traditional left believes that contracting out presents a significant and very serious challenge to both local democracy and community politics. Local flexibility will disappear as authorities' hands become tied in formal contractual arrangements, the very nature of which prevents contractors from responding adequately to the frequently changing needs of the local population. Traditional models of democracy, in which local government is directly accountable to the wishes of the electorate, are challenged as the contractor's independence leaves the public with only indirect influence over service outputs. The relationship between citizens and local government is moulded into a commercial format, closely resembling that which generally exists between a firm and its clients.

Competitive tendering itself poses real dangers to local communities, according to this view. It highlights the distinctions between white-collar and manual workers which had begun to be blurred by a strong trade union movement, thus exaggerating occupational tensions within a given authority. In suggesting to public service employees that they are dispensable, it destroys the special relationship of mutual trust and loyalty which should exist between public servants and their political masters. As a result, all traces of the public service ethos will disappear (even in these areas where contracts have been awarded in-house) and the quality of public service work is likely to deteriorate. The tendering process also suggests that cost-cutting in the name of efficiency is more important to public sector work than effectiveness.[6] It demands that public administrators focus their attention on inputs (costs), rather than on the process (how employees are treated) or its outputs (how well a service is performed). This has serious organisational implications: local employees are no longer part of a team working for the benefit of the authority's client groups, but become part of independent units whose only objective is to complete the specific tasks set out in the in-house tender document within appropriate cost constraints.

This view also emphasises the serious social costs which are often overlooked in authorities' haste to cut spending. These social costs include the impact of redundancies, reductions in pay and conditions, less flexible working hours, heavier workloads and loss of job security.[7] Trade unions have argued that most of these losses must be borne by those individuals least able to afford it and least able to find alternative employment. Ancillary workers in the NHS and manual workers in local government are already at the lowest end of their respective pay scales. Most ancillary workers are women, the great majority of whom work on a part-time basis; many are recent immigrants to Britain or members of minority communities. Local government workers include many individuals who have found it difficult to get jobs elsewhere and have found refuge in public sector jobs. Competitive tendering in both sectors will send older, less 'marketable' and less able individuals to the dole queue; in doing so, it will undermine the public sector's traditional obligation to provide employment for those who cannot find it in the private sector.

Unlike the new right's followers, proponents of this view – including both the Labour Party and the trade union movement – are not convinced that contracting out reflects a major change in citizen preferences. They see the recent initiative as a naked political attack, a carefully crafted part of the Conservative Government's programme to reduce the size and scope of the welfare state. One union publication referred to it as an ideological offensive against the public sector and noted that 'some of the worst aspects of a rundown public service have been deliberately exploited in a propaganda effort to pave the way for dismantling the service and handing large chunks over to the private sector.'[8] According to the left, contracting out has been devised by the Government to remove the foremost obstacles in the path of Conservative ideology: local autonomy and workers' rights. The overtly political nature of the exercise indicates that it has no longer-term or structural significance and that when the attractiveness of the ideology disappears, so too will reliance on private contractors.

The presumption that there is a direct link between the Conservative Government's political or ideological objectives and its tendering initiative is correct. But in emphasising the intensity of the attack and the broad scope of the Government's designs, the left has problems in explaining why the Government did not opt for a mandatory contracting out policy. As noted in Chapter 6, both the contract service industries and Government backbenchers lobbied heavily for such a policy to be implemented at a realistic pace over an extended period. Both groups also suggested to the Government that in allowing local authorities to select their preferred method of provision, the weaker policy of competitive tendering would prevent significant inroads by the private sector and frustrate the objectives of the exercise.[9] Despite these clearly stated preferences for mandatory contracting out, the Government chose the 'gentler' tendering route. This suggests either that the Government's strategy was less ideologically single-minded than the left has claimed or that the Government recognised and attempted to minimise some of the significant social costs accompanying widespread contracting out.

Nor does the historical evolution of competitive tendering accord with the arguments of the left, which link it directly to the Conservative Government's desire to achieve its national political objectives by attacking local political interests. As Chapter 2 demonstrated, the origins of the present initiative lay not in developments at Conservative Central Office or at the Adam Smith Institute but in the events which occurred at Southend, Wandsworth and other local communities. They can also be found in events at the Ministry of Defence, whose very early interest in mandatory competitive tendering could not possibly have been borne of a desire to attack local political interests. Competitive tendering was not created as a means to achieve national political ends. It arose in response to localised developments and needs, becoming part of Conservative policy only after being given considerable exposure by local authorities and the MOD.

An assessment

Although the new right and traditional left views outlined above have played crucial and formative roles in shaping the present debate, neither perspective satisfactorily explains the significance of the debate itself. A more balanced assessment of recent events would look upon contracting out as a natural adjustment to an over-reliance on direct public provision. In order to understand the circumstances prompting this adjustment, it is necessary to consider the nature of in-house or direct provision more closely. Williamson, in analysing why some services are provided in the market (externally) and others hierarchically (internally), has identified five situations in which internal provision offers significant advantages over contracting in the market:

1   Where flexible sequential decision-making is needed to cope with uncertainties in the environment.

2 Where only a small number of competitors are present, and there is a likelihood of opportunistic and predatory pricing behaviour.

3 Where a divergence of expectations is likely to occur between the internal purchaser and the external seller.

4 Where operational or technological information gained from experience is likely to give one external supplier a strategic advantage over all others, thereby reducing competition.

5 Where a transaction-specific 'calculative relation' between parties is inappropriate and 'quasi-moral involvement' between those supplying and organising the service is necessary to effective provision.[10]

The presence of one or more of these conditions may result in a preference for internal provision, even where it is found to be a less cost-effective option than contracting out. Consider the case of major oil companies, many of whom have found that they can purchase oil on the spot market at a lower price than that which it costs them to produce it internally. Though the incentive is there to maximise profits by purchasing large quantities of oil on the open market and reducing the amount produced internally, few companies will do this because of the risks involved in reliance on external suppliers. The quality of the 'external' oil cannot be guaranteed and the firm is likely to lose the flexibility and security associated with being able to have as much oil as it wants when it wants it. Precisely the same risks are associated with the contracting out of certain public sector services. Privatising hospital cleaning, for example, may prevent the health authority from exerting direct control over the quality of the service provided. Some flexibility will be lost, as contractors must adhere to the specific wording of a contract and cannot be expected to change their methods of operation as a result of changes in the needs of either the ward sister or the patient. Security of supply becomes a concern, as contractors may be able to raise prices indiscriminately when it comes to re-tender for the contract or may withdraw during a contract leaving the hospital with no cleaning service.

These illustrations highlight the fact that in-house provision is generally associated with less risk and greater flexibility. But there are also certain dysfunctionalities which may be associated with in-house provision in any organisation. Leibenstein has used the term

'X-inefficiency' to describe the failure of firms to make maximum use of inputs (factors of production) in producing given levels of output. He emphasised the scope which employees have to pursue their own objectives and the fact that such personal utility-maximising behaviour will have a negative overall effect upon the productivity of the organisation as a whole.[11] Competition is important inasfar as it will circumscribe the extent of 'X-inefficiency', though it is unlikely to remove it altogether.

Williamson has also recognised the existence of sub-goal pursuit within organisations. He has outlined four specific distortions or 'biases' that may be associated with hierarchical or internal provision of a service:

1   *The internal procurement bias.* This refers to the tendency of organisations to use their own internal resources without comparing the costs of in-house resources to those on the open market. Where cost comparisons are undertaken, they may take into account only the variable or marginal costs of the transaction and ignore fixed costs altogether

2   *The internal expansion bias.* Because disputes within organisations are often settled by concessions being awarded to sub-units or divisions, the organisation as a whole tends toward continued growth. These expansionary tendencies may be reinforced by the association of financial or status awards with the size of either the unit or its budget.

3   *The programme persistence bias.* In many organisations, there is a strong tendency for established programmes to continue well beyond their useful lives. This usually results from inadequate review procedures, an unwillingness to entertain notions of failure, and a misguided assumption that a large part of the costs associated with the programme are 'sunk' or no longer relevant.

4   *The imperfect communication bias.* Imperfect, irrelevant or inappropriate information may frequently be used in making internal operating decisions. This can be the result of direct manipulation of the information network to promote personal goals; alternatively, it can be an unintentional by-product of interpersonal relationships as in the case of 'telling someone what they want to hear'.

Although these biases are common to internal provision in a range of organisations, the distortions they cause will vary from case to case. In some, the impact will be minimal and will clearly not offset the benefits associated with internalising service provision; in others, the distortions may have a significant and negative impact upon the performance of the organisation as a whole. In any case these problems are likely to become more pronounced as organisations become larger and more complex. Expansion of responsibilities generally leads to new administrative layers within an organisation; this is likely to introduce a higher degree of sub-goal pursuit and further distort existing networks of communication. Size can also bring with it bureaucratic insularity, as managers become somewhat divorced from the needs of the organisation and its clients and as the relationship which exists between senior management and the remainder of the workforce becomes less immediate. It may also result in a loss of discipline, as the personal costs of taking action against an unproductive worker will tend to outweigh the benefits likely to accrue to the firm from improved performance on his or her part.

While both Williamson's and Leibenstein's arguments have been directed specifically at firms in the marketplace, they are also relevant to other forms of hierarchical organisation and are of particular value in analysing service provision in the public sector. Public sector bureaucracies have displayed many of the distortions noted above, and the pursuit of sub-goals by public sector bureaucrats is particularly well documented.[12] Furthermore, the growth in the size and complexity of public sector organisations has indeed appeared to exacerbate the distortions inherent in their internal exchanges. Despite frequent changes of organisational form, particularly at central deparmental level, increasing layers of hierarchy and more complex lines of responsibility and accountability have resulted in very pronounced dysfunctionalities. Among the most visible of these have been severe overstaffing, slack purchasing behaviour, duplication of task and a general fragmentation of the policy-making process.

These inefficiencies, characteristic of many large organisations, have been particularly pronounced in the public sector due to the lack of competition from external sources. Whereas in the 1950s and 1960s a number of health and local authority functions were provided by the private sector, few if any remained in private hands by the early 1980s. The failure to consider private provision where appropriate has led to an over-dependence on direct provision and has allowed the trade unions to act as monopoly suppliers in certain situations, achieving wage rises without concomitant improvements in productivity and thus exacerbating existing inefficiencies. It is no coincidence that the first councils to privatise local services were those with among the worst productivity records and industrial relations problems.

It is in this context that one must view the recent trend away from internal or hierarchical provision. The speed which has characterised the growth of government organisations in this century has increased dependence upon, and thus exaggerated the distortions inherent in, internalised provision. This has spawned interest in contracting out and other private means of service provision, solutions which many believe can help to eliminate these distortions by reducing the size of the bureaucracy and introducing competition to stem efficiency losses. While these new alternatives clearly have certain advantages over direct provision, they are not in all cases preferable and there remain compelling reasons why many public services should be provided in-house (see Chapter 1). The suitability of both internal and external provision will vary from situation to situation, thus each service provision decision must be handled individually. The most likely outcome of this discrete form of decision-making in any organisation – be it public or private – is a mixture of service delivery modes; certain services will be provided internally and others will be resourced externally.[13] The balance between delivery modes may shift from time to time due to changes in the marketplace or to internal organisational changes, but it is unlikely to shift radically.

The concept of a balance between alternative modes of delivery is important, as it helps to explain the real significance of contracting out. Contracting out does not, as the new right suggests, represent a major and long-term shift in public preferences toward private provision. If it did, then the momentum for contracting out in local authorities would not have died as swiftly as it did. Nor is contracting out merely a 'policy boom' created by an ideological national government, as the trade unionists suggest. If so, it would hardly have begun in as motley an assortment of local authorities as it did. Contracting out must instead by seen as a natural adjustment to an over-reliance on public sector provision, a reaction to two decades of poor management and overly powerful trade unions.

Evaluating government policy

It is important to distinguish the rise of contracting out in local authorities from the appearance of compulsory tendering in the health service. Contracting out in local government arose naturally in response to significant and readily identifiable local service problems. It should not be viewed as a radical innovation or change of direction, but as one among many methods that local councils selected to improve the efficiency of their local services; other methods included natural wastage, revised manpower scheduling, revision of the existing bonus schemes and a reduction in the number of cleansing vehicles. The appeal of contracting out was primarily limited to a small number of councils which were unable to undertake these more traditional approaches to efficiency improvements due to a strong trade union presence. In nearly all areas, this union presence had fostered inefficiencies in service provision.

Together with the lack of an alternative remedy, the extent of these pre-existing inefficiencies helps to explain the apparent success of contracting out in nearly all of the local authorities in which it has been implemented. Although a number of councils experienced difficulties in making the switch to private contractors (primarily as a result of trade union action), most have reported improvements in both the standard and the flexibility of the service. Southend's renewal of its contract with Exclusive in 1985 suggests that many of these private arrangements will remain beyond the expiration of existing contracts. But privatising authorities are not the only ones to report improvements in service provision. Equally significant have been the dramatic improvements in the efficiency of in-house services across the country. Many are now in a much better position to compete against outsiders than they were five years ago and will not prove an easy target for private contractors if and when compulsory tendering legislation materialises.

Recent tendering activity in the NHS displays considerably different origins than its local authority counterpart. It is not the manifestation of an underlying trend, but the result of a carefully crafted government policy; indeed without government interference, it is unlikely that the NHS would have witnessed any significant organic growth in tendering activity. Evaluating the Government's initiative is difficult, as many authorities have yet to complete the tendering process and most of the contracts that have been awarded have only been operating a short time. But the difficulties in measuring success go beyond mere temporal constraints. Success can only be judged in terms of a certain set of objectives, and the criteria against which to measure the initiative's outputs are by no means clear. Examined against the Government's 'political' objectives of reducing the size of the state and neutralising the trade unions, the tendering policy appears to have achieved considerable success. Measured against criteria which take into account the standard of service provided to health authorities and the disruption to the hospital environment, the initiative appears somewhat less successful.

One issue which must be addressed in any evaluation of the Government's initiative is that of cost-savings. Mandatory tendering has clearly resulted in savings on a large scale, primarily from reductions in staffing, increased individual workloads, and a major shift from full-time to part-time labour. The actual level of cost savings has varied considerably from area to area. Some areas have cut costs by up to 50 per cent; others have made only incremental savings. Nevertheless, the scope of the health service initiative and the sheer number of hospitals involved are likely to ensure fairly sizeable aggregate savings totals in the less efficient NHS services (such as cleaning) by 1987.

Both individual and aggregate savings figures published by the Government should be handled with care, however. Authority calculations tend to reflect projected savings only, and many of the earlier projections by both health and local authorities have been shown to be hopelessly optimistic. There are also more fundamental problems with these savings figures. They fail to take into account many of the 'relevant costs' associated with the tendering process, including both administrative and transitional costs. The administrative costs of the process, which include the opportunity costs of administrative personnel undertaking tasks associated with individual tendering exercises, are considerable.[14] Transitional costs, both those associated with terminating in-house provision (e.g. interviewing staff, redeployment exercises, calculation of redundancy packages) and those associated with the commencement of a new private contract (e.g. explanation of hospital routines, 'teething troubles', development of new monitoring systems), have also been significant. Although not the only types of costs to be ignored in assessing the financial impact of the Government's initiative, these two alone are of sufficient magnitude and importance to suggest that the aggregate savings figures produced by the Government are not particularly accurate or meaningful.

The inadequate assessment of the relevant costs of the tendering process suggests a much more deeply-rooted problem with the Government's exercise: its overriding preoccupation with savings. The Government very specifically stated that a comparison of costs was to be the primary factor in awarding NHS contracts and demanded that the lowest tender was to be accepted in all but extraordinary circumstances. In doing so, it overlooked the protests of both the larger contractors (who viewed these lowest tender criteria as a recipe for price wars) and public administrators (who realised that such criteria removed a sizeable amount of local discretion). The Government's determination to make this rule apply has been demonstrated by its willingness to intervene in the decisions of authorities which have awarded contracts in-house at prices marginally higher than those proposed by an outside contractor.

This obsession with cost-minimisation, in assigning considerations of the quality and type of service needed a subordinate role in the tendering process, is both dangerous and short-sighted. One American municipal administrator noted:

> The problems of competitive bidding are best illustrated by a story attributed to John Glenn when he returned from the first manned space flight. A reporter asked what was the biggest danger in space travel. Supposedly, Glenn answered that it was being hundred of miles above the earth in a ship made up of 50 000 component parts, each purchased from the lowest bidder.[15]

This anecdote highlights the inevitable tension between cost and quality in purchasing decisions. Predicting changes in the quality of a particular service is clearly more difficult than forecasting changes in its cost, but it is equally important. Although some services lend themselves fairly easily to qualitative measurements, many do not. Domestic service provision in hospitals provides a good case in point. As noted in Chapter 6, NHS domestics have traditionally performed many non-cleaning duties. They have supported ward nurses when they have needed help in dealing with patients, they have provided cups of tea to clinical personnel, and they have contributed on a personal level to making patient stays more comfortable – all in addition to their normal cleaning duties. However, as a result of competitive tendering, the role and contribution of the domestic will change significantly. Domestics' individual routines are likely to become longer, leaving little or no free time for non-cleaning tasks. Hospitals will witness a dramatic shift to part-time work, itself less conducive to the development of patient-cleaner or patient-staff relationships than full-time arrangements. In cases where private contractors take over, the cleaner will no longer be directly accountable to the hospital organisation and is likely to remain somewhat divorced from it.

The hospital cleaning example is useful insofar as it sheds light on some of the confusion surrounding the question of whether contractors provide a 'better' or a 'worse' service. A private contractor taking over a hospital cleaning contract may perform at the standard of service laid down by the specification, but is unlikely to be able to provide the same kind of service as that previously provided by the in-house team. Both the hierarchical and lateral relationships enjoyed by the domestic cleaner will be different and, as a result, so too will his or her behaviour. In theory, this should result in an acceptable level of cleaning at a cheaper price, but without the 'extras'. Such an alternative may appeal to those hospitals which have pressing demands for financial resources in other areas; to others, however, the loss of flexibility and team spirit which contracting can entail will be unacceptable.

The hospital cleaning example raises another important issue concerning the quality of future services. Both competitive tendering and contracting out are likely to have considerable effects upon the public sector organisation as an operating unit. Competitive tendering tends to encourage narrow, short-term and functionally-orientated decision-making and militates against longer term strategic thinking. Where cleaning contracts have remained in-house, service managers are likely to become even more protective of their respective patches and less concerned with the needs of the organisation. Where cleaning contracts have been awarded externally, the needs of the hospital will clearly compete with the needs of the cleaning firm carrying out the contract. Both outcomes suggest a decline in the effectiveness of the hospital's operation as a unit. Although this organisational issue would seem to pose more significant problems for NHS hospitals than for local authorities, it is clearly relevant to both sectors. The best analogy is that of a corporation in which the competition between individual 'profit centres' leads to a sub-optimal level of profit for the organisation as a whole. This danger was emphasised by *The Financial Times* in response to the Government's circular on compulsory tendering for local authorities:

> If a local authority faces an overall financial constraint, its position is somewhat akin to that of a large corporation seeking to maximise overall profit. Large companies could put much of the work done by divisions or departments out to tender and make short-term savings. Often they do not because there are advantages in maintaining in-house expertise. If every activity undertaken by a corporation had to face the 'test of the market', big corporations as such would not exist.[16]

There is another qualitative issue which must be considered when evaluating the Government's initiative. Whereas the previous points dealt with changes in the quality of service outputs as a result of tendering, this third issue concerns changes in the quality of the service decision-making process itself. Mandatory competitive tendering has served to put further constraints upon a local agency's abilities to take realistic and logical decisions about the way its service should be run. Whereas previously service managers were unable to implement necessary changes because of the strength of local trade union interests, key managerial and operational decisions are now even more highly politicised and, as a result, are often based on even less rational criteria than they were before. This is an important change, and to understand it fully it is necessary to consider the impact that the Government's politicisation of the entire issue has had upon the major actors in the tendering drama.

Competitive tendering in the NHS has been viewed as a highly political Conservative crusade by all participants in the process (including the contractors) and the Government itself must take the blame for defining it that way. The ideological nature of the exercise was painfully evident in the hasty way that the policy itself was adopted. No pilot tests or trial runs were conducted, despite repeated pleas for such exercises by the contract service industries. Consultation with NHS administrators was so brief and ineffectual that it served only to insult and alienate large sections of the health service. Suggestions from contractors that an individual approach to each service was required were cast aside in favour of a uniform approach to all three ancillary services. The Fair Wages Resolution was withdrawn in spite of stiff opposition from health authorities, contractors, and trade unions. The highly political nature of the initiative was reinforced during the early stages of its implementation, when the Government publicly demanded timetables from reluctant authorities and attacked the behaviour of those which had adopted fair wages and other 'restrictive' clauses in their tendering documents. It overruled a number of awards to direct labour organisations, in most cases requiring the authority to re-award the contract to the lowest private sector bidder. In conjunction with these rulings, it sent letters to regional authorities informing them that they would be responsible for any 'suspicious' decisions at district level and that no contracts with private firms were to be terminated without prior consultation with the DHSS.

The perception of the Government's tendering initiative as an ideological crusade has had a significant impact upon the behaviour of three of the major interest groups involved in the NHS tendering process – contractors, trade unions and public administrators. The contract service industries felt that they were being 'used' by the Government to achieve its ideological aims; as the Managing Director of one of the most successful cleaning firms noted, 'we're just the meat in the sandwich'. This dissatisfaction with the Government's failure to take into account their needs and capabilities manifested itself in a number of significant ways. Contractors showed little or no interest in certain service sectors (e.g. catering) and became highly selective about their participation in others. Several of the most competent and oldest contract service firms (e.g. Grand Metropolitan and Trusthouse Forte) withdrew from all tendering in certain sectors, leaving public administrators mainly with newer and less experienced firms to choose from and precipitating loss-leader behaviour on a widespread scale. Contractors' dissatisfaction also manifested itself in a continuing stream of complaints to DHSS ministers about both real and perceived biases in the tendering process; this behaviour resulted in constant government intervention in both the procedural and substantive details of local decision-making.

The effects of the Government's political handling of the NHS exercise can also be seen in the activities of the trade unions. Just as the local unions had reacted violently to what they perceived as a localised political attack in Wandsworth, the national unions took a hard-line stance against what they saw as a comprehensive attempt to undermine their position in the NHS. The NHS tendering initiative became the focus of an intense campaign of opposition, one considerably larger and more sophisticated than those mounted to combat other privatisation initiatives in the NHS. A major 'smear campaign' was launched to discredit contractors, one which was fairly effective in 'scaring' public administrators away from private contractors. Union officials refused to cooperate in tendering exercises and localised industrial action was encouraged. These union strategies presented real difficulties for health service administrators, most of whom were keen to work with staff to develop an in-house tender.

The Government's political approach to the exercise had an equally significant effect upon the behaviour of NHS administrators. Although the great majority of functional managers (laundry, catering and cleaning) recognised a certain level of inefficiency in NHS services, few believed that a rigorous and uniform approach to the problem was an appropriate remedy. Their perception of the initiative as both a direct attack on ancillary workers and an indirect attack upon the health service as a whole fostered a more protective attitude toward staff than might otherwise have been the case. Many health administrators and health authority members who would normally have dismissed union opposition as an inevitable consequence of efficiency improvements took a conciliatory and sympathetic stance during the tendering exercises. This protective attitude manifested itself in two specific ways. Some individuals worked unusually hard to involve the in-house force in the tendering process, lobbying for extensions to the tendering deadline or devising elaborate consultative procedures. Others exhibited a subtle bias to retain in-house provision and gently manipulated the process in favour of that outcome. In both cases, the paternalistic feelings which arose in response to the Government's dictatorial approach caused health administrators to lose a measure of objectivity.

These three developments – dissatisfaction among contractors, intense trade union opposition, and the protective attitude shown by administrators – can all be traced back to the Government's political handling of the entire initiative. Together, they have had a significant effect upon the nature and outcome of NHS tendering exercises. Very few exercises have been carried out in a pragmatic, administrative fashion; most have involved considerable deviations from the 'normal' practice described in Chapter 5. In some cases, the authority has gone to considerable effort to placate the unions and put together a viable and acceptable in-house tender; in Hammersmith, for example, the authority twice delayed award of the contract to a private contractor in hopes that an in-house compromise could be reached. In other cases, the rules governing the tendering process or the specification itself have been adjusted to improve the competitive position of the in-house team; in North West Hertfordshire, for example, the decision to ask contractors to quote for work done on their own premises ensured higher bid prices from contractors than if they had been allowed to quote for work done on hospital premises with existing equipment. And in a third set of cases, the Government has intervened to overrule the award made by the authority's adjudication panel; in Norwich, for example, the authority's decision to award a major cleaning contract in-house was overruled by the minister on the grounds that the 'compelling reasons' put forward by the authority for keeping the service in-house were unacceptable.

In summary, the events which have occurred in the NHS flatly contradict Government claims that tendering has been carried out in a commercial fashion. The Government's ideological approach and highly political methods of implementation have resulted in a collection of tendering exercises governed not by the rules of the tendering process but by the dynamic interaction of local interest groups, personalities, political preferences and government intervention. Many authorities which have contracted out took this path because the in-house team would not cooperate, and *not* because private provision offered a more cost-effective alternative.

Similarly, many of those that have awarded contracts in-house have done so for political reasons, *not* because direct labour proved the more cost-effective option. Only in a minority of cases have the service needs of the health authority or the true economics of the situation been the primary factor in determining the outcome of tendering decisions. Not only does this behaviour totally undermine the foundations upon which the tendering initiative has been based, but it also suggests that health authorities may yet be selecting methods of service provision that are not consistent with their technical needs.

The changes in the nature of NHS decision-making which have resulted from the Government's initiative are illustrated most clearly by examining recent events against the theoretical framework laid out earlier for organisational decision-making of this type. It has been argued that no one method of service provision is inherently better than another and that the effectiveness of both internal and external provision will depend upon the circumstances in which they are employed. Each organisation, and indeed each service that comes under that organisation's umbrella, may require a slightly different approach. Selecting that approach requires a careful consideration of both the nature of the organisation and the needs of the service at hand, as well as a realistic assessment of both the advantages and disadvantages of alternative modes of provision.

To a large extent this is self-evident, and it is indeed the approach that was taken in health authorities in Britain in the years preceding the growth of public sector union militancy. Reference has already been made to the fact that many authorities (including the Royal Bethlem and Maudsley SHA) at one time or another found in-house provision unsatisfactory and switched – for some very good reasons – to private contractual arrangements. These informal but realistic comparisons between in-house and external provision stopped in the mid- to late 1970s and inefficiencies appeared in many NHS services. This spawned government interest in competitive tendering as a means to reduce inefficiency. But those who viewed the Government's espousal of competitive tendering as the vehicle that would allow them to return to the days of greater flexibility, stronger management, and more appropriate service provision solutions have been bitterly disappointed. The NHS initiative has simply replaced union-imposed constraints with government-imposed ones. The criteria to be used in service provision decisions have been tightly circumscribed; in some cases the decision-making process itself has been pre-empted by central interference. The high level of politicisation surrounding the initiative has prompted sharp political reactions at local level and has resulted in a series of decisions that say more about the relative strength of local interest groups than they do about the needs and objectives of individual health authorities.

Concluding remarks

Two significant conclusions can be drawn from the events documented in previous chapters. The first is that both contracting out and competitive tendering appear to work most smoothly (in terms of both procedures and outputs) in non-political environments. Their success has been visible in America, where both Republican and Democratic-controlled cities have treated the techniques as technical tools in solving local service problems, and in Britain, where a number of authorities have been successfully tendering and contracting out for many years. But Britain has also witnessed the dangers of highly politicised tendering processes. Events in both Wandsworth and the NHS suggest that once these techniques are adopted as political rather than as technical solutions, their perceived objectivity disappears and with it goes much of their effectiveness. The great irony of the British local government experience is that it has generally been the highly politicised areas that have been most desperate for the efficiency improvements that the tendering process can bring.

A second and related conclusion is that both competitive tendering and contracting out are most effective when they arise naturally in response to local needs. There is considerable evidence that competitive tendering has been more effective in local authorities, where the initiative for tendering came primarily from the 'bottom-up', than it has been in the NHS, where the motivation for tendering came from the 'top-down'. Not only have projected savings in the local authority sector been considerably higher than those in the NHS, but local authority exercises have generally been much less disruptive to administrative life than those in the health service. Both local authorities which awarded contracts in-house and those which awarded them externally are satisfied with the current standard of service and report no long-term undesirable effects upon the organisation. Although it is too early to draw conclusions about the quality of recent NHS service provision decisions, it is already obvious that the organisational effects of both tendering and contracting out have been significant in many areas. As one hospital administrator reported: 'Morale has gone way down and there's no leadership. People are out to get what they can for themselves.'

These two conclusions suggest that centralised policy initiatives are unlikely to offer comprehensive answers to local problems, particularly when implemented in an overtly political and ideological fashion. Although local decision-making is itself politicised, pre-empting the right to take these decisions locally *will inevitably* make decisions more controversial. It follows that local solutions, while not always ideal, are likely to be more effective than nationally imposed ones. Local agencies have different priorities, generated by different citizen preferences and needs; as a result they will want to make different trade-offs between cost and quality, for example, or between efficiency and effectiveness. These preferences will only be manifest if the authority has the right to select the type of service it believes best meets the needs of the community.

The highly political nature of competitive tendering in Britain suggests that its future as government policy will be determined by the outcome of the next general election. If a Conservative government is returned to power, it is likely that compulsory tendering in local authorities will be implemented with much the same gusto as the NHS initiative. But this second major tendering programme is likely to be characterised by considerably less controversy than that which accompanied its predecessor. Not only has more care been given to the responses to the DOE's consultative document, but local authorities have had more time to prepare for these exercises than their NHS counterparts did. Preliminary soundings from local government sources suggest that authorities are already 'putting their house in order' in anticipation of the relevant legislation.

It is less clear what will occur if either a Labour or a SDP/Liberal Alliance government wins the next election. In the few pioneering local authorities that have seen a switch from Conservative to Labour control, the trend has been to bring privately contracted services back in-house. This is relatively easy to do on a small scale but much more difficult to carry out on a national scale, particularly when thousands of health service contracts are involved. It is thus unlikely that even a radical Labour government would attempt such a programme. A Labour administration might instead attempt to boost the competitive position of direct labour forces by encouraging alternative forms of provision (such as workers' cooperatives or joint ventures) or by allowing direct labour organisations to compete for work in the private sector – something that the Conservative Government has consistently refused to sanction.

Whatever the result of the next election, it is unlikely that competitive tendering will disappear as rapidly as it arose. Financial constraints on local authorities are likely to remain, and pressures for cost-savings will continue to exist. Even authorities who prefer to maintain in-house control may find tendering the easiest way to keep a check on the efficiency and relative productivity of their in-house force. Contracting out is also likely to remain, not as a permanent substitute for direct provision, but as an alternative. American municipal administrators with significant experience of managing private contracts reportedly live by the creed: 'Anything a city is doing in-house ought to be contracted, anything contracted should be done in-house, and every five years you should switch.'[17] The point is not that there is any inherent advantage in alternating modes of provision, but that services which remain unchanged for long periods of time are likely to become inefficient and unresponsive to citizen needs.

Competitive tendering activity in Britain has confirmed that considerable scope for improvement in local services did indeed exist and that new approaches to service delivery were needed. But it has not served to demonstrate the virtues of the private sector over the public sector, as many Government supporters had hoped it would. Instead it has highlighted the need for more flexible and realistic approaches to service provision at local level, ones which take into account both the nature of the providing organisation and the needs of the community it serves. The real significance of Conservative policy lies not in the economic savings it has produced, but in the lessons it has taught about the need for better and stronger management in both the health service and local government.

Guide to Further Reading

Contracting out and competitive tendering

Most of the literature on contracting out has been published by interest groups active in the present debate and is therefore highly partisan. Three publications in support of contracting out have come from the Adam Smith Institute in London: *Privatization* by M. Pirie (1985); *Reservicing Britain* by M. Forsyth (1980); and *Reservicing Health* by M. Forsyth (1982). A fourth pamphlet which advocates tendering and contracting out in the health service was published by the Tory Reform Group in 1984; see *High Noon in the National Health Service* (London: Tory Reform Group, 1984). Two pamphlets presenting opposing views are *Public or Private* (London: Labour Research Department, 1982) and *Privatisation: Who Loses? Who Wins?* (London: Labour Research Department, 1983). For a survey of initial health authority reactions to the government's initiative, see *Contracting Out 'Ancillary' Services: The Health Authority View* (London: NHS Unlimited, 1984). A comprehensive summary of contractors 'failures', as defined by the trade unions, can be found in *Contractors' Failures: The Privatisation Experience* (London: TUC, 1984). Less partisan views on the issues surrounding contracting out and competitive tendering can be found in *Contracting Out in the Public Sector* (London: RIPA, 1984). The best guides to the tendering process in local authorities and the NHS respectively are *Management Guide to Contracting Out Services in Local Government* (London: CIPFA, 1984) and Thornton Baker, *Health Services Management*, (London: Nuffield Provincial Hospitals Trust, 1984).

The American experience

Useful works on approaches to local services delivery include S. Sonnenblum, J. Kirlin and J. Rees, *How Cities Provide Services: An Evaluation of Alternative Delivery Systems* (Cambridge, Mass.: Ballinger, 1977) and E. S. Savas, *The Organisation and Efficiency of Solid Waste Collection* (Lexington, Mass.: Lexington Books, 1977). Two publications by the Urban Institute offer comprehensive surveys of existing practices; see D. Fisk, H. Kiesling and T. Muller, *Private Provision of Public Services: An Overview* (Washington, D.C.: The Urban Institute Press, 1978) and *A*

Review of Private Approaches for the Delivery of Public Services by H. Hatry (Washington, D.C.: The Urban Institute Press, 1983). For a practitioner's guide to municipal contracting out, see H. E. Wesemann, *Contracting for City Services* (Pittsburgh: Innovations Press, 1981).

The contract service industries

Information on the contract cleaning industry can be found in *Contract Cleaning: Keynote Report* (London: Keynote Publications, 1985). The best sources of information about the textile maintenance industry are two Monopolies and Mergers Commission reports, *The British Electric Traction Company PLC and Initial PLC: A Report on the Proposed Merger*, Cmnd 9444 (London: HMSO, 1985) and *The Sunlight Service Group and Johnson Group Cleaners PLC and Initial PLC and Johnson Group Cleaners PLC: A Report on the Proposed Mergers*, Cmnd 8868 (London: HMSO, 1983). Comprehensive data on the contract catering industry is not available due to the number of small catering firms, but estimates of market size and a description of some of the major catering firms can be found in *Contract Catering: Keynote Report* (London: Keynote Publications, 1985). Further information on individual contractors can be found in their respective annual reports and in records kept at Companies House in London.

The NHS

A good introduction to the history and structure of the NHS and to issues facing the health service can be found in *Understanding the NHS in the 1980s* (London: Office of Health Economics, 1984). Further discussion of these issues is contained in the *Sixth Report from the Social Service Committee*, Session 1984–5 (London: HMSO, 1985). Statistical information about health service expenditure and manpower is available in the *Compendium of Health Service Statistics, 5th Edition* (London: Office of Health Economics, 1984), in *Health Service Costing Returns*, published annually by the DHSS and Welsh Office, and in *Joint Manpower Watch Returns*, published quarterly by the Joint Manpower Watch Group.

Local government

The subject of local government expenditure is addressed comprehensively in K. Newton and T. J. Karran, *The Politics of Local Expenditure* (London: Macmillan, 1985). Statistics on local expenditure can be found in *Finance and General Statistics* produced annually by CIPFA in London.

Local policy-making processes and trends in British local government are placed in an analytical framework in P. J. Dunleavy, *Urban Political Analysis* (London: Macmillan, 1980). For a critical assessment of local service provision, see Coopers & Lybrand, *Service Provision and Pricing* (London: HMSO, 1981). More detailed information about trends in refuse collection services is available in *Securing Further Improvements in Refuse Collection*, Audit Commission (London: HMSO, 1984).

Current developments

The best sources for monitoring the contracting out debate are also the most highly partisan. *Public Service Action*, a monthly newsletter published by SCAT Publications (London), presents the trade union viewpoint on contracting out and a range of other privatisation issues. *Public Service Review*, which is published by the Public Service Research Centre (London), has followed the format of *Public Service Action* and presents the views of the new right and contractors on developments in this area. Less partisan sources of information about recent developments include the weekly journals *Local Government Chronicle*, the *Health Service Journal* (formerly *Health and Social Service Journal*) and *Laundry and Cleaning News*, as well as a quarterly journal entitled *Contract Services*.

Notes and References

1 An Introduction to Contracting Out

1. M. Pirie, *Privatization* (London: Adam Smith Institute, 1985), p. 21.
2. Information on asset sales can be found in *Privatisation in the United Kingdom*, Background Briefing (London: HM Treasury, 1985).
3. Pirie, *Privatization*, p. 90.
4. See D. Heald and G. Morris, 'Why Public Sector Unions Are on the Defensive', *Personnel Management* (May 1984), 30–4.
5. See S. Sonnenblum, J. Kirlin and J. Ries, *How Cities Provide Services: An Evaluation of Alternative Delivery Systems* (Cambridge, Mass.: Ballinger, 1977).
6. P. J. Dunleavy, 'Explaining the Privatisation Boom: Public Choice versus Radical Approaches', *Public Administration*, 64 (Spring 1986), 13–34.
7. A further description of the changes in American municipal government in the 1970s can be found in H. E. Wesemann, *Contracting for City Services* (Pittsburgh: Innovations Press, 1981).
8. Competitive tendering was pioneered in Phoenix, Arizona where city agencies competed against private firms for custodial services, trash collection and street landscaping. In several cases, the city was divided up into districts which were bid for separately. H. P. Hatry, *A Review of Private Approaches for Delivery of Public Services* (Washington, D.C.: The Urban Institute Press, 1983).
9. Information on the Connecticut study can be found in P. Kemper and J. M. Quigley, *The Economics of Refuse Collection* (Cambridge, Mass.: Ballinger, 1976). The Columbia University study findings are summarised in E. S. Savas, 'Policy Analysis for Local Government: Public versus Private Refuse Collection', *Policy Analysis* (Winter 1977), 49–74.
10. The earlier St Louis study was described in W. Z. Hirsch, 'Cost Functions for an Urban Government Service: Refuse Collection', *The Review of Economics and Statistics*, 47 (February 1965), 87–92. For details of the later study, see J. N. Collins and B. T. Downes, 'The Effects of Size on the Provision of Public Services: The Case of Solid Waste Collection in Smaller Cities', *Urban Affairs Quarterly*, 12 (March 1977), 333–47.
11. W. J. Pier, R. B. Vernon, and J. H. Wicks, 'An Empirical Comparison of Government and Private Production Efficiency', *National Tax Journal*, 27 (December 1974), 653–6.

12. Many of the studies undertaken in the US, including the study undertaken by Hirsch in 1965 and the Pier, Vernon and Wicks study completed in 1974, do not themselves distinguish between the various types of non-governmental collection (contract, franchised or private). A fairly recent study of a large sample of US cities with populations over 2500 showed that 37 per cent relied on municipal collection, 21 per cent on contract collection, 7 per cent on franchised collection and 38 per cent on private collection. E. S. Savas *The Organization and Efficiency of Solid Waste Collection* (Lexington, Mass.: Lexington Books, 1977).
13. M. Forsyth, *Reservicing Health* (London: Adam Smith Institute, 1982), p. 14.
14. Hatry, *A Review of Private Approaches for Delivery of Public Services* pp. 18–19.
15. *Hospitals*, 58 (1 September 1984), 50.
16. D. Fisk, H. Kiesling and T. Muller, *Private Provision of Public Services: An Overview* (Washington, D.C.: The Urban Institute, Press 1978).
17. Further details of this study are given in Hatry, *A Review of Private Approaches for Delivery of Public Services*, pp. 16–17.
18. Ibid., p. 24.
19. A study covering 48 Canadian cities with populations above 10 000 showed that municipal collection was generally more expensive than collection by private firms. H.M. Kitchen, 'A Statistical Estimation of an Operating Cost Function for Municipal Refuse Collection', *Public Finance Quarterly*, 4 (January 1976), 56–76.
20. See J. T. Marlin, *Privatisation of Local Government Activities: Lessons from Japan* (London: Aims of Industry, 1984).
21. Forsyth, *Reservicing Health*, p. 15.

2 Conservative Policy: Development and Dimensions

1. *British Hospital and Social Service Journal* (24 January 1964), p. 109.
2. Circular 72(56), issued in 1972, announced that contractual arrangements were to be seen as an integral part of providing hospital services. *British Medical Journal*, 284 (3 April 1982), p. 1060.
3. Forsyth included in his definition of hotel services the following areas: catering, portering, cleaning, linen services, personnel, estate management, security, building maintenance, pest control, engineering, plumbing and architectural services. See M. Forsyth, *Reservicing Health* (London: Adam Smith Institute, 1982).
4. The Ministry of Defence experience suggested savings of 20 per cent, but the DHSS study team noted that the health service could realistically expect only 10 per cent savings. For further details see *High Noon in the National Health Service* (London: Tory Reform Group, 1984), pp. 18–20.
5. *Health & Social Service Journal*, XCIII (24 February 1983), p. 229.
6. *Contracting Out 'Ancillary' Services: The Health Authority View*, Memorandum 7 (London: NHS Unlimited, 1984), p. 2.

7. *The Challenge of Our Times*, Election Manifesto (London: Conservative Party, 1983).
8. *Contracting Out 'Ancillary' Services: The Health Authority View*, p. 55.
9. WHC (83) 24 is the Welsh Office equivalent of HC (83) and was issued simultaneously. The Scottish Office did not issue a similar directive at this time. Instead it asked regional health boards to test the efficiency of various services and report back to Minister John Mackay in March 1984.
10. Exclusive's tender suggested that it would charge the council an additional £15 for each 100 new properties built. Six months into the contract, in October 1981, the company announced that this figure was a mistake and that it would charge £15 per new house. The cost of this error was calculated to be £6000 per annum or £30 000 over the lifetime of the contract. *Public or Private* (London: Labour Research Department, 1982), p. 20.
11. The Director of Technical Services at West Lindsey District Council (Independent control) reported to his authority that Exclusive's savings figure of £492 000 in Southend was exaggerated by a factor of 10 and that the true savings came to approximately £45 000. He added that if the council had doubled its waste charges to commercial clients, as Exclusive had done, direct labour would have proven marginally cheaper than the contractor. Ibid., p. 20.
12. The 5 per cent return on capital target was to be based on current cost accounting methods. Under powers given in the Act, the proportion of DLO work for which tendering is required has been progressively increased. As of 1985, councils were required to invite competition for 100 per cent of all new building works over £50 000 and all maintenance jobs over £10 000, for 60 per cent of new works under £50 000 and maintenance under £10 000, and for 30 per cent of all general highway work.
13. For details of the effect that the 1980 legislation had upon local council's direct labour forces, see *Public Service Action*, 6, 9, and 13 (February and August 1984, February 1985).
14. UK examples used by Forsyth in *Reservicing Britain* included privatised window cleaning in Hull schools, private cleaning contractors in Salisbury District Council's offices, and privatised refuse collection in Southend. M. Forsyth, *Reservicing Britain* (London: Adam Smith Institute, 1980).
15. Coopers & Lybrand, *Service Provision and Pricing* (London: HMSO, 1981).
16. There were several reports that Coopers and Lybrand's endorsement of a flexible approach to service provision came as a disappointment to the Government. The *New Statesman* reported that the Conservative Party had delayed the document's publication and sent only 25 copies to the press for this reason. *New Statesman*, 103 (5 February 1982), p. 6.
17. *Hansard*, vol. 57, 27 March 1984, col. 137–8. DOE officals report that

they were surprised by the Prime Minister's comment, as the necessary legislation would not be particularly technical or complex.

18. *Hansard*, vol. 57, 3 April 1984, col. 820–7.
19. *Local Government Chronicle*, 6046 (29 March 1985), p. 372.
20. This view was specifically put forward by the Association of District Secretaries in their response to the consultative document. *Local Government Chronicle*, 6055 (31 May 1985), p. 604.
21. *The Financial Times*, 15 February 1985.
22. *Guardian*, 15 February 1985.
23. *Hansard*, vol. 74, 4 March 1985, col. 746. The deadline for tendering of catering services is April 1988.
24. These figures are incomplete and should therefore be treated as indicative only. It is unclear, for example, whether departmental catering run by CISCO (Civil Service Catering Organisation) is treated as direct or indirect provision.
25. This includes savings from some efficiency improvements as well, the largest of which is a £2 million annual savings from new work procedures implemented at the Postal Sorting Office at Kew.
26. For details of manpower 'savings' across the civil service, see *Treasury and Civil Service Committee Report 1985*, n. 6, p. 22.
27. Unions are being consulted on all aspects of the policy's development and the Treasury is in the process of formulating standard consultative procedures which will apply across all departments.
28. *The Economist*, 288 (17 September 1983), p. 53.
29. *Omega Project Report on Local Government* (London: Adam Smith Institute, 1983).
30. This pamphlet argued that the Government should change its policy to one of mandatory contracting out because 'the contest is being systematically rigged against contractors in favour of the in-house tenders' and 'contractors are becoming discouraged and will soon become more selective about tenders'. *High Noon in the National Health Service*, p. 4.
31. A motion supporting privatisation in these circumstances was passed at the 1983 Liberal Party conference in Harrogate. Similar views were put forward at this time by David Owen, leader of the Social Democratic Party, who noted: 'There is no reason why British Rail catering services should not be put out to competition and there is no need to assume that the NHS has to run all its own laundries.' *Public Service Review*, 1 (1983), p. 3.

3 The Contract Service Industries

1. *Flooring and Carpet Specifier*, 15 (August 1970), p. 14.
2. *Purchasing Guide*, 28 (August 1971), p. 43.
3. Ibid., p. 43.
4. A recent report on the contract cleaning industry by Keynote Publications concluded that: 'Owing to the lack of statistical evidence it is not

possible to conclude whether the market is expanding, static or shrinking.' *Contract Cleaning: Keynote Report* (London: Keynote Publications, 1985).

5. A survey of the health care section of the CCMA in 1983 revealed that 52 per cent of the member companies claimed national coverage, while 48 per cent were limited to specific regions. Of those with regional coverage only, 72 per cent were based in London and the South-east.

6. W. Goldsmith and D. Clutterbuck, *The Winning Steak* (London: Weidenfeld and Nicolson, 1984), p. 78.

7. The National Federation of Launderers became the Institution of British Launderers in the 1930s, and the Institute of British Launderers in 1955. The name was later changed to the Association of British Launderers and Cleaners (ABLC) which merged with the British Textile Rental Association (BTRA) to form the Association of British Laundry, Cleaning and Rental Services (ABLCRS) in 1984.

8. A summary of the history of three of the leading companies in the textile maintenance industry – Sunlight, Initial and Johnson – can be found in Monopolies and Mergers Commission, *The Sunlight Service Group PLC and Johnson Group Cleaners PLC and Initial PLC and Johnson Group Cleaners PLC: A Report on the Proposed Mergers*, Cmnd 8868 (London: HMSO, 1983).

9. The most recent review of activities in these markets is contained in Monopolies and Mergers Commission, *The British Electric Traction Company PLC and Initial PLC: A Report on the Proposed Merger*, Cmnd 9444 (London: HMSO, 1985).

10. Sunlight itself had attempted to take over Spring Grove. It lost out to Pritchard Services, but later acquired the St George's division of Spring Grove from Pritchard. While its attempted takeover of Spring Grove was underway, Sunlight itself was the subject of a takeover move by Brengreen. Referred to as 'probably the toughest battle recently in the cleaning industry', the attempt left Brengreen with only a 14 per cent acceptance rate. *Laundry and Cleaning News* (17 August 1984), p. 9.

11. A more comprehensive analysis of the contract catering industry can be found in *Contract Catering: Key Note Report* (London: Keynote Publications, 1985).

12. Trusthouse Forte is well-known for its dedicated approach to training and management development. All management training is tied directly to the achievement of business objectives, and all courses are assessed rigorously to ensure that they closely reflect corporate needs. Further details of its approach are given in K. Ascher, *Management Training in Large UK Business Organisations* (London: Harbridge House, 1983), p. 61.

13. At the start of the Government's competitive tendering initiative in 1983, contract caterers serviced the Bethlem Royal and Maudsley Hospitals in London and Beckenham, Kent respectively (Bethlem Royal and Maudsley SHA) and the Ellen Terry Home in Reigate (Merton and Sutton Health Authority).

14. In November 1985 the Government raised the national insurance threshold from £35.50 to £38 per week. Contract cleaners paying NHS wage rates of £1.90, for example, could thus employ workers for up to 20 hours a week (at basic rate) without being eligible for national insurance payments. *Autumn Statement 1985* (London: H.M. Treasury, 1985), p. 32.

15. Academy Cleaning and I.C.C., for example, were dismissed from school cleaning contracts in late 1984 only months after their respective contracts in Merton and Birmingham had begun. Hospital Hygiene Services was dismissed from a cleaning contract at Bromley Hospital in Bromley Health Authority; Allied Medical Catering withdrew from its catering contract at Farnham Hospital after only three months.

16. Much of the information contained in the following section can be found in the annual reports of the respective companies.

17. Goldsmith and Clutterbuck, *The Winning Streak*.

18. In 1984–5, the Hawley Group was ranked 390 in the Times Top 1000 listing, having risen from a rank of 703 in 1983–4. *The Times Top 1000*, (London: Times Books, 1984).

19. The Monopolies and Mergers Commission approved BET's acquisition of the outstanding 58 per cent share of Initial on the grounds that any detrimental effects upon competition caused by BET's control over both Initial and Advance already existed because of its 42 per cent shareholding in Initial, and that increasing this to 100 per cent would not have any further negative impact upon the public interest.

20. A detailed description of the activities of both Initial and Advance can be found in Monopolies and Mergers Commission, *The British Electric Traction Company PLC and Initial PLC: A Report on the Proposed Merger.*

21. For a comprehensive summary of Sunlight's development see Monopolies and Mergers Commission, *The Sunlight Service Group PLC and Johnson Group Cleaners PLC and Initial PLC and Johnson Group Cleaners PLC: A Report on the Proposed Mergers*, ch. 3.

22. *Cleaning Companies*, Philips & Drew Industry Research (March 1984), p. 15.

4 The Trade Union Response

1. For a general description of industrial relations in the UK following World War II, see chapter 1 in Colin Crouch's *The Politics of Industrial Relations* (London: Fontana Collins, 1979).

2. David Heald and Gillian Morris, 'Why Public Sector Unions are on the Defensive', *Personnel Management* (May 1984), 30–4.

3. See R. F. Elliott and J. L. Fallick, *Pay in the Public Sector* (London: Macmillan, 1981), p. 158–9.

4. *Annual Reports*, Trades Union Congress, 1970 and 1975.

5. *Health and Social Service Journal*, xcii (3 June 1982), p. 664.

6. *Local Government Chronicle*, 6042 (18 March 1983), p. 300.

7. *Annual Reports*, Trades Union Congress, 1982 and 1984.

8. The laws governing redundancy entitlement in the NHS can be found in Section 111 of the Employment Protection Consolidation Act 1978. Workers who accept a job in the NHS within four weeks of being made redundant are not entitled to redundancy payments; those who accept a job with the contractor remain eligible. Payments are determined by the length of service and age of employee.

9. This survey, conducted by Michael Meacher (Opposition Spokesman on Social Services), showed that estimated savings per employee stood at £3400, but that the loss of tax and cost of additional social service benefits per individual totalled £7000, both on an annual basis.

10. In 1979, the Government's Chief Inspector of Audit noted: 'Many bonus schemes have become little more than a complicated and expensive method of calculating a man's pay and have weakened local authority's financial control over an important part of their budget.' The Audit Commission, *Securing Further Improvements in Refuse Collection*, (London: HMSO, 1984), p. 19.

11. Conditions for part-time workers in the NHS are calculated in the proportion which their part time hours are to 40.

12. *Hansard*, vol. 70, 21 December 1984, col. 746.

13. *Local Government Chronicle*, 6158 (21 June 1985), p. 708.

14. A detailed explanation of the union's approach can be found in 'Privatisation: A Negotiator's Guide to Specifications and Tenders', COHSE (9 May 1985).

15. *The Truth on the Smear Campaign Against Contract Cleaning* (London: Aims of Industry, 1985), pp. 2–5.

16. P. Ainsworth, 'Contracting Out ... The Only Way Forward', *Crossbow* (Winter 1984/85), p. 21.

17. The document reported that nine firms had filed no accounts, another nine filed accounts which broke the law, six were not registered as companies, and three did not trade. *Would You 'Approve' This Lot?* (West Midlands Regional TUC Health Service Coordinating Committee, 1984).

18. One example of this testimony was published by London Health Emergency in 1984. Entitled 'I Was a Mole in Mediclean', it recounts the experiences and impressions of a member of the Health Emergency Steering Committee during her stint as an employee on Mediclean's contract at St Helier Hospital (Merton and Sutton District Health Authority).

19. Details of the Basingstoke campaign can be found in *Public Service Action*, 1 (March 1983). Information on the Coventry alliance is contained in issues 5 and 9 of *Public Service Action*, (November/December 1983 and August 1984).

20. *Nursing Times*, (30 May 1984), p. 19.

21. *Public Service Action*, 5 (November/December 1983), p. 4.

22. COHSE, 'Campaign Bulletin Privatisation – 1' (8 March 1984), p. 1.

5 The Mechanics of Competitive Tendering

1. See K. Hartley, 'Policy Towards Contracting Out: The Lessons of Experience', *Fiscal Studies* 5 (February 1984), 98–105.

2. *Health Services Management*, prepared by Thornton Baker Associates for the Nuffield Provincial Hospitals Trust (London) in 1984, gives a detailed breakdown of the NHS tendering process and focuses specifically on the responsibilities which should be assigned to functional areas and general management. A similar guide for local authority officals, entitled *Management Guide to Contracting Out Services in Local Government*, was produced jointly by the Chartered Institute of Public Finance and Accountancy (CIPFA) and the Public Sector Economics Research Centre at the University of Leicester in 1984.

3. *Health and Social Service Journal*, XCIV (27 June 1985), p. 807.

4. See H. E. Wesemann, *Contracting for City Services* (Pittsburgh: Innovations Press, 1981), p. 61.

5. It should be noted that the 'avoidable costs' which form the basis of an in-house tender are not the costs of the *existing* service, but the costs of the *projected* one. Any savings that can be made on present practices, particularly in the area of labour deployment, would therefore be taken into account. The issue of avoidable costs is examined in greater depth in CIPFA's *Management Guide to Contracting Out Services in Local Government* (London: CIPFA, 1984).

6. A good discussion of the conceptual and practical difficulties involved in calculating capital costs can be found in 'Contracting Out: Relevent Costs and Decision Criteria', an article by Cyril Tomkins in *Contracting Out in the Public Sector* (London; Royal Institute of Public Administration, 1984).

7. Although the Government began refunding VAT on service contracts to health authorities in 1983, it must continue to pay the European Community levy of 1 per cent and has suggested that authorities take this into account in calculating the financial effects of contracting out.

8. Wesemann, *Contracting for City Services*, p. 83.

9. *Notes on Monitoring and Specifications for Domestic Service Contracts*, Domestic Services Management Branch, DHSS (March 1985), p. 1.

10. Wesemann, *Contracting for City Services*, p. 81.

11. DHSS, *Notes on Monitoring and Specifications for Domestic Service Contracts*, p. 1.

12. The DHSS has asked authorities to follow the guidelines outlined by the Treasury in its publication *Investment Appraisal in the Public Sector*; this recommends the depreciation of major assets over a 20-year period. Because these guideliness are not mandatory, there is a move afoot within the health service to incorporate capital costs into district authority accounts. In a paper produced in 1985 and entitled 'Managing Capital Assets in the NHS', the Association of Health Service Treasurers suggested that regions charge districts for the use of capital assets to bring NHS investment criteria into line with the private sector.

13. DHSS, *Competitive Tendering in the Provision of Domestic, Catering and Laundry Services*, HC (83) 18, Annex to Appendix 1.

6　Competitive Tendering in the NHS

1. A comprehensive account of the 1974 reorganisation can be found in Ruth Leavitt's *The Reorganised National Health Service* (London: Croom Helm, 1976).

2. *Understanding the NHS in the 1980s* (London: Office of Health Economics, 1984), 19. This booklet offers a useful summary of the history and current structure of the NHS.

3. Information on domestic production and government expenditure can be found in *United Kingdom National Accounts: 1985 Edition*, Central Statistical Office (London: HMSO, 1985) and *The Government's Expenditure Plans 1986–87 to 1988–89, Volume II*, Cmnd 9702–II (London: HM Treasury, January 1986) respectively. For more detailed statistical data concerning the NHS, see *Compendium of Health Statistics, 5th Edition* (London: Office of Health Economics, 1984).

4. *Sixth Report from The Social Services Committee*, Session 1984–85 (London: HMSO, 1985), p. 39.

5. This would represent approximately 75 000 whole-time equivalent (adjusted for Scotland, Northern Ireland and Wales), based on figures in *Health and Personal Social Services Statistics for England – 1985 Edition* (London: HMSO, 1985), p. 48.

6. *British Hospital and Social Service Journal* (24 January 1964), p. 106.

7. The Nuffield Orthopaedic Centre was among the first to put its domestic services out to contract in 1961. Its specification was inadequate and plagued by ill-defined wording. When it came to re-tendering in 1983, according to one senior sister at the hospital, 'An adminstrator decided that we had to start from scratch. The old format was not even considered.' *Nursing Times* (8 August 1984), p. 59.

8. This figure is calculated from estimates of whole time equivalents, adjusted according to the ratio of full-time to part-time workers. See *High Noon in the National Health Service* (London: Tory Reform Group, 1984).

9. It is interesting to note that in 1983 the minimum daily provisions allowance for a contract caterer in a private hospital was £4.50 and the maximum allowance was £12. *Hospital Equipment & Supplies*, 29 (November 1983), 23–5.

10. This 'contribution return' figure reflects the fact that income from staff catering covers the marginal costs of food and additional catering staff and makes a contribution towards the fixed costs of the hospital (e.g. machinery, heat and light). Ibid., p. 25.

11. *Health and Social Service Journal*, xcv (26 September 1985), p. 1201.

12. A comprehensive survey of health authority views, with particular reference to those opposed to mandatory tendering, was published by Frank Dobson, MP, and NHS Unlimited in 1984. *Contracting Out*

'Ancillary' Services: The Health Authority View (London: NHS Unlimited, 1984).

13. The best sources for information on contract awards are the 'Privatisation Fact Sheets' published by NUPE (London) and a regularly updated summary put together by the CCMA (London) entitled 'NHS Cleaning Contracts – List A'.
14. *Sixth Report from the Social Services Committee*, xx. The relevant sections of this report provide a useful insight into the attitudes of both parliamentary backbenchers and the government.
15. Three model contracts were produced by the DHSS. The first two, *Provision of Catering Services: Invitation to Tender* and *Provision of Domestic Services in the NHS: Specimen Contract for Competitive Tendering*, were issued on 22 November 1983. Model contract documents for the laundry area, entitled *Provision of Laundry Services: Specimen Tender and Contract Documents*, were not issued until 9 March 1984.
16. Tory Reform Group, *High Noon in the National Health Service*, p. 13.
17. Only 1000 pieces were sent out to private contractors; this compared to the authority's weekly processing output of 149 000 pieces. The cost of laundering these 1000 pieces privately came out of the service's annual budget, which was based directly on the in-house tender figure.
18. For a closer insight into the attidues of the health authority's administrators, see L. Paine, 'Contracting Out in the Bethlem Royal and Maudsley Hospitals' in *Contracting Out in the Public Sector* (London: RIPA, 1984).
19. Ibid., p. 54.

7 Contracting Out in Local Authorities

1. See H. P. Hatry, *A Review of Private Approaches for Delivery of Public Services* (Washington, D.C.: The Urban Institute Press, 1983).
2. The arguments of American trade unions were put forward clearly in a book by John Hanrahan entitled *Government for Sale: Contracting Out – The New Patronage* and published by the American Federation of State, County and Municipal Employees (Washington, D.C.) in 1977.
3. This excludes additional income from trading services, which constitute an increasingly important source of local authority finance. For trends in local government expenditure and employment, see K. Newton and T. J. Karran, *The Politics of Local Expenditure* (London: Macmillan, 1985) and P. J. Dunleavy, *Urban Political Analysis* (London: Macmillan, 1980), Chapter 3.
4. Dunleavy, *Urban Political Analysis*, p. 61.
5. Four out of five part-time workers, from the 1950s right through until the present time, have been female. Newton and Karran, *The Politics of Local Expenditure*, p. 28.
6. In 1965, NALGO had 338 000 members and NUPE had 240 000. By

1980, these totals had increased to 753 000 and 692 000 respectively. *Annual Reports*, Trades Union Congress, 1965 and 1980.

7. Health service unionisation increased from 39 per cent to 61 per cent over this same period. Dunleavy, *Urban Political Analysis*, p. 66.

8. Wages and salaries constitute 19 per cent and 35 per cent of total current expenditure of central government and public corporations respectively, but make up roughly 50 per cent of comparable expenditure in local government. Newton and Karran, *The Politics of Local Expenditure*, p. 87.

9. Finance and General Statistics, published annually by the CIPFA Statistical Information Service in London, provides a comprehensive breakdown of local government service expenditure.

10. *Refuse Storage and Collection*, Ministry of Housing and Local Government (London: HMSO, 1967), p. 90.

11. If potential changes in the standard of service are considered, savings could amount to £50 million per annum. Audit Commission, *Securing Further Improvements in Refuse Collection* (London; 1984), pp. 11 and 20–1.

12. For a comprehensive description of the ROSS System see *ROSS: The Complete Refuse Service Management System* (London: LAMSAC – Local Authorities Management Services and Computer Committee 1979, revised 1985).

13. *Local Government Chronicle* 6055 (17 June 1983), pp. 655–62.

14. *Local Government Chronicle* 6107 (22 June 1984), pp. 704–8.

15. In June 1984, Ealing's Director of Technical Services reported to the Council's Policy and Resources Committee that during the period 17 October 1983–27 May 1984, Exclusive performed at between 57 per cent and 79 per cent of the rate expected by the Council. The Council relaxed the required standard of performance to 'not less than 75 per cent of the specified standard' and adapted its criteria so that 'partially completed work can qualify for the appropriate payment'. *Public Service Action*, 9 (August 1984), p. 3.

16. *Public Service Action*, 4 (October 1983), p. 2.

17. 'Cleaning Standards in Dudley Schools' (Dudley: Dudley National Union of Teachers, 1984).

18. A complete list of 'failures', as defined by the trade union movement, can be found in *Contractors' Failures: The Privatisation Experience* (London: TUC, 1984).

19. *Local Government Chronicle*, 6107 (22 June 1984), p. 704.

20. 'The Local Government Annual Privatisation Survey', Supplement to *Local Government Chronicle*, 6160 (5 July 1985).

21. Both refuse collection and street cleaning were administered by the City Engineer's Department. These two services were clearly linked; once refuse collection employees reached age 50, they were offered jobs on the less demanding street cleaning side.

22. T. Williams, *Fighting Privatisation: The Victory in Gloucester* (London: NUPE/IWC pamphlet, 1984) describes events surrounding the tendering exercise in Gloucester in more detail.

23. Bonus payments decrease with each default notice that is issued within a given week. For example, one default notice results in a 5 per cent bonus deduction, two notices lead to a 10 per cent deduction, three notices lead to a 20 per cent deduction, and so on.
24. The perspective of the Wandsworth trade unions is clearly articulated in D. Benlow and I. Scott, *Fighting Privatisation: the Struggle for Wandsworth* (London: NUPE/IWC pamphlet, 1983).
25. *Public Service Action* 1 (March 1983), p. 6.
26. Benlow and Scott, *Fighting Privatisation: The Struggle for Wandsworth*, p. 23.

8 An Overview of the Debate

1. This view has been put forward by W. A. Niskanen in *Bureaucracy and Representative Government* (New York: Aldine-Atherton, 1973). Similar approaches to bureaucracy can be found in T. E. Borcherding (ed.), *Budget and Bureaucrats* (Durham, N.C.: Duke University Press, 1977) and G. Tullock, *The Politics of Bureaucracy* (Washington, D.C.: Public Affairs Press, 1965), among others.
2. P. J. Dunleavy, 'Explaining the Privatisation Boom: Public Choice versus Radical Approaches', *Public Administration*, 64 (Spring 1986), 13–34.
3. K. Hartley, 'Why Contract Out' in *Contracting Out in the Public Sector* (London: RIPA, 1984), p. 11.
4. Dunleavy argues that bureaucrats generally maximise their own personal utilities (rather than some unspecified collective utility) and that the utility curves of individuals will not exclusively be based on financial or budget-maximising considerations. He suggests that senior bureaucrats will only maximise budgets up to the point where the net personal utility of an expenditure decision equals the advocacy costs associated with it and that 'bureau-shaping' considerations – those designed to improve the individual's work environment – will be more important to this group. P. J. Dunleavy, 'Bureaucrats, Budgets and the Growth of the State: Reconstructing an Instrumental Model', *British Journal of Political Science*, 15 (July 1985), 299–328.
5. This view is put forward in *Public or Private: The Case Against Privatisation* (London: Labour Research Department, 1982). See also *Privatisation: Who Loses? Who Profits?* (London: Labour Research Department, 1983) and S. Hastings and H. Levie, *Privatisation?* (Nottingham: Spokesman, 1983).
6. Efficiency has been defined as the ratio of resource inputs to a given level of output by the organisation; effectiveness relates to the quality of the organisation's outputs in relation to their impact upon the community. K. Spencer, 'Assessing Alternative Forms of Service Provision', *Local Government Studies*, 10 (March/April 1984), p. 17.
7. *Jobs at Risk: Privatisation in the NHS* (Birmingham: West Midlands TUC Health Services Committee, 1984).
8. *It's Not for Sale* (London: Council of Civil Service Unions, 1984).

9. *High Noon in the National Health Service*, published by the Tory Reform Group early in 1984, argued that tendering was too soft a policy and recommended 'a new programme of action' which would see: (1) all NHS domestic and laundry services contracted out over a three- or five-year period; (2) a fixed number of catering contracts in all authorities contracted out on a management fee (as opposed to a fixed price) system within the next year; and (3) all linen hire contracted out over a period of five years. *High Noon in the National Health Service* (London: Tory Reform Group, 1984), p. 71.

10. See O. E. Williamson, *Markets and Hierarchies: Analysis and Antitrust Implications* (New York: The Free Press, 1975).

11. H. Leibenstein, 'Allocative Efficiency and X-Efficiency', *American Economic Review*, 56 (1966), 392–415. Also see 'Aspects of X-Efficiency Theory of the Firm', *The Bell Journal of Economics*, 6 (1975), 580–606. A summary of Leibenstein's work can be found in D. Heald, *Public Expenditure* (Oxford: Martin Robertson, 1983), pp. 88–9.

12. See G. Tullock, *The Politics of Bureaucracy* (Washington, D.C.: Public Affairs Press, 1965).

13. Williamson suggests that internal provision should be seen as a 'syndrome of characteristics' – which includes both strengths and weaknesses. The suitability of internal provision in a particular case can only be determined by comparing these relative strengths and weaknesses against those associated with market-organised exchanges.

14. One Hammersmith administrator reported that the first competitive tendering exercise undertaken at the hospital occupied approximately one-third of his time over the course of a year. Although his experience was somewhat extreme, the sheer volume of exercises within each authority and the number of staff they involve suggests that the aggregate administrative costs of the policy must be substantial.

15. H. E. Wesemann, *Contracting for City Services* (Pittsburgh: Innovations Press, 1981), p. 59.

16. *The Financial Times*, 15 February 1985.

18. Wesemann, *Contracting for City Services*, p. 105.

Index